The Political ı   Party since 1945

D1424007

The Political Thought of the Conservative Party since 1945

Edited by

Kevin Hickson

School of Politics and Communication Studies,
University of Liverpool

First published 2005 by
PALGRAVE MACMILLAN
Houndmills, Basingstoke, Hampshire RG21 6XS and
175 Fifth Avenue, New York, N.Y. 10010
Companies and representatives throughout the world

PALGRAVE MACMILLAN is the global academic imprint of the Palgrave Macmillan division of St Martin's Press LLC and of Palgrave Macmillan Ltd.
Macmillan® is a registered trademark in the United States, United Kingdom and other countries. Palgrave is a registered trademark in the European Union and other countries.

ISBN-10   1–4039–4907–7 hardback
ISBN-13   978–1–4039–4907–3 hardback
ISBN-10   1–4039–4908–5 paperback
ISBN-13   978–1–4039–4908–0 paperback

This book is printed on paper suitable for recycling and made from fully managed and sustained forest sources.

A catalogue record for this book is available from the British Library.

A catalogue record for this book is available from the Library of Congress

10   9   8   7   6   5   4   3   2   1
14   13   12   11   10   09   08   07   06   05

Printed and bound in Great Britain by
Antony Rowe Ltd, Chippenham and Eastbourne

Contents

Acknowledgements

I wish to acknowledge first and foremost the contributors themselves, without whom this book could not have been produced. An edited volume such as this benefits considerably from the participation of a number of distinguished academics, journalists and politicians, each bringing their own perspectives and areas of expertise. They have worked tirelessly and with enthusiasm and have allowed me to pester them considerably when they had many more pressing things to do! I have also benefited in my knowledge and understanding of the Conservative Party and its ideas from discussions with several of those involved.

I would also like to thank Alison Howson and the staff of Palgrave Macmillan who have provided much practical support.

I would also like to state my considerable appreciation for the help, advice and encouragement from Andrew Gamble, who has allowed me the benefit of his considerable knowledge of the Conservative Party.

Finally, I would like to thank the lecturing and support staff and my students in the School of Politics and Communication Studies at the University of Liverpool for their friendship and encouragement.

Kevin Hickson

Notes on Contributors

Arthur Aughey is senior lecturer in politics at the University of Ulster. He has published widely on the Conservative Party, conservative political philosophy and Ulster unionism. Relevant publications include *Conservatives and Conservatism* with Philip Norton (1981) and *The Conservative Political Tradition in Britain and the United States* with Greta Jones and William Riches (1991).

Norman Barry is Professor of Social and Political Theory at the University of Buckingham and researches in political philosophy, in particular on the New Right, Hayek and welfare. His publications include *Hayek's Social and Economic Philosophy* (1979), *The New Right* (1987) and *Welfare* (2nd edition, 1999).

Mark Garnett is senior research fellow in politics at the University of Leicester. He has written extensively on the Conservative Party and has produced a number of biographies of leading Conservative politicians such as Keith Joseph and William Whitelaw. Recent publications include *Whatever Happened to the Tories* with Ian Gilmour (1997) and *The Conservatives in Crisis* edited with Philip Lynch (2003)

Andrew Geddes was recently appointed Professor of Politics at the University of Sheffield and previously taught at the University of Liverpool. He has written extensively on the European Union, especially on Britain's relationship with the EU. His recent publications include *The European Union and British Politics* (2004).

Damian Green has been Conservative MP for Ashford since 1997 and previously worked as a journalist and in the Prime Minister's Policy Unit (1992–94). He has held a number of frontbench positions. He is Vice President of the Tory Reform Group and Chairman of Parliamentary Mainstream. He has produced a number of publications on One Nation Conservatism.

Simon Heffer is a columnist at the *Daily Mail* and previously served as Deputy Editor of the *Daily Telegraph* and worked for the *Evening Standard*, the *Spectator* and *The Times*. His books include *Tory Seer: The Selected Journalism of T.E. Utley* with Charles Moore (1989), *Like the Roman: The*

Life of Enoch Powell (1998) and *Nor Shall My Sword: The Reinvention of England* (2000).

Kevin Hickson is lecturer in politics at the University of Liverpool. His main research interest is in British political ideologies and political economy. His books include *New Labour, Old Labour: The Wilson and Callaghan Governments of 1974–79* edited with Anthony Seldon (2004), *The Struggle for Labour's Soul* edited with Raymond Plant and Matt Beech (2004) and *The IMF Crisis of 1976 and British Politics* (2005).

Francis Maude has been MP for Horsham since 1997 and was previously MP for North Warwickshire (1983–92). He held a number of ministerial positions prior to 1997. He has since served as Shadow Chancellor and Shadow Foreign Secretary. He was Chairman of the Government's Deregulation Taskforce from 1994–97. He is Chairman of Conservatives for Change.

Philip Norton is Professor of Politics at the University of Hull and Director of the Centre for Legislative Studies. He became a Conservative peer in 1998. He is a widely recognised authority on the British constitution and has published 25 books. He chairs the House of Lords Committee on the Constitution and also chaired the Commission to Strengthen Parliament, which reported in 2000. He is Chairman of the Conservative Academic Group.

Bruce Pilbeam completed his PhD on contemporary conservative political thought at the University of Sheffield and has recently been appointed as lecturer in politics at London Metropolitan University. He has published a number of articles in journals and his book *Conservatism in Crisis? Anglo-American Conservative Ideology after the Cold War* was published in 2003.

John Redwood has been Conservative MP for Wokingham since 1987. He has held a number of ministerial positions including serving as Secretary of State for Wales from 1993 to 1995 and is currently Shadow Secretary of State for Deregulation. He was Head of the Prime Minister's Policy Unit prior to 1987. His books include *Popular Capitalism* (1987) and *Singing the Blues* (2004).

David Seawright is senior lecturer in politics at the University of Leeds. He has published widely on Britain's relations with the EU and is currently conducting research on the One Nation tradition within the Conservative Party. His relevant publications include *Britain For and Against Europe?*

British Politics and the Question of European Integration edited with David Baker (1998).

Andrew Taylor has recently been appointed Professor of Politics at the University of Sheffield. He has written extensively on the trades unions both in a British and comparative context and also on the history and politics of the Conservative Party. His relevant publications include *From Salisbury to Major: Continuity and Change in Conservative Politics* with Brendan Evans (1996).

Introduction

Kevin Hickson

The Conservative Party is often seen as a party concerned with power, one that is prepared to adapt to changing times and changing electoral demands in a pragmatic, if not ruthless, way. It is usually regarded as having done this successfully, at least in the twentieth century when the Party was in power for much of the time. There would seem to be little scope for ideology in such a political party. The need for a book devoted to the political thought of the Conservative Party would therefore seem a little odd even to some who are more versed in the politics of the Conservative Party. Indeed, many Conservative politicians have argued that they are non-ideological and see this as something that is desirable in politics. Ideology is something to be left to opponents and is something to be critical of therefore.

For this reason the political thought of the Conservative Party has been little studied. This is certainly the case with the pre-Thatcherite Conservative Party, which is often said to have been non-ideological. However, Thatcherism is said to have brought ideology into the Conservative Party and there are many more studies of the New Right. With the decline of the Conservative Party's electoral position since 1997 there has again been little academic attention on the Party in opposition. Attention has naturally focused more on New Labour.

However, the Conservative Party does contain several ideological perspectives and competing views on things such as the constitution, Europe and the wider role of Britain in the world, economic policy, welfare and social morality. The thought of the Conservative Party is therefore something to be studied. This also raises interesting discussions as to whether there is a 'true' Conservative tradition and whether there is a core value that unites all Conservatives.

This book aims to provide a comprehensive analysis of the political, economic and social thought of the Conservative Party since 1945. In so doing it seeks to provide fresh perspectives. It allows for a comparison of the main ideological positions within the Conservative Party and a discussion of how these positions approached a range of political issues that have been present in Britain since 1945. A particular feature of the book is that it allows for a discussion of the intellectual development of the Party from differing perspectives and with a wide range of academic interests and specialisms.

Ultimately the book offers no one single interpretation of or argument about Conservatism. Instead, the reader is encouraged to reflect on the different arguments made in the book and to reach their own opinion. This is one key advantage of an edited volume such as this.

Structure of the book

The book is divided into three parts. The first analyses the four broad ideological positions within the Party since 1945: traditional Toryism, New Right, centre and 'One Nation'. The aim of these chapters is to outline the key aspects and the main thinkers and politicians associated with these perspectives, then to offer an evaluation of the broad position. Arthur Aughey seeks to analyse the nature of traditional Toryism. The core idea he argues is for a minimal state, in which people will be 'let alone' and which will preserve individual freedom within traditional social structures. This idea is underpinned by attitudes towards human character and British (or essentially English) national identity. However, there is also a fatalistic element within traditional Toryism, which stresses that the traditional way of doing things is about to be lost forever, if not already.

The political and economic thought of the New Right is analysed by Norman Barry. Barry argues that the New Right is inherently a conservative doctrine, which shares ideas with key conservative philosophers. The emphasis here is more on efficiency and freedom and the need to reverse the post-war drift to state intervention. Barry argues that the Conservative Governments after 1979 held to New Right ideology but that there are also several contemporary problems that can be resolved by the application of New Right ideas.

The chapters on the centre by Mark Garnett and the 'One Nation' tradition by David Seawright show the fluidity of Conservative thought. The centre contains both a pragmatic, party loyalist tradition imbued with a public service ethos and also an ideological element that seeks to find unity by connecting ideas often associated with the left and the right of the Party. Seawright's main focus is on the One Nation dining group.

He analyses the extent to which the ideas of this group accurately reflect the ideas of Disraeli. The group contained both more interventionist and free market ideas and so he argues the position should not be seen as a 'left-wing' position, although there were strong links between some in the 'Nation' with more clearly defined progressive groups such as Pressure for Economic and Social Toryism and Tory Reform.

The second part deals with a number of cross-cutting themes and issues. Philip Norton discusses the constitution, saying why Conservatives see it as important and also how they respond to constitutional change. Norton raises the question of how Conservatives should deal with the constitutional reform agenda of New Labour when they return to power. The constitutional question is also important in relation to the Conservatives' approach to Europe, discussed by Andrew Geddes. This often hinges on the constitutional principle of sovereignty. Some see sovereignty as something that can be 'pooled' meaning that closer integration is desirable. However, others see sovereignty as an 'absolute' meaning that closer integration should be avoided or even that Britain should seek to withdraw itself from various elements of the EU (or withdraw from the EU completely).

Europe is also an economic question. Some see free markets as desirable and identify more with the political economy of the United States. Attitudes to the economy are addressed by Andrew Taylor, who sees economic attitudes as a tension between order and chaos, identifies a range of opinions on the economy since 1945 and discusses how these competing positions impact on current policies. He says that there is now little debate on economic policy, as there is an essentially free market consensus. Instead, debate is limited to social questions. This theme is developed by Bruce Pilbeam who examines the potential for conflict between those of a more conservative or a more liberal stance on issues of social morality. Pilbeam identifies a range of issues over which these tensions have been played out in the past and examines the extent to which the Conservative Party has become more socially liberal.

Although many of these themes and issues suggest conflict within the Conservative Party, Kevin Hickson asks if a common principle can be found which unites Conservatives. He argues that such a unifying principle can be found with the idea of 'inequality'. Conservatives oppose the idea of 'equality', which they see as an ideological construct of the left, but also defend the notion of inequality positively, albeit for different reasons and to different extents.

The final part consists of personal commentaries written by those often associated with the position they seek to defend. Each argues that their position can best be used to restore the electoral fortunes of the Conservative Party. Simon Heffer argues that there is widespread support for traditional Toryism, based on defence of the constitution, English nationalism and traditional social morality. John Redwood argues that the idea of 'popular capitalism' and the emphasis on individual freedom by the New Right was popular in the 1980s and is still relevant and popular today. Francis Maude argues that the Conservative Party should not seek to move to the left or the right but should defend its core principles, most notably the interrelated ideas of individual liberty and community. Damian Green also argues that a more compassionate conservatism should be developed and that Conservatives should adopt a more positive attitude to the state, seeing state intervention in social issues as desirable in cases where markets or voluntary action are insufficient.

By way of conclusion, Kevin Hickson argues there is still much to be debated within the Conservative Party over many areas of policy.

Part One
Positions

1
Traditional Toryism

Arthur Aughey

In May 1912, at the height of the Irish Home Rule crisis, the *Ballymoney Free Press* expressed in particular circumstances a universal truth of traditional Toryism. 'The statement of Unionist Ulster', it announced, 'is that it merely wants to be let alone.' Unfortunately, it continued, 'since Satan entered the Garden of Eden good people will not be let alone'.[1] The desire at the heart of traditional Toryism has been this same desire to be let alone in order to enjoy whatever vocation or customary pursuits may be freely chosen. It is explicit in Lord Hugh Cecil's preference for the known, which is safe, to the unknown, which is likely to be dangerous. 'Why not let it alone? Why be weary instead of at rest? Why rush into danger instead of staying in safety?'[2] It is implied in Lord Hailsham's celebrated passage where he argued, like most other conservative writers, that meddling in politics is very much a second order activity. For the Tory, life is elsewhere and, in a phrase that now conveys the assumptions of a lost world, the 'simplest among them prefer fox-hunting – the wisest, religion'. Indeed, for Hailsham the person who would put politics first 'is not fit to be called a civilised being'.[3] There is an innocence, an authenticity, a piety in those non-political preferences and this attribution of value has consequences for conservatism itself. As the Third Marquess of Salisbury once argued, the Conservative Party is rather like a policeman. If there were no criminals around there would be no need for it, even though the existence of the Party was no guarantee of protection.[4] Unfortunately, Conservatives will not be let alone, there will always be criminals around and the tranquil disposition is forever under threat. In recent history both interference and threat have been associated with the state since the modern state has the potential to deprive good people of property, savings and now even fox hunting. Traditional Tories, then, inhabit a world that is both enchanted and disenchanted. Like the people of Ballymoney they possess a deep sense of what the good life is and this life can be enchantingly and sentimentally described in conservative literature, the sort of 'poetics of the civil life' at which Michael Oakeshott excelled.[5] Commentators seduced by his description of Conservatism as a preference for the familiar to the unknown, 'the tried to the untried, fact to mystery, the actual to the possible, the limited to the unbounded, the near to the distant, the sufficient to the superabundant, the convenient to the perfect, present laughter to utopian bliss' often fail to note that Oakeshott thought this attitude inappropriate 'in respect of human conduct in general'.[6] He, like the people of Ballymoney, also knew that the possession of that enchanted world can never be secure and its enjoyment can never be certain. Such is the Tory tragedy and the fall into politics involves a detestable, disenchanted, unsentimental but unavoidable fate.

The origin of traditional Toryism, then, is a dream of reconciliation – of order and liberty, of legitimacy and power, of justice and discipline. It is the origin but cannot be the conclusion since experience is not as the ideal would have it. The reconciliation is reconciliation within Conservative thought, not reconciliation in reality, and this creates a damnable conundrum. As Roger Scruton acknowledged, once the Conservative has fallen into politics 'he has set himself apart from things' and helped to 'instil the world with doubt' (Satan has entered the Garden of Eden). Having struggled to be articulate, the only recourse for the Conservative is to 'recommend silence'.[7] This echoed Angus Maude's opinion that the part of Toryism 'that is not articulate is by far the best and most enduring' since most of the rest is meaningless sloganising.[8] Unfortunately, silence, like being let alone, is no longer an option. Both aspects of the Tory condition – the enchanted and disenchanted – were captured by Lord Salisbury when, at the height of political success in 1897, he warned that 'the dangerous temptation of the hour is that we should consider rhapsody an adequate compensation for calculation'.[9] The rhapsodic, enchanted ideal and the calculating, disenchanted politics are two sides of Conservative fate and the relationship between them has never been straightforward. On the one side, traditional Toryism has an elegiac tone which explains its appeal to intelligent, sensitive and romantic young people, something that Disraeli well understood. It appears to hold, like the Italian poet Leopardi, that to enjoy life, a state of despair is necessary.[10] The temptation today is to dismiss this style of Toryism as a mere affectation, a sort of Young Fogeyism, especially now that it has become detached from its aristocratic roots, though there are those who still defend it with style.[11] Moreover, its elegiac tone is thought to be a characteristic that makes it inappropriate for a modern politics that requires imagination, experiment and 'reflexivity'.[12] On the other side, traditional Toryism has a combative character. As A.J.P. Taylor once remarked of Salisbury: 'He fought for victory; he expected defeat.'[13] The expectation of (long term) defeat did not mean the absence of (short and medium term) victories. Moreover, what constitutes victory, what constitutes defeat for Toryism has never been self-evident and so the struggle itself may be worth it. For those of a nostalgic frame of mind, the fall into politics is already proof of defeat. For those of a sanguine disposition there remains much to play for. This question of Tory fatalism requires further consideration.

Toryism and fate

Politics is about deliberation and a weighing up of the odds. It is disposed towards action either in the promotion of change or in resistance to change. Fatalism, therefore, would appear to be a disposition at odds with the political. A strictly fatalistic view is that any given situation can have only one outcome. This is one way of understanding Scruton's recommendation of silence and also one way of making sense of that innate Tory suspicion of what has recently been called the 'chattering classes', those who are always opening up things for pointless discussion. That sort of fatalism seems at first sight to be at odds with another characteristic commonly attributed to the Tory, a bloody-minded mentality of resistance. Resistance in every particular means that one's enemies exhaust themselves challenging the inessentials and so delays the final assault on the citadel. However, rhapsodic fatalism and calculating resistance can share a simple world-view. The surface may change but the currents are remorseless. Things will not change for the better, only for the worse and pessimism (the world is going to the dogs) is married to complete defiance (no surrender). Even the fatal certainty of defeat provides a barrier against complexity and political ambiguity. This is especially the case if you believe that your future is behind you. Why, as Lord Hugh Cecil might phrase it, get involved in schemes for one's own undoing? Why move when movement can only be in a hostile direction? Here is a view of the world that believes all schemes for political improvement to be futile and follows Schopenhauer in always qualifying the noun 'optimism' with the adjective 'unscrupulous'. 'No rose without a thorn. Yes, but many a thorn without a rose.'[14] Of course, that mentality

– at least since J.S. Mill's remark at the Conservative Party's expense – has been associated with incorrigible Tory ignorance. Yet it should be stressed that this is not necessarily an unintelligent response to the world. Insofar as political wisdom emerges from what experience obliges one to believe, Tories often do perceive a world of decadence and decline. And yet, like the Conservative Party itself, they survive. So it is not necessarily the case that fatalism is without its political dividends since being able to endure in what appears to be a hostile world encourages a form of self-esteem. Unfortunately, fatalism also provides a ready excuse for political failure and political indolence (and the two may be related). It can be an enchanting rhapsody that excuses a lack of disenchanted calculation (nothing could be done).

This is not of merely historic relevance since every generation of Tories, especially following electoral defeat, experiences that fatalism in large or small measure. In the 1970s, Elie Kedourie feared that Tories had become gripped by an 'iron Fate' that locked them into surrender to the politics of state aggrandisement. Though the Party may continue as a 'great' institution, he wondered 'what, under such conditions, Conservatives will come to understand by Conservatism'.[15] The Party will survive as the party of government, in other words, but Toryism is likely to perish. Without self-understanding and a sense of political purpose, Conservative pragmatism is a demoralising and debilitating experience. Writing about the Party in 2004, after seven years of Opposition, one sympathetic journalist detected a collapse of Tory nerve and a tendency amongst some in the Party to turn defeat into defeatism.[16] The Party may not survive as a party of government, in other words, and Toryism is still as likely to perish. In this case, what is the point in being Conservative at all?

While both sorts of fatalism have indeed their place in Tory history they have never been (at least for any length of time) the Party's leading characteristics. 'Stern and unbending Toryism', according to Lord Blake, 'has never paid dividends to the Conservative party, nor in practice when in office has the party ever taken that line.'[17] Wisdom suggested that it was best not to provoke confrontations and to avoid dividing society unnecessarily. Here was a politics of modesty that was not averse to looking after Tory interests but often did so 'by round-about ways'.[18] What the Conservative Party has generally taken from a reading of its own history, sometimes erroneously, is an aversion from projects that seem to be ultimately self-defeating. (Of course, what some may take to be an example of a self-defeating course of action, for instance a policy of withdrawal from the European Union, may be seen by others as a principled alternative to the fatalistic acceptance of 'inevitability'.)

Instead, the lesson has been that one must make the best of the hand which fate has dealt, and this disposition is sometimes known as Conservative realism.[19] This game is not a game of political poker but a game of political tarot. It involves readings, interpretations, meanings and divinations in which fate may just possibly be made to bend some way to one's will. The trick is to make the best of things and the task of Conservative leadership is to encourage both Party and country to accept its reading of the cards. This political game, as R.A. Butler once put it, is the art of the possible, a dialogue between fatalism and possibility.

One historian has attempted to capture this Conservative dialogue in terms of what may be called the Lampedusan paradox.[20] Taken from Lampedusa's novel *The Leopard*, set in 1860, it recounts the process by which the Sicilian Prince of Salina accommodates himself to the new political regime. The paradox states: 'If you want things to stay the same things will have to change.' The aim of the Prince's generation is to survive and any 'palliative which may give us another hundred years of life is like eternity to us'. In this he proves successful although he is 'burdened with the truly onerous responsibility of bequeathing a once vital past to a future that seems to have no place for it'.[21] What is envisaged is not a future of 'liberty, security, lighter taxes, ease, trade' (the enchantment of ideology) but a future of petty compromise, manipulation and manoeuvre in which decent values and old standards will be lost (the disenchantment of politics). It involves a process of settling for what today would be called gently managing decline. How could this not be when the modernising Piedmontese administration (for all the world the confident voice of New Labour), believes that Sicily 'is only now sighting the modern world, with so many wounds to heal, so many just desires to be granted?' That is the process which Fforde traces in Britain, a process in which 'Conservatives not only offend their more conservative associates but end up by changing themselves'.[22] He argues that this process 'had a vampire effect: it drew out the true Tory blood'. Hence the irony that 'the Conservative Party came to be an integral part of the means by which Liberalism and Socialism progressed – it was a political carrier of previously resisted proposals'.[23] Academic research here repeats one of the enduring Tory complaints about Party policy, one that may be traced back at least as far as Disraeli – Tory men and Whig measures.

Lord Coleraine, for instance, thought the problem for the Conservative Party was never that it would prove too reactionary but that it would be carried too far along the road of change and would lose the capacity to make its distinctive contribution to national life. Indeed, for most of the twentieth century, he thought, all the Party had to offer 'was a reformulation of the fashions of the day'.[24] With his delicate register of Tory sensibility, T.E. Utley observed that most Conservative politicians have assumed that their opponents represent the future. 'Is it not the great merit of English Conservatism', he asked, 'that it comes to terms with reality and the great merit of the Tory party that it confines itself to the role of a midwife to history?' For Utley, this represented 'a kind of sophisticated timidity', an attitude that led a politician to decide 'what he loves best and then consider how he can preside most elegantly and judiciously over its destruction, making that process as painless as possible, saving what he could from the wreckage'. Lampedusa could not have phrased it more elegantly. This policy had become the politics of controlled surrender, though such was Utley's unfailing insight that he could also acknowledge how far this was from being a 'contemptible creed'. He accepted that its practical wisdom had often stood the party in good stead.[25] Concession, surrender and transformation are indeed the lot of intelligent Conservatism but that is only one side of the truth (even if a version of that one-sided truth informed Mrs Thatcher's successful, though possibly temporary, Tory renaissance). That fatal gift of Tory statesmanship is not the whole of the Party's inheritance for, as Fforde himself goes on to admit, much of 'the British "liberal tradition" is rooted in Conservatism and its political sense'.[26] The Lampedusan paradox would be of little interest if it only illuminated a process of change. By contrast, from the perspective of Tory opponents, the remarkable thing about British politics is the extent to which Conservative interests *have been* let alone. That has been the enduring complaint of radicals and they too have their own version of the paradox.

It was the traditionalism and Conservatism of British political culture that puzzled Marxist commentators and the reason appeared to lie in the sophisticated timidity of the Labour Party. Here, if traditional Tories cared to look, was the dividend from faithful subscription to the Lampedusan paradox. The Conservative Party had helped to fashion an opposition that believed if you wanted things to change things would also have to stay the same. The Labour Party, as one critic put it, became committed 'to the fundamental civic values of British political culture' which just happened to be Tory, a 'manifestation of the institutional integration characteristic of British society'.[27] Another was absolutely convinced that British political culture was one in which Conservatism 'swims like a fish in the sea'. The national culture '*is* a Tory culture' and the Conservative Party is a '*necessary* embodiment of the central core of this Tory culture'. Moreover, 'there are some ways in which it exists more as this embodiment than it does as a political party'.[28] This was written in the 1980s, not the 1880s, and it goes to show how many on the left accepted Tory myths as political truths. Of course to Tory activists, engaged in the disenchanted business of getting out the vote, much of this was academic nonsense. Few of them really felt comfortable with modern Britain and for one of them it was luck, rather than a dominant Tory culture, that made the Conservative Party the 'Great Survivor'. And like all good Tories he felt its luck would soon run out.[29]

The acceptance of their respective sides of the Lampedusan paradox by Tories and by Socialists helps to explain the distinctive experience of right versus left in British politics in the last century, an experience very different from continental Europe's. No ruler, as Schopflin neatly puts it, is going to share power 'if he thinks that those who are to be newly assumed into power will use it to string him up from the nearest lamp-post'.[30] The conciliatory intelligence of Tory politics meant that power was ceded but it also meant that no one was lynched (in Great Britain at any rate, if not in Ireland). And while it is true that post-war academics and in-house historians reinterpreted the Conservative past to conform to 'mid-twentieth century assumptions about the purposes of politics' with which many traditionalists in the Party felt uneasy, this should not conceal the extent to which many things close to the hearts of traditionalists remained secure.[31] Conciliation was not without the ability to resist effectively. It is possible to argue that it is Conservatism which has had a vampiric effect, drawing out the true Socialist blood from the Labour Party, making it a political carrier of previously resisted proposals, Whig men and Tory measures. In 1950, A.J.P. Taylor thought it rather amusing to suggest that 'We are all Tories nowadays.'[32] Almost 50 years later Lord Blake observed that one is unlikely to say of British politics that 'we are all conservatives nowadays'. But, he thought, 'it would be true, all the same'.[33] Well, up to a point. If this were the result of accident as much as of design, it has had an ironic effect on the current popularity of the Party. Despite, or even because of, Conservative electoral successes between 1979 and 1997, Tory fatalists may today think of the Party like the stuffed carcass of the Prince of Salina's faithful hound and recall former glory in the throws of ultimate dissolution. What remained of Bendico was flung into a corner of the yard and during 'the flight down from the window its form recomposed itself for an instant; in the air there seemed to be dancing a quadruped with long whiskers, its right foreleg raised in imprecation. Then all found peace in a little heap of livid dust.' The enchantment of a glorious past exists with the disenchanted prospect of political futility.

New Labour has harvested, for the moment at least, the fruits of the so-called 'Conservative century' and one of the reasons, some feel, is that Tories have lost touch with the people. For the Tories to lose touch with the people is the condition that every great survivor fears. The Conservative Party has always prided itself on being the national party in both its geographical appeal and in its attraction to all classes. However, as one psephologist observed, the tendency now is for people to think of the Party as 'alien and somehow "other"'.[34] The question that every successful Party leader must ask is: who are the Tory people? This is not so much a sociological question as an imaginative one, not so much a psephological question as a conceptual one. It is about seeing, as it was claimed Disraeli once saw, angels in the block of marble. Upon the answer to that question depends the policies to be formulated and the platform to be constructed.

Toryism and the character of the people

Traditional Toryism assumed a distinctive form of popular appeal and an important aspect of it was a sort of snobbery that crossed class boundaries. This was, and in some cases remains, a fact of life for those many working class and lower middle-class conservatives who think it best to maintain distinctions of social rank.[35] In this case, the 'people' is not some abstract sociological category but the British people in their regional and social variety, their customary beliefs, particular affections and long-standing prejudices. The purpose of Conservative politics is to defend traditional allegiances since they are thought to be the source of identity and individuality. Toryism assumes it is more in tune with the common sense of the people than the rationalism of political radicals. This distinctive populism remains strong in contemporary Conservative politics since the Party lays claim to being the true defender of the people against petty tyrannies imposed by an unrepresentative metropolitan elite (the shorthand for these tyrannies today is 'political correctness'). This traditional argument follows a recognisable pattern. On the one hand, there is the destructive influence of universal, abstract thinking and 'the moment abstraction enters the mind of politicians, the blood and substance of the people they govern is sucked out, and they decline into ideological poster-people'. These 'eviscerated subjects' then become the subject of state manipulation, to be persuaded or cajoled 'into the plans of their rulers'.[36] Liberalism has been attacked for carrying within it the death of liberty and socialism, the death of independence. On the other hand, there is the partiality of such abstract thinking since whenever 'the modern liberal tries to make concrete the ideal of freedom that he proposes he finds himself always constrained to endorse (whether wittingly or not) the habits and predilections of a particular way of life – the way of life of the emancipated urban intellectual'.[37] That way of life may be sweet but it is not the only way of life. To think that it is and to try to impose it on, for example, traditional rural communities (like the ban on fox hunting) reveals the limit of liberal tolerance.

Once more, radicalism will not let good people alone and Conservative politics presents itself as the protector of social variety, a role that is sometimes described as defending 'freedom'. That description is not entirely convincing. As Cowling honestly put it, what Tories want is 'the sort of freedom that will maintain existing inequalities or restore lost ones, so far as political action can do this', an objective that appeals to large numbers of citizens who, 'while not partaking in the benefits, recognize that inequalities exist and, in some obscure sense, assume that they ought to'.[38] That proposition closes the argumentative circle. Radicalism confuses the interests of the people with its own cultural prejudices. The cultural prejudices of traditional Toryism embrace the real interests of the people. Like the eighteenth-century notion of virtual representation, the people may not find that the Party faithfully reflects their diversity in its own composition but does, in its wisdom, take account of its diverse interests. The Tories, then, are always subject to the 'populist temptation' but only within that specific and circumscribed sense of the (naturally conservative) will of the people.[39] Unfortunately for the Party, the conservatism of the people is not necessarily translated into support for Conservatism. One 'should beware', Pugh noted, 'of assuming an immutable connection between deference and Conservatism'.[40] Certainly, to leave matters in the enchanted condition of popular Toryism would again be only one part of the story.

The other part is a disenchanted suspicion of popular intentions. If traditional Toryism should not be confused with libertarian thinking, neither should it be confused with populism. Though it does share some of the populist rhetoric common on the right, Toryism has been concerned to limit the impact of ideas like the popular will or popular sovereignty on the conduct of government. Populism, with its tendency to deny limit and constitutional constraint, has been thought to be just as subversive of good government as any other species of radicalism. Traditional Toryism's suspicion of political enthusiasm of all kinds makes it uncomfortable with the fickleness of popular opinion. In this light, the task of the Conservative Party has been to educate a democratic citizenry in the necessity of limiting collective power and of containing the effect of democracy. As Lord Salisbury candidly put it, for a Tory the best form of government in a democratic age is one where the masses have little power, and seem to have a great deal. Public sentimentalism is always threatening to subvert reasoned judgement and the decency of civilised life continues to be challenged by plebeian barbarism. If the political class cultivates the wrong sort of public culture then it undermines its own authority. 'If the political establishment decides the people can do without the Serjeant at Arms, hereditary peers, the Lord Chancellor, the Royal Ulster Constabulary, etc, it can hardly be surprised that, increasingly, the people seem inclined to the view that they can also do without the political establishment.'[41] In short, an idealised people coexists in the Tory imagination with very real fears of (to use another of Lord Salisbury's expressions) public disintegration. What reconciles these two very different perspectives is the notion of 'character' and it plays a substantial part in Tory self-understanding.

The notion of 'character' has suffered ridicule at the hands of those 'emancipated urban intellectuals' who, in return, have been the object of Tory ridicule. The association of 'character' with public school sadism or with the unquestioning stoicism that led soldiers to their death in the First World War has had a lasting political effect, even if some Tories could still put in a good word for Colonel Blimp, 'a far more faithful and reliant servant' to the country than 'the unstable and brittle intellectuals who derided him'.[42] The weakening of 'character' is thought to have coincided with the decline of those 'vigorous virtues' that so concerned the intellectual supporters of Mrs Thatcher.[43] Mrs Thatcher herself chose to call them 'Victorian values' and that alone was to condemn her social vision as a return to the morality of the workhouse. Like the Victorians, she did believe that weakness of character would lead to a dependency culture and encourage individuals in ever greater numbers to make claims on the state.[44] And in this opinion Mrs Thatcher was not at all alien to the Tory tradition, as her critics frequently claimed, and she could trace a distinguished lineage in the Party's history.[45] Not only did Mrs Thatcher believe that there was a natural Conservative majority. She also believed that there was a definite 'character' to the people that would be 'the basis of a non-socialist British political, social and economic order'.[46] At least she did believe that, if it were not much in evidence under Labour, this character could be rediscovered under Tory leadership.

The philosophy of that 'character' can be found in the work of Oakeshott. Indeed, Oakeshott can be read as the philosopher of the instinct to be 'let alone'. He understood contemporary political differences in terms of two distinctive character types. The first, an 'individual *manque'*, fears the challenges and responsibilities of individuality; the second, an independent soul, relishes those challenges and understands the world as an adventure. The first looks to the state to provide a kind of 'warm, compensated servility', in a 'therapeutic corporation' devoted to remedying their 'so-called alienation', a Utopia bristling 'with inspectors and overseers'. The second, having plans and projects of their own, want nothing more than to be let alone and look to the state to provide a stable, non-managerial set of rules that allows self-determined individuals to seek 'the satisfaction of their wants in self-chosen transactions with others of their kind'.[47] This was not a romantic celebration of the individual will or an invitation to solipsism, for the 'character' of Oakeshott's individual was revealed in the negotiation of 'the current of moral activity' and the knowledge 'of how to behave well which belongs to our way of living'.[48] His was not a character ill-disposed to make concessions to others or to find in experience only the reflection of his or her own desires. It was a character who had learnt to be at home in this commonplace world and knew the danger of the 'encounter of dreams'.[49] One of Oakeshott's sympathisers, Shirley Letwin, reworked these insights into an idea of 'conservative individualism'. The conservative individual wants the security that is not to be found in a constantly interfering government but 'can only be found in an order that rests on tradition and authority'. Such individuality does not mean being opinionated, the felt-need to have a view on everything (like the chattering classes). 'On the contrary, the more civilized men are, and the better they can appreciate their individuality, the readier they will be to recognize that they do not know and to defer to those who do.' This deference is to personal 'quality' not to the state as a 'moral manager'. This sort of individualism may not be exciting but 'we need not feel ashamed of enjoying a quiet independence'.[50] And it has been Shirley Letwin's son, Oliver, who has attempted to translate this into the practical politics of 'civilised Conservatism'. The traditional Tory connection of freedom and tradition, he proposes, enables society 'to make the journey into the modern with confidence and success'. This politics is thought to be popular because people will hear in its advocacy by the Conservative Party 'the echoes of the felt, the experienced, the familiar, the inherited, the cherished, the fundamental, the sound, the right and the British'.[51]

This celebration of character is only one part of Tory thinking. As we know, the enchanted idea calls forth the practice of a disenchanted politics. This disenchanted politics is concerned with law and order, social discipline and family values since they are necessary to the cultivation of self-reliance, honour and trust. People of good character need protection from those who would invade their quiet independence and their enjoyment of individuality. Criminals are one source of immediate threat but the prevailing concern has been with the alliance of individuals *manques* and ambitious politicians. People of good character will not be let alone but witness their schools undermined by 'progressive' education, their liberties constrained by bureaucratic interference and their taxes squandered by unaccountable government agencies. Tory fatalism often thinks that character has been so weakened by generations of social engineering that the conservative cement of society will no longer hold. This has produced 'the sort of people whose only skill is in getting something for nothing out of the state', a nation of 'selfish hedonistic pagans' who 'no longer possess recognisably conservative values'. Tory faith resides still, however, in the natural conservatism of the people, now defined as the 'ever-growing middle and upper working class' who own their own homes, have some shares, provide for their own pensions and want choice in public services. These are not individuals *manques* but Conservative individualists who love their country and despise the 'cultural nihilism' of the New Labour elite. Their 'love of liberty is not a love of weightless freedom' but of responsible independence. Here is the challenge for Tory leaders. 'If the Conservative Party cannot tell their story, there is no point to it.'[52] In response to the politics of character, the Party's opponents consciously cultivate the politics of another persona – 'sophisticated, upwardly mobile, multicultural, tolerant, urban' – with whom, it is claimed, the people of Britain 'consciously or subconsciously aspire'.[53] That characterisation of 'the people' has become the real terrain of contemporary political battles cannot be doubted. If traditional Toryism was good at telling a popular story it was the story of patriotism. Electorally, this proved to be a very profitable story for the Tories. It associated the Party with the very spirit of the country, with the proper governance of Britain and the competence of its political leadership with the security of the people. Unfortunately for Conservatives, some commentators have argued that by 1997 New Labour had stolen the Tories' patriotic clothes and left the Party without a story to tell.[54] This has provided the Party with another significant challenge.

Toryism and the nation

What distinguishes Tory patriotism is its belief in the exceptional character of British political experience. It was exceptional not only in the sense of being different but also in the sense of being uniquely virtuous. Though the heart and mind of this patriotism is British, its soul is English. This is not the familiar condition of blessed confusion between England and Britain so frequently observed in Conservative discourse. It is actually a *distinction* between what is English and what is British. One (Australian-born) commentator remarked that Toryism is a very specific and locally rooted view of politics, one so specific that it was difficult for outsiders to feel if not to understand.[55] One insider argued that the advantage of the name Tory over the title Conservative is that 'it is not a name for foreign imitation'. It indicated (despite being an *Irish* word) the Party's English origin and made clear that 'Toryism is not for export.'[56] And Utley was not being completely mischievous when he wrote that 'there are absolutely no authentically Conservative Scotsmen, Irishmen or genuine Welshmen'.[57] This suggests (to the rationalist in politics) the logical consequence of English nationalism and some have advocated it eloquently.[58] That sort of formal logic, however, has never been a characteristic of Tory patriotism and the leadership has been careful to repudiate it in favour of a larger British patriotism. For example, Mrs Thatcher in her stormy relationship with Scotland was compelled to admit that 'the Tories are seen as an English party' and that she herself was regarded 'as a quintessentially English figure'. While she was proud of the second point, she denied the first. 'The Tory Party is not, of course, an English party but a Unionist one.' England, because of its population, just happened to be the prominent partner in the Union. If the Scots wanted special treatment they would have to persuade the rest of the United Kingdom, particularly the English, of its merits. 'It was understandable', conceded Mrs Thatcher, 'that when I come out with these kind of hard truths many Scots should resent it' but that had nothing to do with her Englishness. It was just a fact of British political life.[59]

Englishness and Britishness was reconciled in Toryism by an imaginative extension of constitutional blessings. The secret of England's greatness is – as it is often inscribed on Orange Order banners – its Parliament, its Monarchy and its defence of the Protestant faith, and became part of a common British inheritance. Those who subscribed to that view, according to Geoffrey Elton, thought that English history (and by extension British history) 'most convincingly demonstrated how man should order his existence on earth'. Elton called this the 'Froude complex', a belief that England was somehow peculiarly blessed in God's creation.[60] This was an attitude that irritated outsiders. In 1953, for example, Eric Voegelin commented that most Oxford political philosophers assumed that 'the principles of right political order have become historical flesh more perfectly in England than elsewhere at any time'. Happy the political philosopher, then, who finds that these principles are 'identical with those of his own civilisation'.[61] Voegelin's view was shared by intellectuals contemptuous of this English parochialism, a tradition that generally preferred, as Disraeli once said, government by Parliament rather than by logic, intellectuals who ought to have known that political stability is to be preferred to philosophical excitement.[62] Such patriotic complacency was, in this case, relatively innocent but Toryism also had its nasty and racist aspects. Again it has often been the case that what 'is not articulate is by far the best and most enduring' since most of the rest is rather banal. Nonetheless, sophisticated exponents generally avoided these traps and, while drawing sympathetically on a wide philosophical inheritance, remained in no doubt about the unique value of the country's constitutional tradition. Oakeshott, for one, stated the case concisely. He argued that 'British democracy is not an abstract idea but a way of living and a manner of politics which first began to emerge in the Middle Ages.' In that era 'almost the whole outline of this way of life and manner of politics was adumbrated, an outline which has since been enlarged by experience and invention and defended against attack from without and treason from within'. It was 'not the gift of nature but the product of our own experience and inventiveness'. British liberty, guaranteed by law, represented a method of social integration, 'the most civilized and the most effective method ever invented by mankind'.[63] That was Tory patriotism in all its self-esteem and the contrast with European experience appeared to confirm it. This method of social integration translated the English political tradition into a British one in order to secure the multinational integration of the United Kingdom. The appeal of this social and multinational integration relied in good measure upon the relatively stable identity which (Tory) England gave to Britain.[64] It is the Britishness of England and the Englishness of Britain that makes the Tory nation.

Tory patriotism has the power to enchant and, when it is poetically phrased, can be emotionally intoxicating. It is this patriotic story, rather than yet another 'big idea', that distinguishes for traditional Tories the real substance of Conservative politics. Enoch Powell was able to express the enchantment, the poetry and the emotional intoxication of this Tory patriotism in his famous Royal Society of St George speech in 1961. Powell traced England's patriotism from its soil to the laws, disciplines and freedoms emanating from 'a thing called "Parliament"' that dispensed the same justice to all the people of England. What one finds, he claimed, is that 'the continuity of her existence was unbroken when the looser connections which had linked her with distant continents and strange races fell away'. Patriots today 'at the heart of a vanished empire, amid the fragments of demolished glory, seem to find, like one of her own oak trees, standing and growing, the sap still rising from her ancient roots to meet the spring, England herself'. The English could now recognise more clearly than before 'the homogeneity of England', one brought about 'by the slow alchemy of centuries'.[65] Powell was a complicated man and his patriotism was equally complicated. He was telling his audience that what had been taken to represent 'England's glory' – the Empire – had now gone and that a whole tradition of sentimental education should be abandoned. He was also inviting his audience to keep faith with the national spirit which was British as much as it was English. There was also that distinctively Tory melancholy of anticipation. The idea of Britain as a great power – even though he knew it was not so – would not die for him 'until I, the carrier of it, am actually dead'.[66] That elegiac note is just as characteristic of Tory patriotism as national bombast.

Powell's enchantment was not the only one on offer. However, it did, in suggesting a way to resolve Conservative anxieties about the nation, identify the big questions that haunt the patriotic Tory. The questions are these. What if those institutions that served Britain so well have become disenchanted? What if those institutions are prepared to alienate the alchemy of centuries, estrange themselves from the people and confound the homogeneity of the country? What if that most civilised and the most effective method of governance has itself undermined British civilisation? The disillusion implied in these sorts of questions presents a serious challenge for traditional Toryism since the very thing that it desires to conserve can appear to be no longer capable of conservation. This is a condition of disenchantment in which all the old Tory pieties appear to be mocked by experience. Roger Scruton has written recently of a 'disenchanted' England which the people no longer believe to be theirs. This England was once understood in terms of 'the physiognomy, the habits, the institutions, the religion and the culture' of a very distinctive way of life. 'Almost all have died.' This way of life depended on 'England being somewhere and a home' but that 'somewhere' and that 'home' have been slowly dismantled. Interestingly, Scruton brings together all the elements of traditional Toryism because he relates this disenchantment to the weakening of the ideal of character. When 'people discard, ignore or mock the ideals which formed their character,' he thinks, 'they no longer exist as a people, but only as a crowd'.[67] This disenchantment within is complemented by subjection from without by the rules of the European Union and 'this political disenfranchisement is also a disenchantment of their country'.[68] The disenchantment is all the more powerful since the enchantment of the patriotic story continues to be so strong.

And who has been responsible for this disenchantment? The simplest partisan target, of course, is New Labour which could do nothing else but betray Mrs Thatcher's reassertion of the key elements of Tory patriotism: the uniqueness of parliamentary sovereignty and Britain's distinctiveness in Europe. In Heffer's view, the Blair Government is 'probably the most anti-British and certainly the most anti-English in history' and, with devolution of powers to Scotland, Wales and Northern Ireland and its insidious policy of English regionalism, it has shown itself to be a dangerous constitutional vandal. The ancient institutions that Tories revered, that the English invented and that the British together worked so well in the past have been 'wrecked in the interests of political expediency and democracy has been perverted'.[69] New Labour also stands accused of seeking to abolish British sovereignty for good by its willingness to accept a constitution for Europe that must entail 'the greatest alteration in the rights and powers of government in this country since 1688'.[70] This European constitution will delegitimise democratic institutions by frustrating their ability to act in the national interest. One finds in this critique strong echoes of Edmund Burke's hostility to the 'rational despotism' of the French revolutionaries.

The larger view believes there has been an insidious victory by what Elton (in contrast to the Froude complex) called the 'New Statesman complex', a view that assumes everything is for the worst in Britain. Some have identified an inverted patriotism in which 'the majority of modern commentators on the constitution appear to assume as a matter of course that foreigners generally do it better than we do, especially if they are our partners in the European Union'.[71] To describe the contemporary version of this tradition, Scruton has invented the term 'oikophobia'. The loyalty that the British people needs to find reflected in the reporting of public life 'is constantly ridiculed or even demonised by the dominant media and educational system'. Oikophobia is the repudiation of inheritance and home and it has found its niche in state institutions that offer the oikophobes 'the power base from which to attack the simple loyalties of ordinary people'. The consequences have been assaults on national values and the constitution, the weakening of traditional institutions, the promotion of subsidised immigration and the propagation of rule from Brussels.[72] The disenchanted visions of both Heffer and Scruton demand a correspondingly disenchanted style of Tory politics with tough policies on immigration, Europe and Britain's international obligations.

However, a more insidious answer to the question may be found within the Conservative Party itself rather than outside it. Those opposed to further European integration believe that the defence of representative government, accountable to the British people, is what Tory patriotism is all about. It *is* the popular story that will deliver electoral success and there is frustration at the caution and reserve of the leadership in acknowledging its truth. The suspicion lurks that Europe is another example of Tory men and Whig measures and that, despite all the rhetoric of patriotism, the Party's leadership will eventually funk the challenge. As one of Mrs Thatcher's former advisers put it, 'the pillars of Conservatism, English-Britishness, the Protestant Religion and the limited State have gone, to be replaced by the deracinated cornucopia State'. Powers have been passed to Brussels by Conservative Governments in the past and will continue to be ceded in the future. The 'national' Party has been reduced to debating 'how far they dare allow the process to proceed, not how to reverse it'.[73] And as Bulpitt alleged, the 'turn' towards Europe has had a lot to do with the political elite's lack of confidence in the British political system. As a consequence of political weakness rather than a deliberate intention to betray, he thought that 'future resistance to Euro-Union amongst both Conservative MPs and leaders will be minimal'.[74] In this instance, hard-nosed Tory realism that rejects all sorts of pious humbug is married to that familiar fatalism which expects betrayal and loss. In thinking so, it is not too distant from public opinion in general which also tends to think – whether it approves or not – that there is an inevitability to the process of European integration which is beyond its power to control. Traditional Tories would not expect or accept that their own Party should facilitate 'ever closer union' for, like Lord George Bentinck's sentiment at the repeal of the Corn Laws, this would mean 'being sold'. This would be a contemptible fate. Better, even if expecting defeat, to fight for victory.

Conclusion

Traditional Toryism has often appeared to be either something of an affectation or something marginal to the march of history. In one recent understanding, the advancing 'forces of modernisation' were conducting a comprehensive rout of the retreating 'forces of conservatism'. Insofar as we have lost faith in the 'grand narratives' of the last two centuries – like socialism – and insofar as we are now all supposed to be postmodern then the Tory disposition no longer appears so outlandish. Since Conservatism never subscribed to the grosser forms of the modernist faith then its failings come as no surprise to it and Tories can take some satisfaction in the fact that the deluge let them alone and swept away many of the mantras of their ideological foes. 'We should all become conservatives now' argued Anthony Giddens.[75] Giddens did not imply by this declaration a subscription to Tory limits. He was merely proposing that useful bits of Conservative thought could be abstracted to help shape a radical political programme. Tory themes would now be put to work in the design of a new social democracy, one that would destroy traditional Toryism. And here is potentially the irony of recent British history. If the twentieth century was Europe's age of 'armed doctrines', or as Eric Hobsbawm called it, the 'age of extremes', then Britain's twentieth century was, by contrast, the 'Conservative century'.[76] In a twenty-first-century Europe that could become a chastened age of conservatism, then in Britain it could become the 'Labour century'. That has been the Blair objective, it has been temporarily successful and it continues to trouble Tory fatalists.

That prospect is not entirely without its attraction to those who do not associate a conservative disposition with the politics of the Conservative Party or for whom traditional Toryism is a taste that they could never acquire. Yet they also know deep in their hearts that whatever limitations circumstances may place upon radicalism in politics, New Labour has no intention of letting them alone. That desire to be let alone remains the key to understanding Toryism and it is also the key to how Conservatives can formulate an intelligent response to their opponents. Their response would acknowledge the character of contemporary individualism and locate it within a modest, if self-confident, patriotism. If the Conservative Party must subscribe to any faith, it should be the faith that it alone can properly translate the needs of individuals and of the country into a popular set of public policies.

Notes

1. Cited in P. Bew, *Ideology and the Irish Question* (Oxford: Clarendon Press, 1994), p.7.
2. H. Cecil, *Conservatism* (London: Home University Library, 1912), p.10.
3. Lord Hailsham, *The Conservative Case* (Harmondsworth: Penguin, 1959), pp.15–16.
4. P. Smith (ed.), *Lord Salisbury on Politics* (Cambridge: Cambridge University Press, 1972), p.92.
5. T. Fuller, 'The Poetics of the Civil Life', in J. Norman (ed.), *The Achievement of Michael Oakeshott* (London: Duckworth, 1993), pp.67–81.
6. M. Oakeshott, *Rationalism in Politics and Other Essays* (Indianapolis: Liberty Press, 1991), p.415.
7. R. Scruton, *The Meaning of Conservatism* (Harmondsworth: Penguin, 1991), p.191.
8. A. Maude, 'Scepticism and faith', *The Spectator*, 22 March 1963.

9. Cited in A. Roberts, *Salisbury: Victorian Titan* (London: Weidenfeld and Nicolson, 1999), p.2.
10. G. Carsaniga, *Giacomo Leopardi: The Unheeded Voice* (Edinburgh: Edinburgh University Press, 1977), p.43.
11. See, for example, P. Worsthorne, *In Defence of Aristocracy* (London: HarperCollins, 2004).
12. A. Giddens, *Beyond Left and Right* (London: Polity Press, 1994), pp.80–7.
13. A.J.P. Taylor, *Essays in English History* (London: Book Club Associates/Hamish Hamilton, 1977), p.128.
14. A. Schopenhauer, *Studies in Pessimism: A Series of Essays*, trans T. Bailey Saunders (London: Swan Sonnenschein and Company, 1892), p.138.
15. E. Kedourie, *The Crossman Confessions and Other Essays in Politics, History and Religion* (London: Mansell, 1984), p.46.
16. J. Daley, 'Tories must defeat their defeatism', *Daily Telegraph*, 6 October 2004.
17. R. Blake, *The Conservative Party from Peel to Major* (London: Arrow Books, 1998), p.411.
18. B. Coleman, *Conservatism and the Conservative Party in Nineteenth Century Britain* (London: Edward Arnold, 1988), p.206.
19. See K. Minogue, 'Introduction: On Conservative Realism', in K. Minogue (ed.), *Conservative Realism: New Essays on Conservatism* (London: HarperCollins, 1996).
20. M. Fforde, *Conservatism and Collectivism 1886–1914* (Edinburgh: Edinburgh University Press, 1990).
21. Saccone, E. 'Nobility and Literature. Questions in Tomasi di Lampedusa', *MLN*, 106: (1991), pp.159–78, p.169.
22. Fforde, *Conservatism and Collectivism 1886–1914*, p.43.
23. Ibid., p.165.
24. Lord Coleraine, *For Conservative Only* (London: Tom Stacey, 1970), p.63.
25. C. Moore and S. Heffer (eds), *A Tory Seer. The Selected Journalism of T.E. Utley* (London: Hamish Hamilton, 1989), pp.73–4, 88.
26. Fforde, *Conservatism and Collectivism 1886–1914*, p.166.
27. B. Jessop, *Traditionalism, Conservatism and British Political Culture* (London: George Allen and Unwin, 1974), pp.76–7.
28. R.W. Johnson, *The Politics of Recession* (London: Macmillan, 1985), pp.234–5.
29. J. Bulpitt, 'The Conservative Party in Britain: A Preliminary Paradoxical Portrait', paper presented to the PSA annual conference, Lancaster, 1991, p.7.
30. G. Schopflin, *Nations, Identity, Power: The New Politics of Europe* (London: Hurst, 2000), p.30.
31. Coleman, *Conservatism and the Conservative Party in Nineteenth Century Britain*, p.3.
32. Taylor, *Essays in English History*, p.21.
33. Blake, *The Conservative Party from Peel to Major*, p.416.
34. T. King, 'Can Howard rally his party and steer it out of the doldrums?', *Daily Telegraph*, 4 October 2004.
35. R. Scruton, *England: An Elegy* (London: Chatto and Windus, 2000), pp.149–58.
36. Minogue, 'Introduction: On Conservative Realism', p.4.

37. R. Scruton, *The Meaning of Conservatism* (Harmondsworth: Penguin, 1986, 2nd edition), p.44.
38. M. Cowling, 'The Present Position', in M. Cowling (ed.), *Conservative Essays* (London: Cassell, 1978), pp.9–10.
39. G. Peele, 'The Character of Modern British Conservatism', in Z. Layton-Henry (ed.), *Conservative Politics in Western Europe* (London: Macmillan, 1982), p.44.
40. M. Pugh, 'Popular Conservatism in Britain: Continuity and Change, 1880–1987', *Journal of British Studies*, 27:2 (1988), pp.254–82, p.272.
41. M. Steyn, 'It's dangerous to get rid of men in tights', *Daily Telegraph*, 21 September 2004.
42. A. Bryant, 'In Defence of Colonel Blimp', *Illustrated London News*, 23 June 1951, in M. Bryant (ed.), *The Complete Colonel Blimp* (London: Bellew Publishing, 1951).
43. S. Letwin, *The Anatomy of Thatcherism* (London: Fontana, 1992).
44. See S. Collini, 'The Idea of Character in Victorian Political Thought', *Transactions of the Royal Historical Society*, 5th Series (1985), pp.29–50.
45. W.S. Rodner, 'Conservatism, Resistance and Lord Hugh Cecil', *History of Political Thought*, IX:3 (1988), pp.529–51.
46. R. Harris, 'Tories at war – still', *Prospect*, September 2004.
47. M. Oakeshott, *On Human Conduct* (Oxford: Clarendon Press, 1991), pp.185–326.
48. Ibid., p.130.
49. Ibid., pp.436–7.
50. S. Letwin, 'On Conservative Individualism', in Cowling, *Conservative Essays*, pp.67–8.
51. O. Letwin, 'Time the Tories came home', *The Spectator*, 19 June 1999, pp.18–19.
52. C. Moore, 'There's no point in voting Labour now, but can the Tories cash in?', *Daily Telegraph*, 2 October 2004.
53. R. Liddle, 'The Tories are at rock bottom – and falling', *Sunday Times*, 3 October 2004.
54. P. Lynch, *The Politics of Nationhood: Sovereignty, Britishness and Conservative Politics* (London: Macmillan, 1999), p.66.
55. Minogue, 'Introduction: On Conservative Realism', pp.5–6.
56. J. Biggs-Davison, *Tory Lives* (London: Putnam and Company, 1952), p.5.
57. Moore and Heffer, *A Tory Seer*, p.76.
58. S. Heffer, *Like the Roman: The Life of Enoch Powell* (London: Phoenix, 1999).
59. Oakeshott, *On Human Conduct*, p.624.
60. G. Elton, *Return to Essentials: Some Reflections on the Present State of Historical Study* (Cambridge: Cambridge University Press, 1991), pp.110–11.
61. Cited in N. O'Sullivan, *European Political Thought since 1945* (Basingstoke: Palgrave, 2004), p.21.
62. See, for example, the attitude of Canetti recorded in P. Conradi, *Iris Murdoch: A Life* (London: HarperCollins, 2002), p.324.
63. M. Oakeshott, 'Contemporary British Politics', *Cambridge Journal* (1947–48), pp.474–90.
64. J. Stapleton, 'Englishness, Britishness and Patriotism in Recent Political Thought and Historiography', *British Journal of Politics and International Relations*, 1:1 (1999), pp.119–30.
65. Cited in Heffer, *Like the Roman*, pp.334–40.

66. E. Powell, 'Commentary', in B. Brivati and H. Jones (eds), *What Difference Did the War Make?* (London: Leicester University Press, 1995), pp.14–16, p.15.
67. Scruton, *England: An Elegy*, p.67.
68. Ibid., pp.244–57.
69. S. Heffer, *Nor Shall My Sword* (London: Phoenix, 2002), p.15.
70. N. Malcolm, 'A federal constitution with the heart of a manifesto', *Daily Telegraph*, 28 July 2003.
71. N. Johnson, 'Then and Now: the British Constitution', *Political Studies*, 48:1 (2000) pp.118–31, p.127.
72. R. Scruton, *The Need for Nations* (London: Civitas, 2004), pp.36–7.
73. A. Sherman, 'A Coincidental Resemblance: Conservatism and the Conservative Party', *The Salisbury Review*, Winter 2000, p.20.
74. J. Bulpitt, 'Conservative Leaders and the "Euro-ratchet": Five does of Scepticism', *Political Quarterly*, 63:3 (1992), pp.258–75, p.267.
75. Giddens, *Beyond Left and Right*, p.49.
76. E. Hobsbawm, *The Age of Extremes: The Short Twentieth Century 1914–1991* (London: Abacus, 1995) and A. Seldon and S. Ball (eds), *The Conservative Century: The Conservative Party since 1900* (Oxford: Oxford University Press, 1994).

2
New Right
Norman Barry

Undoubtedly the many changes that conservatism in Britain has undergone since 1945 culminates in the preponderance of 'classical liberal' or New Right thinking, despite significant hostility to it. Of course, the long reign of Margaret Thatcher as Prime Minister, in which some of the main features of that paradigm were implemented, and adherents of the post-war collectivist consensus were gradually removed from leadership roles in the Party and lost influence as opinion leaders, was decisive. But that success represented a change in thinking widespread in the West. Indeed, the collapse of communism from 1989 was presaged by significant alterations in the public mood and official policy stances of even mildly collectivist governments. In this the Thatcherite Conservatives can take much credit for pioneering some ideas, especially privatisation and the attempt to reduce the size of government, which became the prevailing features of modern conservatism wherever it is found. Equally significant is the fact that even socialists have significantly modified their collectivism and admitted certain features of classical liberalism into their doctrine. The true ancestor of modern conservatism might be the great nineteenth-century liberal, and man of principle, William Gladstone, rather than his rival, the deliberately non-ideological and unprincipled Benjamin Disraeli.

Regardless of its rhetoric, New Labour under Tony Blair has retained many of the innovations of Thatcher's regime: conservatism may not have prevailed but the market certainly has. The older, pragmatic Conservatives might well say that the changes were a necessary response to the perilous state Britain was in prior to Thatcher's electoral victory in 1979 rather than redolent of a new philosophical adventure. Did not the much revered eighteenth-century thinker Edmund Burke once say that 'a state without the means of change is without the means of its preservation'? But this response involves two mistakes. Firstly, it underestimates the intellectual significance of the Thatcher 'revolution' and the departures it made from post-war orthodoxy. And secondly, it elides the fact that Burke was not in any way moderate about the market but was a committed follower of Adam Smith's economics.[1] His traditionalism was not reactionary but a spirited opposition to political events, notably the French Revolution. Free market economic liberals have a greater claim to be part of the pantheon of conservative *traditionalists* than those tame adherents, such as Edward Heath, of the post-war consensus. The latter accepted meekly the degree of state intervention introduced by the 1945–51 Labour Government and its ruinous extension between 1974 and 1979. The Thatcher era was not some kind of aberration, it saw the adoption of an agenda consistent with tradition.

Nevertheless, at the philosophical and practical levels some conservatives have clung to a previous, mistaken approach and have persistently claimed that this represented a more accurate form of conservatism and that the advent of classical liberal thinking with its new emphasis on the market, capitalism and individualism was simply a form of rationalism and ideology to which traditional conservatism had been resolutely opposed. Conservatives were always non-doctrinaire, pragmatic and capable of adjusting to the exigencies of the moment. It is the task of a writer on post-war Conservative thought to elucidate exactly where the New Right fits into traditional conservatism.

Main elements in Conservative thinking

A distinction might be made between two sorts of conservatism – *dispositional* and *substantive*.[2] The former refers to an attitude towards the past that demands its preservation at all costs and a resistance to anything that might upset it. It trades on a traditional conservative fear of the unknown and distrust of innovation. The past must be preserved no matter how bad it might be. It is the kind of disposition that characterised a hardline communist who resisted economic change even though his own world was visibly falling apart or an Islamic fundamentalist who is prepared to tolerate immense human suffering in order to preserve what he believes to be the truth. There are some very mild versions of this attitude in those Conservatives who resisted Thatcher's reforms in the 1980s and clung desperately to an already discredited consensus. But even Thatcher herself evinced elements of this attitude. Notice her repeated statement that the National Health Service was safe in Conservative hands when all her economic and social values suggested that it required radical reform, if not abolition.

A substantive conservative has a reverence for the past but it is not a blind, unthinking commitment. He distils from history certain institutions and policies which have proved their value in a utilitarian sense and can be elaborated and made serviceable for the future. This conservative certainly does not make a god of reason, or is under the illusion that a society can be reshaped according to its dictates, but is prepared to make analyses of the successes or failings of institutions and policies according to rational argument. Those conservatives who were attracted to market economics were of the substantive type for their understanding of economics convinced them of the *limitations* of those consensus policies that go against the grain of human nature. A substantive conservative would endorse the liberal economist Lionel Robbins' account of his own subject: it is concerned with the 'necessities to which human action is subject'. Thus you cannot have an egalitarian wage policy and preserve liberty and efficiency; if money is printed in excess of productivity inflation will result and if you do not pay the factors of production their marginal products a misallocation of resources will occur. The Thatcher revolution amounted to the ruthless application of these truths even if recent tradition indicated otherwise.

It is therefore a little misleading for Anthony Quinton to say that 'conservatism does not depend on a substantive theory about universal human nature issuing universal political principles, such as the lists of the rights of man'.[3] It is the case that the substantive conservatives object strongly to dogmas about human rights but this does not mean that they reject all universal principles as guides to action. Like many traditionalists they take a pessimistic view of human nature. It is just that the New Right conservatives maintain that human greed and selfishness are moderated by market principles subject to the rule of law. A more accurate rendition of conservatism is better captured by Noel O'Sullivan's comment that conservatism 'is just as capable of being defended in the light of a philosophical view of the nature of man, of society and of the world as a liberal or socialist one'.[4] Thus elements of classical liberalism began to be articulated by conservative thinkers in the twentieth century when the demise of the Liberal Party left them with a more formidable enemy – socialism. Elements of the doctrine of the market, capitalism and private property had always been present in conservative thought but earlier there had been little need to theorise them. And conservatives often got economics completely wrong. A spectacular example was the defence of the landed interest. There had always been a conservative predisposition to value land over commercial wealth and this reached its apogee with the Corn Laws in the nineteenth century. But it was a conservative, Robert Peel, the first genuine 'moderniser', who got rid of this economic absurdity in 1846. It was indeed the partial freeing of conservatives from their association with the land that allowed it to absorb the market almost painlessly. The Corn Laws merely advanced the self-interest of landowners.

A traditional conservative casualty in the rise of the New Right was the belief in the 'organic society'. Traditionalists had always maintained that society is a myriad of informal habits, rules and practices which cannot be reduced to contract. Individuals had an obligation to society and the state which cannot not be reduced to a utilitarian calculus. While this organicism has not been entirely eliminated from conservative thought – even some New Right thinkers sometimes prudently preserve its metaphorical advantages – it certainly suffered from the penetration of society by market relationships in the 1980s. Indeed, Mrs Thatcher gave some credence to this with her controversial claim that there is 'no such thing as society'.

From philosophy to politics

The two most important conservative political philosophers after 1945 were Michael Oakeshott (1901–1990) and Roger Scruton, and although like most conservative theorists they both disdain any direct application of their ideas to actual politics, they reveal implications of how Conservative Government ought to be conducted. In Oakeshott in particular there are certain ideas that are directly related to the New Right. Scruton's conservatism deliberately distances itself from free market economics but there are hints that some connections might be made.

Oakeshott is a product of Cambridge but he spent much of his professional life as Professor of Political Science at the London School of Economics where he was surrounded by left-wingers (though between the wars the economics department there provided the main opposition to Keynesian interventionist ideas). His unpopularity never deterred him from articulating a strong conservative case. Amongst his myriad of philosophical works two books are important for politics, *Rationalism in Politics*[5] and *On Human Conduct*.[6] The former is, superficially, an unpromising book for New Right politics. Its elimination of 'reason' from political argument and his distrust of any kind of abstract theorising would seem to preclude the kind of critical thinking that New Right spokesmen regularly do today. His suggestion that political theorising should be restricted to the 'pursuit of intimations'[7] within a given political tradition could be disabling for anyone intent on subjecting collectivism to a rigorous critique. In the volume Oakeshott condemned Friedrich von Hayek's *The Road to Serfdom*, which had already become the bible of some conservative economic thinking, as another exercise in rationalism: 'A plan to beat all planning may be better than its opposite but it belongs to the same style of politics.'[8] But to dismiss Oakeshott from the New Right category is too abrupt a verdict. Oakeshott had already written some sprightly popular essays in criticism of the post-war Attlee Government, with its extended welfare state and pledge to capture the 'commanding heights of the economy'. Also, in *Rationalism in Politics* there is an extended review[9] of a book by the Chicago free market economist, Henry Simons, in which Oakeshott expressed a clear preference for free market capitalism. One feels that at the time Oakeshott hadn't worked out a social theory in which a justification for the market and limited government could be cogently expressed in conservative terms.

This came with *On Human Conduct* which, despite its philosophical obscurity, is a theoretical framework for New Right ideas on the need for markets and a minimal state. Here Oakeshott makes an important distinction between a *civil association* and the *enterprise state*. The former is a loose collection of individuals who do not have a common purpose but pursue their private goals within the context of adverbial rules. The latter do not tell us what to do but provide us with guidelines for the pursuit of whatever it is that we want to do. An enterprise state, however, aims at the realisation of communal goals and individual interests and private property are subordinated to that ambition. Law operates through a series of commands in which individual goals are suffocated by the demands of a 'national plan'. It is not just economic planning that is condemned by Oakeshott's reasoning but milder versions of social democracy, such as the welfare state. Indeed, he once described the National Health Service as a harbinger of totalitarianism. Oakeshott sees European history as a conflict between these two rival conceptions of social order.

Although Scruton regards socialism as the great menace of our times, his critique owes almost nothing to the free market, limited state tradition associated with the New Right. Indeed, some of the communitarian aspects of socialism might have a limited appeal to him. In his book, *The Meaning of Conservatism*,[10] which he describes as a work of 'cultural dogmatics', Scruton declares early on that his principal enemy is liberalism 'with all its attendant trappings of individual autonomy and the rights of man'.[11] Scruton does not make a distinction between classical liberalism, which is concerned with the market, property and the limited state, and contemporary liberalism, especially the American variety, which has little interest in economics (except redistribution from the rich to the poor) but protects only civil liberties: he would regard both liberalisms as connected in that they emanate from similar philosophical roots, namely individualism and freedom.

For Scruton, unlike the New Right, freedom must be subordinate to something else – authority and the preservation of a social order based on a kind of natural hierarchy. And it is an arrangement that transcends the contractual basis of some New Right thinking. And Scruton's dogmatics envisage a bigger role for the state than the New Right. Whereas that school of thought, following Hayek,[12] sees a constitution as a set of formalised constraints on government, Scruton does not stress this. A constitution for him is not a book of rules but a transcendent source of authority that validates those necessary actions of the state that are revealed by history and tradition. Whereas classical liberals and New Right theorists restrict it to the production of those goods which, for technical reasons, cannot be supplied by the market,[13] for Scruton the role of the state cannot be merely a mechanical device. It is a source of authority and fulfils man's need to be governed.

There is very little of the individualism of the New Right here and reverence for capitalism and the market. Indeed, rather like some historical conservatives, Scruton openly asserts that there is no identity between capitalism and conservatism. There is an economic role for the state and no conservative can let individuals be subject to the vagaries and whims of an unregulated market, and 'without the state's surveillance, destitution and unemployment could result at any time'.[14] There is certainly no theoretical objection to Keynesianism and Scruton claims that when the Conservative Party, under Margaret Thatcher, 'abandoned the conception of the state's economic role, and took up the banner of liberal economics it was deserted by the electorate ...'.[15]

But nevertheless there are some explicit suggestions in Scruton which resonate with classical liberals. He is angered by the 1968 Rent Act[16] which prevented owners charging a market rent for letting their property: a clear breach of property and a serious attenuation of the common law right to contract. His attack on social justice[17] which necessitates forced redistribution from the wealthy to the deprived (the state does not itself own anything) is quite consistent with anything said by Hayek.[18] Scruton contrasts social justice with 'natural justice' or the rules of fairness which emerge from common law. However, the welfare state is a 'social and political necessity'.

But welfare must not go too far and it must be distinguished from egalitarianism. Yet he never indicates how far; presumably that is a matter of wise judgement informed by history. He is not prepared to do the careful analysis of welfare policy[19] that has characterised the New Right in Britain and the United States. To do that kind of work would be to surrender to liberalism and its rationalistic social science. Yet whatever success Conservatism had in the 1980s was due to the fact that it could counter the left with superior analysis and accurately costed recommendations. Cleverness beat wisdom. Oakeshott did not do that analysis either but his distinction between the enterprise state and the civil association is a theoretical framework from which such work might begin.

Background to the rise of the New Right

The emergence of the New Right to a prominent position in the Conservative Party was not originally an ideological conversion but more a response to events. The taste for theorising among Conservatives tends to come after stark political facts have compelled a rethinking of ideas. Although there have always been free marketers in the Conservative Party, they did not come into prominence until the depredations of even a mild form of socialism became too obvious to ignore. There has also been that paternalist tradition in conservatism which has placed a duty on government to relieve suffering. And Disraeli's plea for 'One Nation' Toryism, unprincipled though it was, has always had a resonance among Conservatives. But the truth is that in the nineteenth century, Conservatives did not have to theorise much about economics because socialism was not an immediate threat. Also, they did not have to think too much about the unintended consequences of state intervention, a favourite New Right concern, since the interventions were usually too small to threaten the viability of capitalism. Any serious market thinking was done by Liberals but with the replacement of them by Labour, with an uncompromising socialist agenda, partially implemented in 1945–51, pro-capitalist thinking was forced on them.

One important fact that made it difficult for classical liberalism and pro-market thinking to get a foothold in the Conservative Party was that the latter had been involved in the post-war 'settlement' of 1945–51 and was anxious to accept some of the rearrangements Labour had introduced. The Great Depression had a serious impact on all Western countries and led to doubts about the viability of capitalism. Mass unemployment was bound to lead to the demand for planning and the indignity of means testing for meagre benefits was certain to produce a demand for a comprehensive welfare state. Of course, Conservatives did not want socialism but they thought that minor inoculations of collectivism would prevent a major outbreak of the socialist disease. As New Right thinkers were to point out much later, these minor inoculations were themselves responsible for a significant move to wholesale collectivism. And some Conservatives, Churchill included, were very much influenced by Hayek's *The Road to Serfdom.*

The book that had great influence on Conservative thinking throughout much of the twentieth century was Harold Macmillan's *The Middle Way,* first published in 1938.[20] Though supposedly an attempt to save capitalism from itself and to fend off socialism, it is predicated on the assumption that the free market is a combination of misery and inefficiency. To replace the anarchy of the market a plethora of planning boards and economic strategies are proposed, all of which are designed to overcome the problem that the market is not self-correcting but requires constant government attention. There is no evidence that Macmillan ever departed from these views even when he became Prime Minister in 1957: hence his desire to placate labour unions in any industrial dispute. It was this attitude that led to the delusion among members of the National Union of Mineworkers that they were immune from economic laws. Indeed, that was a feature of the consensus period; the belief that political leaders were free to pick and choose policies as if certain adverse consequences were not predictable.

Given the economic legacy of the 1930s it is not surprising that welfare reform should be top of most politicians' agendas and Conservatives were heavily involved in the Beveridge Report of 1942[21] which envisaged a comprehensive post-war welfare state in which almost everybody would be insured against the contingencies of life such as unemployment and sickness. The more economically inclined Conservatives could accept Beveridge *in principle* since it would be self-financing and workers would be entitled to their benefits through a lifetime's contribution. Only a small part of it, National Assistance, was to be unfunded. Only a minority of Conservatives were aware of the fact that national insurance never works out as intended and the bulk of expenditure ends up as pure 'welfare', that is, not funded by contributions but by tax. It became therefore heavily means tested and subject to the usual problems of that system, notably the discouragement to save. Also the ambitious National Health Service with its promise to provide treatment 'free at the point of consumption' was not financed by insurance but by tax and this led to serious underfunding, certainly in comparison to France and Germany where health is financed by social insurance and delivered by competing suppliers. Apart from the small minority who pay for private insurance, the health care system in Britain is completely in the hands of a monopolist, the National Health Service.

But these problems were to emerge much later, perhaps not completely until the 1970s. At the time the above measures were passed the Conservatives were complicit in a national consensus. The Labour Party, in or out of office, promised not to do any more serious nationalisation and the Conservatives agreed that they wouldn't privatise things essential to national well-being. Only steel remained controversial and it passed in and out of public ownership. There was a consensus on macroeconomic policy, that full employment had to be preserved at any cost. The economic policies of both parties were called 'Butskellism', a neologism constructed from the names of Rab Butler, the Conservative Chancellor, and Hugh Gaitskell, the Labour leader in the 1950s.[22] Keynesian economics, which required an active role for the state in economic management, had clearly captured the Conservative Party.

But the 1950s was a curious decade for Conservatives. It began with a revulsion against the wilder planning experiences of the Attlee Government. Some Conservatives felt that the experiment of socialism had produced inefficiency and a loss of personal liberty. Most were influenced by the aforementioned Hayek with his fears of a 'road to serfdom' effect from planning, but the philosopher Karl Popper's book, *The Open Society and its Enemies*[23] was securing increasing support from thinking Conservatives. As a result, in the parliamentary party a new group of MPs interested in freedom became significant. This was the One Nation group which, despite its Disraelian name, produced a stream of pamphlets which argued the case for free markets within the prevailing consensus.[24] They argued for less centralised control and more liberty for individuals to take decisions.

They were also interested in social policy and while they did not challenge the post-war welfare settlement, they did question indiscriminate welfare spending in a pamphlet called *One Nation*, published in 1950. They thought it would have a detrimental effect on the economy in that much-needed money for industrial development would go on welfare. They questioned whether too much welfare spending would increase the autonomy of individuals: it would more likely make them wards of the state. There were many debates in the Conservative Party between 1950 and 1957 which presaged the controversy between 'wets' and 'drys' in the 1980s. In the 1950s the drys wanted a strict economic policy which would cut out waste and reduce the size of government. The wets were much more relaxed, just as in the 1980s. However, a boost was given to the wets with the appointment of Harold Macmillan as Prime Minister in 1957, for he showed that he had not changed much since the publication of *The Middle Way*. The government interfered at the micro level (something excluded by the original application of Keynesianism) and harried the private sector. Also, public spending increased and this led to the resignation of three free market members of the government, Peter Thorneycroft, Enoch Powell and Nigel Birch, from the Treasury in 1958. It was the last gesture for liberty until Mrs Thatcher's era.[25] Intervention steadily increased and in a dreadful portent hints were made in 1961 that a prices and incomes policy would be eventually be introduced. Then it was called a 'pay pause'[26] but it heralded a disastrous episode in British economic history.

The Harold Wilson Labour Government of 1964, with its creeping interventionism and inept attempts at economic planning, instigated some economic rethinking among Conservatives and the return of a Conservative administration under Edward Heath in 1970 looked extremely promising for the drys, or economic realists, as they would prefer to be known. The Heath Government certainly had a free market agenda known as 'Selsdon man', named popularly after a hotel where a meeting was held in 1969. It promised a freer market, less government control, even some minor privatisation, trade union reform and no prices and incomes policy. These last two aims were obviously linked because it was union obduracy which had partially caused the failure of Labour's economic policy and led to the humiliating defeat of Barbara Castle's proposal of union reform, *In Place of Strife*, in 1967.

But these grandiose schemes came to nothing and Heath's Government was an unmitigated disaster; the worst in conservative history.[27] Trade union militancy had bedevilled all governments of the 1960s and it was getting worse. In most cases governments had succumbed to wage demands, but the Heath Government promised something different. It delivered on that promise, it produced unprecedented industrial chaos. At the first sign of difficulty for big firms the government intervened through nationalisation and financial aid. Despite the stated claim that it would not come to the assistance of 'lame ducks' and would let the market perform its reallocative function, it replenished them, thus ensuring further trouble for the future. As soon as unions realised that their excessive wage demands would not lead to bankruptcy and redundancies their militancy intensified. Thus Rolls-Royce was nationalised and the government caved in balefully to union occupation of the threatened Upper Clyde Shipbuilders. Worse, it passed the 1972 Industry Act which gave the government vast financial and regulatory powers over the economy. It was a legacy to the 1974–79 Labour Government which Tony Benn gratefully exploited.

And then there was inflation. Desperate governments in an advanced democracy, whose time preferences rarely extend beyond the next election, will always be tempted to play on the monetary instrument at the onset of unemployment. Once the Bretton Woods agreement, an international scheme which guaranteed fixed exchanges, had collapsed in 1971 there was little restraint on money creation. We had not developed an internal mechanism for curbing government monetary profligacy, as the Germans had with their independent Bundesbank. Under the Chancellor, Anthony Barber, the Conservatives lost all credibility in its capacity to curb inflation so that by 1974 it was approaching 20 per cent annually.

But there was something else which at the time was not especially controversial but which was to prove the most divisive issue in conservative politics – Europe. No doubt some Conservatives would say that despite his manifest economic failures Heath at least got Britain into the then European Economic Community (EEC). At the time many Conservatives of proven free market credentials were favourable to our entry into Europe. The continent was more successful economically than Britain, largely because most countries there had been less afflicted with Keynesian demand management economics and most had a more sympathetic attitude to capitalism: although France had experimented mildly with something called 'indicative planning', its largely capitalist system still flourished and West Germany had been revolutionised by Ludwig Erhard's market economics. But perhaps the most important reason why some Conservatives gave a cautious welcome to the EEC was fear of the depredations to the market economy a future Labour Government might do. The unions were becoming even more militant and the intelligentsia and opinion leaders more left-wing. Our much-vaunted parliamentary sovereignty had allowed the Attlee Government to socialise the country, the common law had been undermined by statute and the absence of any kind of restraint on government bode ill for the future. To prevent more socialism the economic absurdity of the Common Agricultural Policy was a price worth paying. Only Enoch Powell was definitely hostile to the end of sovereignty and our national identity. It was not generally realised at the time that the superficially more market-oriented EEC would mutate into the regulatory socialism of the later European Union. Nor did pro-business thinkers understand that the best prospects for international capitalism would be a system of competitive jurisdictions, in which a nominally sovereign state is able to offer its own tax and regulatory arrangements. Capital and labour would then flee to the most propitious regime, compelling, for economic reasons, others to reduce taxes and regulations.

The emergence of Thatcherism

The Conservative Party was restored to office in 1979 after the previous Labour Government had brought the country to its knees with basically a continuation of Heath's policies with worse results. A series of very damaging strikes, especially from the National Union of Mineworkers, culminating in the 'Winter of Discontent' of 1978–79, had left the country ungovernable, or only so with the permission of the unions. The emergence of a welfare mentality in which people found it easier to be on benefits than to get a job had a detrimental effect on the economy and on the morality of society. Indeed, under Conservatives a traditional concern for the poor and deprived had become a licence not to work and lax family law had encouraged the break-up of traditional families.

Clearly something had to be done, and although the 1979 manifesto was not particularly radical, a serious rethinking of conservative ideas and policy had been going on throughout most of the 1970s. Margaret Thatcher had defeated a thoroughly discredited Edward Heath for the Conservative Party leadership in 1975 and had begun to imbibe some radical ideas about economic management which were to come to fruition as her reign progressed. Although they had some provenance in conservative history their cutting edge had been blunted by the years of the consensus. The crucial question for historians of ideas is whether Mrs Thatcher really was a conservative or had she imported an ideology, classical liberalism, into conservatism? Had she added a squally individualism to the normally tranquil lagoon of traditionalist thought, as Scruton implies? Perhaps it was the Conservatives who had adjusted unthinkingly to an ephemeral and quickly fading consensus who were aberrant? Had not their opportunism led to the abandonment of genuine traditional values?

The leading figure in the Conservative reorientation was Sir Keith Joseph who, like Thatcher herself, had been a prominent figure in the Heath Government. They were to overturn everything that he stood for and effected a genuine revolution in Conservative theory and practice. Joseph himself was more successful as a thinker and opinion former than as a minister and it is to his intellectual influence that we can attribute the success of Thatcherism.

Joseph[28] went through a Damascene, publicly expressed, conversion from an exponent of the moderate consensus to the proponent of free market individualism. Joseph and Thatcher became associated with 'monetarism', but the correct meaning of the term is rarely understood. As a scientific economic theory, monetarism merely states that if the supply of money increases ahead of productivity, inflation, or a general rise in prices, must result. There is no such thing as 'cost-push' inflation, where the rise in cost of a particular factor of production, normally labour, causes an overall increase in prices. For all their faults, trade unions cannot cause inflation because they do not control the monetary lever, government does. Inflation can never be defeated by prices and incomes policies while government retains its monetary power. Of course, there is a number of factors which lead to monetary laxity and one of these is excessive public spending, but monetarism as a pure theory has nothing to say about government economic policy in general. A government could spend 100 per cent of national income and still successfully pursue a non-inflationary monetary policy. As many Conservatives, Joseph included, stressed that 'monetarism is not enough', a thorough attack on the consensus required a battery of economic policies, including reducing the size of the state, privatisation, lower taxes, less regulation, trade union reform and a modified welfare system. Equally important it needed a government with a will to resist pressure group demands for subsidies and relaxation from the rule of law when things get a little difficult in the short run. Joseph had learnt from studying the Chicago economist Milton Friedman, and the Austrian (though naturalised Briton) Friedrich von Hayek, that the attempt to fix a short-term problem with even modest intervention would be productive of long-term disaster.

Joseph was worried about the social, as well as economic, effects of an expanding welfare state. The disincentives to work was producing cycles of deprivation when single mothers raised children who grew up expecting to live on welfare, with only a future of relative poverty to look forward to. Joseph outraged the 'liberals' (not classical liberals) with his suggestion that there was an increasing birth rate among the deprived which will lead to a decline in the proportion of the intelligent in the population.

He also wanted trade union reform which would detach ordinary union members from their more militant and left-wing leaders. In effect, a reform that would restore unions to their true 'owners', the members. Sympathy strikes, where unions supported another union in an issue that did not concern them, would have to be outlawed, as would 'wildcat' strikes, strikes without even union authorisation. Thatcher's step-by-step union reform throughout the 1980s and her defeat of the miners' strike in 1984–85 were perhaps her finest achievements.

But Joseph was significant in dispelling the illusion that there is some virtue in always seeking the 'centre' in politics. This was the key to moderation and 'wisdom'. The Conservative should not be out of step with the people as this would not only put them out of office for the foreseeable future but would also leave them at the mercy of extremists, and free marketers and welfare state reformers were regarded as such by the Heath hierarchy. But Joseph pointed out that this strategy necessitated the Party adopting policies it knew to be detrimental to British interests. There is a kind of a 'ratchet' effect in politics whereby the acceptance of one unsound policy after another locked the country into an endless downward spiral. In contrast to the search for the middle, Joseph argued that there is a 'common ground'; policies that are in the interests of most of the people but which are not revealed in surveys of opinion on particular issues or by the latest by-election result. What Joseph was objecting to was the inordinate influence that pressure groups had on British Government. They were not in any sense representative of the people but spoke successfully for minorities seeking privileges from the state.

In summary, Joseph's intellectual ambition and Thatcher's Governments represented the complete destruction of what Oakeshott called the enterprise state and called for the restoration of civil society. While the establishment of economic prudence was the first essential of Thatcher's Government it must be remembered that Thatcherism, perhaps best articulated by Joseph, was a theory of society as well as economics. And what was important here was the connection between economics and civil liberty, for modern liberalism had bifurcated liberty into the economic and the social and ranked them – the civil liberties always being placed above economic. But to the Joseph–Thatcher view of the world there was an intimate connection between the two; in fact, our civil liberties would become senescent without economic freedom. The liberty to use our talents to be, say, entrepreneurs, was as important as freedom of speech and that liberty had been 'cribbed, cabined and confined' by taxes and regulations throughout the years of the consensus.

The Thatcher years

So Mrs Thatcher took office in 1979 with, if not a fully-fledged ideology, at least a coherent programme to meet the immediate crisis and a strategy to deal with the long-term problems of the British economy and society.[29] It meant turning back at least 80 years of history. Thatcher had secured the services of enough people favourable to her ideas to serve in her first administration. Geoffrey Howe was Chancellor of the Exchequer (though later he departed significantly from her over Europe and money) and with him at the Treasury was Nigel Lawson, a gifted economist who had been campaigning, mainly as a journalist, for a free market for years. At the Department of Trade and Industry was Keith Joseph. Also there was the combative Norman Tebbit who was to become instrumental in the long battle with the trade unions. But there were still members of the Conservative *ancien régime* who opposed her radicalism and yearned for a better yesterday. They had to be replaced before her programme could be regarded as safe in her own party.

The first thing that had to be done was the reestablishment of monetary stability and this was a traditional Tory aim which had been badly neglected by the ersatz Conservatives of the consensus era. However, before the attack on inflation could be effective Howe did something which revealed that the Thatcher Government was serious about economic change – he abolished exchange controls in October 1979. All sorts of arcane arguments had been produced to show that they were necessary for a country's economy when the slightest acquaintance with what had once been conventional economics showed this to be quite false. But their abolition revealed something very important: that Thatcher cared about liberty and wanted to release citizens from the irksome interventions of the state.

The Thatcher Government had inherited high inflation from Labour (and Heath) and pursued a strict monetarist line with the adoption of the Medium Term Financial Strategy which Howe faithfully steered through Parliament and a reluctant Civil Service. Within a few years inflation was down to 5 per cent at the cost of a rise in unemployment, which rose eventually to 3 million. But Thatcher stuck to her principles and aroused the wrath of the Keynesian intelligentsia. Howe's budget of 1981 actually raised taxes in the midst of a recession while orthodoxy recommended a tax cut: 364 economists wrote a famous letter to *The Times* in protest. But Thatcher and Howe knew that there was an intimate connection between public spending and the money supply and that government exorbitance had to be curbed if monetary stability were to be restored.

It was the duty of the Treasury and the Bank of England to keep a strict watch on the money supply figures, rather like the Bundesbank, and keep inflation under control. A measure of money, known as the 'broad' money rule, was rigorously followed. In spite of some complaints by even market economists that monetary targets were often being missed, it largely worked. It is better to be roughly right than exactly wrong. Of course, it was accompanied by a necessary rise in unemployment, but it was a striking feature of the theory that Thatcher had adopted that it was not the duty of either the Treasury or the Bank of England to do anything about unemployment. This would ultimately be unaffected by macroeconomic policy but was a part of microeconomics, the market. To admit this was quite unprecedented for a Conservative of the consensus era. It certainly breached Roger Scruton's responsibilities for a traditionalist government. Yet it worked and unemployment gradually fell from its high point in the early Thatcher years.

But as it reached a kind of fruition it all went terribly wrong. And its errors emerged not from something in Thatcherism which would have been spotted and exploited by critics of the experiment itself but from disagreements within the Thatcher camp. They might be thought of as merely technical but they had a lasting impact on Conservative governments. In 1984 Geoffrey Howe was replaced as Chancellor by Nigel Lawson. Now there is no doubting the latter's credentials as a Thatcherite. He was indeed as much an inflation hawk as she. The problem was that he had a different way of dealing with the problem from Howe. The latter had coped by closely monitoring the internal price mechanism, but Lawson did it by watching the exchange rate, particularly by tracking the German currency, the Deutschmark. There are good reasons why he should have done this. After all, this had been the most successful European currency, along with the Swiss franc, and there seemed to be less of a danger of overshooting the money supply as had occurred under the broad money rule. Unfortunately, the times were not propitious for such a strategy. The British economy was beginning to improve, the international value of the pound was rising and eventually the German economy was badly affected by the costs of the country's reunification. Hence, to follow the Deutschmark in such circumstances would mean the lowering of interest rates, something definitely not required in British circumstances. But interest rates were lowered and inflation resulted. This led to a great argument about who had caused the ill-advised cut in interest rates, Mrs Thatcher or Nigel Lawson? Because of doubts about the strategy of tracking exchange rates, Thatcher had already installed Alan Walters, a strict monetarist, as her economic adviser. Lawson always maintained that Thatcher had authorised the cut in interest rates because she was worried about house prices and unemployment, but the edifice of Conservative economic unity was broken and Lawson and Walters resigned.

Whatever the truth about that episode, it led to Britain joining the European Exchange Rate Mechanism with catastrophic results. The very high interests that were required led to an overvalued pound and a serious economic dislocation. Many small businesses did not survive and some homeowners had their properties repossessed. The Conservatives lost their credibility for economic management and consequently lost two elections.

The revitalisation of the real economy

Away from money, Thatcher realised that if Britain were to be rejuvenated the dead hand of the state had to be removed from the economy and entrepreneurship made the motor of change. Return on capital was much lower in the public sector than the private and when she took office the nationalised industries, which covered great swathes of the economy, were indebted to the tune of £4 billion. Hitherto, all attempts to make them more efficient consisted of expensive and useless reorganisations which had the primary goal of saving jobs; British Leyland, the car company, being the classic example. It occurred to only a few people that the solution was simply to get rid of them. From 1983 Thatcher embarked on a massive scheme of privatisation with the sale of British Telecom to the public the following year. This was a huge success, against the predictions of many 'experts'. It was followed by British Airways and other titans of the public sector hitherto thought to be untouchable. Eventually, even the public utilities, including gas and electricity, which many people thought should be publicly owned because they were technically 'public goods'[30] that could not be supplied by the market, were put into private hands and subject to competition. The public-good argument turned out to be bogus.

But perhaps the most significant privatisation was that of council houses. Now this was not done for efficiency reasons alone, for sitting tenants were offered significant discounts on the price according to how long they had been in occupation. More money could have been raised if the market price had been charged. But just as important for Thatcher was the expansion of freedom that private ownership produced. She realised that liberty did not depend only on the removal of government restraints on personal choices, which the permissive legislation of the 1960s on homosexuality and abortion had achieved (in fact she might have thought all this was an ersatz form of liberty) but was better expressed in the personal responsibility for action that property ownership brought and the freedom from irksome governmental control that privacy entailed.

Privatisation was one crucially important part of a widespread programme to set the nation free and to end that sloth and inefficiency that had almost ruined it in the consensus years. Other elements were tax reform and the further spread of private share ownership through the offer of Personal Equity Plans (PEPs) free of all tax. Both these policies were pioneered by the Chancellor, Nigel Lawson: whatever his faults at the macro level, he was a radical tax reformer who managed to get taxes down from an unproductive 83 per cent (a rate which was also an affront to Thatcher's sense of justice) at the highest to two simple rates, 23 per cent for the standard earners and 40 per cent for those at a higher level. His removal of tax on small shareholdings was again an aspect of the strategy of making individuals independent of the state and more capable of taking care of their own futures.

John Redwood correctly described all this as 'popular capitalism'.[31] As an academic he had made extensive studies of nationalised industries and was aware of the fact that they were inefficient behemoths successful only at absorbing public money, and as a professional in the City of London he knew of all the financial intricacies of privatisation. Redwood succeeded in demonstrating that capitalism was more than glamorous multibillion-dollar deals on Wall Street or in the City of London, it was also about the ownership of small amounts of capital by millions of people, and entrepreneurship was a concept that described all market activities from a rich and adventurous corporate raider down to a humble but self-employed window cleaner. Redwood correctly asserted that capitalism is the 'democracy of the marketplace', where you cannot be outvoted. And it was about more than economics, it was also an expression of liberty. For Thatcherite Conservatives, economics and liberty are intimately related.

But this perhaps frenetic free market activity, at the practical and theoretical level, was certain to produce conservative opposition. This was not genuine conservatism, it was said, but an alien ideology, often of foreign origin, especially the Chicago school of free market economics under Friedman and the Austrian school under the exiled Hayek. They were certainly welcomed at Downing Street but it must not be forgotten that the Thatcher revolution was an indigenous product that emerged out of the catastrophic circumstances that faced a once proud nation in the 1970s. Certain philosophers could not accept the overriding claims of economic liberty. Scruton wrote that 'freedom is comprehensible as a social goal only when subordinate to something else, to an organisation ... which defines the individual aim'.[32] By this he meant authority. But all market theorists have admitted that capitalism is nested in law, and they agreed that there is a necessity for some state activity. But the state is not to be venerated uncritically and the character of its actions must be analysed as much as its extent. The state in 1970s Britain had become huge (in 1979 it spent more than 50 per cent of gross domestic product), cumbersome, the plaything of interest groups, inflation-prone and potentially, if not actually, oppressive. It would have been unconservative not to have demanded at least its retrenchment.

At the political level, opposition to Thatcher's strident free market individualism came from the left and the Conservative 'One Nation' ideologues. Peter Walker, once a Cabinet minister in Heath's Government, was formerly a successful businessman but he could not accept the capitalism of the Thatcher regime. He wrote that 'a system of free enterprise often fails and a centralised bureaucracy has in practice done better. It is not a question of ideology but a balance of advantages.'[33] But it was a question of theory and Thatcher had advisers who knew very well that markets worked and government failed when acting outside its proper role. A former Thatcher minister, Ian Gilmour, wrote a book[34] expressing his disenchantment with the Thatcher experiment. He thought her government was the victim of an outdated economic theory and was presiding insouciantly over unemployment of 3 million. He thought that a Tory Government is responsible to citizens and has a duty to act in their economic interests. Politics come before economics and Tories have a duty 'to kill off *laissez-faire*'.[35] He did not consider the possibility that the politicisation of the British economy might have caused the nation's decline. He wrote in 1983, just as the despised economic theory was having its therapeutic effect and unemployment was beginning to fall. A disaffection for theory is an unfortunate tradition in Conservatism, and the belief that we can get by with hunch, wisdom and intuition is too prevalent.

The impact of Margaret Thatcher and post-Thatcher Conservatism

With the obvious exception of Winston Churchill, and then only for war, Margaret Thatcher's premiership was the most important Tory reign of the twentieth century. And she had her war too, the Falklands. Despised by the bulk of the intelligentsia, not overwhelmingly loved by the electorate (she never secured more than 44 per cent of the poll) and earning no more than a grudging respect from some important members of her Party, she nevertheless changed the face of Britain and much of the Western world. Indeed, Thatcherite policies are pursued more enthusiastically elsewhere than in Britain. If she did not quite 'see off' socialism, she unwittingly created New Labour. In Australia and New Zealand it was Labour parties that initiated market reform and free trade.

A curious tribute to the influence of her ideas is the very paucity of original Conservative thought since her demise. Compared to the originality and energy that characterised Conservative thinking in the 1980s, the ideas of the 1990s and years of defeat since 1997 have produced very little. The only ideas of intellectual merit have come from that gloriously unreconstructed Thatcherite, John Redwood,[36] and from David Willetts. The Party itself seems still intellectually immobilised by the now rather tame debate as to whether it is classical liberal or traditionalist conservative.

Yet there are two issues which have absorbed Conservatives in recent years: the state of the public services (especially health and education) and Europe. On the first question the New Right has made the significant intellectual contributions, often from free market think tanks rather than the Party itself. On Europe there at last appears to be an emerging Eurosceptic consensus, though some important Europhiles remain.

Post-Thatcher Conservatism

It was part of the consensus that Conservatives would not undermine the agreement that there should be a role for the state in the provision of welfare. Conservatives would be in breach of their duty of care to the deprived in a society, to which people are organically linked, if they left the poor and the sick to fall by the wayside. But historically Conservatives never did. Mrs Thatcher herself said 'it is no part of my Party's thinking to dismantle the welfare state'.[37] However, what Conservatives failed to do was to distinguish between necessary aid and a system in which the state offered incentives to people to become dependent on benefits with little encouragement to leave the world of welfare and join the world of work. Thatcher's failure here was blatant and the number living off benefits was no different from before her revolution.

But she had one real achievement: the partial privatisation of the pension system. After Labour was defeated in 1979, the incoming Conservative Government had immense problems, some of which have already been alluded to. One of them was the pensions crisis bequeathed by Barbara Castle. She had introduced, with scarcely a thought to its cost, the State Earnings Related Pension Scheme (SERPS). It was a supplementary pension, in addition to the basic state minimum, based on a lifetime's earnings.[38] People who were already in private schemes could opt out of SERPS. Economists calculated that, as SERPS was unfunded, its future costs would be horrific. But Thatcher, via her Secretary of State for Social Security, Norman Fowler, introduced an Act in 1986 which reduced the generosity of SERPS and offered incentives for people to go private. It worked so well that by the end of Thatcher's era more than half of all workers were in private schemes.

But the pensions problem has been immeasurably worsened by Labour so that there is a need for a thinker who can combine the traditional conservative virtues of economy in government with care for the deprived. Fortunately, the MP David Willetts has provided a string of pamphlets enquiring into pensions and all other aspects of welfare. He is one of the most astute and original of post-Thatcher thinkers.

However, Conservatives have been bedevilled by the National Health Service with all its emotive appeal. Despite matching, indeed exceeding, Labour in expenditure on it, Conservatives have never evaded the charge that they would let people who could not afford to pay privately die on the streets. But conservative think tanks have demonstrated that before the NHS there were numerous voluntary organisations, mainly Friendly Societies, that catered for people's health needs. Thatcher managed to separate the supply of health services from their financing but never seemed to realise that real choice in health is inconceivable without prices, so that the NHS remained in its original form accompanied by the meaningless mantra (in the context of endless queues) 'free at the point of consumption'. But here Thatcher herself was something of a dispositional conservative, fearing that radical reform would be electoral suicide. It is this fear of the unknown, and the still vibrant conservative tradition of paternalist care, that prevents rational New Right policies on welfare being adopted. They have become almost the exclusive property of conservative think tanks.[39]

There are signs of convergence between traditionalists and the New Right on Europe.[40] As mentioned above, free market Conservatives had been mildly in favour of Europe as a counterbalance to British socialism. This was once true of Mrs Thatcher. As Prime Minister she signed the Single European Act (1987) because in theory it widens the market and allows obdurate member states' anti-market laws to be overridden. But very soon that Act led to a mania for uncompetitive harmonisation and gradual dominance of a form of regulatory socialism: benign but inefficient. New Right theorists who had at one time despaired of parliamentary sovereignty now value it as a method of avoiding a centralising Europe. New Right thinkers and traditionalists like Scruton now regard European law as a bigger threat to the treasured common law than statute ever was.

Interestingly, the unending crises over Europe resulted in a new Tory affection for something it had historically opposed – direct democracy via the referendum. This was often disdained as a licence for mob rule but its successful endorsement of conservative views in Europe has made it more alluring to traditionalists. Indeed, if they had looked a little closer they would have noticed that Switzerland, the most successful conservative and free market economy in Europe, makes extensive use of the referendum at federal and cantonal levels. Indeed, it is still largely a genuine federal state with the cantons spending more than the central government. Many conservatives blithely assume that federal systems either become heavily centralised or break up (for cultural reasons). But Switzerland's exceptionalism is a result of direct democracy; the voters regularly rebuff blandishments from their leaders about the joys of Europe. There is a lot of untapped conservatism in a *proper* democracy.

To conclude with the vexed question as to whether the New Right is classical liberal or genuinely conservative, Mrs Thatcher was preceded by a Conservative Government that had all but destroyed the currency, undermined private property, allowed sectional groups to act as a quasi-government, damaged the rule of law and nearly destroyed the economy. To put this right with New Right ideas is hardly to be unconservative. The tragedy is that these ideas became less fashionable for Conservatives under John Major just as they were beginning to work very well. That might explain the lost 2 million votes in 1997.

Notes

1. See N. Barry, 'The Political Economy of Edmund Burke', in I. Crowe (ed.), *Edmund Burke: His Life and Legacy* (Dublin: Four Courts Press, 1997), pp.104–14.
2. See N. Barry, *The New Right* (London: Croom Helm, 1987), pp.86–101.
3. A. Quinton, 'Conservatism', in P. Pettit and R. Goodin (eds), *A Companion to Contemporary Political Philosophy* (Oxford: Blackwell, 1993).
4. N. O'Sullivan, *Conservatism* (London: Dent, 1976), p.31.
5. M. Oakeshott, *Rationalism in Politics and Other Essays* (London: Methuen, 1962).
6. M. Oakeshott, *On Human Conduct* (London: Oxford University Press, 1975).
7. See M. Oakeshott, 'Political Education', in Oakeshott, *Rationalism in Politics*, pp.133–6.
8. Oakeshott, *Rationalism in Politics*, p.21.
9. M. Oakeshott, 'The Political Economy of Freedom', in Oakeshott, *Rationalism in Politics*.

10. R. Scruton, *The Meaning of Conservatism* (Basingstoke: Palgrave Macmillan, 2001, 3rd edition).
11. Ibid., p.5.
12. F.A. von Hayek, *The Constitution of Liberty* (London: Routledge and Kegan Paul, 1960).
13. See N. Barry, 'The Rationale of the Minimal State', in A. Gamble and A. Wright *Restating the State* (Oxford: Blackwell, 2004), pp.11–23.
14. Scruton, *The Meaning of Conservatism*, p.106.
15. Ibid., p.106.
16. Ibid., p.27.
17. Ibid., p.75.
18. See F.A. von Hayek, *The Mirage of Social Justice* (London: Routledge and Kegan Paul, 1976).
19. See N. Barry, *Welfare* (Buckingham: Open University Press, 1999, 2nd edition); C. Murray, *Losing Ground* (New York: Basic Books, 1994, 2nd edition).
20. H. Macmillan, *The Middle Way* (London: Macmillan, 1938).
21. For a summary, see Barry, *Welfare*, pp.40–1.
22. S. Brittan, *Steering the Economy* (London: Secker and Warburg, 1969).
23. K. Popper, *The Open Society and its Enemies* (London: Routledge and Kegan Paul, 1945).
24. See D. Willetts, *Modern Conservatism* (London: Penguin, 1992), chapter 3.
25. Ibid., p.41.
26. Ibid., p.42.
27. Ibid., pp.42–6.
28. Important works of Joseph are *Stranded in the Middle Ground* (London: Centre for Policy Studies, 1976) and with J. Sumption, *Equality* (London: John Murray, 1979).
29. A detailed and thorough account of Thatcher's era is S. Letwin, *The Anatomy of Thatcherism* (London: Fontana, 1992).
30. See Barry, 'The Rationale of the Minimal State'.
31. J. Redwood, *Popular Capitalism* (London: Routledge and Kegan Paul, 1988).
32. Scruton, *The Meaning of Conservatism*, p.8.
33. P. Walker, *The Ascent of Britain* (London: Sidgwick and Jackson, 1977), p.23.
34. I. Gilmour, *Britain Can Work* (Oxford: Martin Robertson, 1983).
35. Ibid., p.218.
36. See his *Singing the Blues* (London: Politicos Publishing, 2004).
37. Quoted in Alistair B. Cooke, *In Defence of Freedom* (New York: Prometheus, 1985), pp.12–13.
38. See N. Barry, 'The State, Pensions and the Philosophy of Welfare', *Journal of Social Policy*, 14:4 (1985), pp.468–90.
39. Especially Civitas, the Institute of Economic Affairs, the Centre for Policy Studies and the Adam Smith Institute.
40. For New Right analyses of the governance of Europe, see N. Barry, 'Constitutionalism, Federalism and the European Union', *Economic Affairs*, 24:1 (2004), pp.13–16 and M. Ricketts, 'Economic Analysis and Inter-jurisdictional Competition', *Economic Affairs*, 24:1 (2004), pp.28–33. See R. Lea, *The Essential Guide to the European Union* (London: Centre for Policy Studies, 2004).

3
Centre
Mark Garnett

'It is not I who has changed; it is the party.'[1]

It is hardly surprising that the Conservative 'centre' has been neglected by students of the Party. It is too easily dismissed as the bit which is left over once the interesting people have been discussed. Conservatives of the centre are also hardest to pin down. The 'left' and the 'right' obligingly identify themselves by associating with ginger groups – One Nation, the Monday Club, No Turning Back, the 92 Group, and so on. But, to paraphrase Margaret Thatcher, no one ever went on crusade under the banner of centrality. Or rather, if they do raise that standard they have probably lost their battle already, like the short-lived Centre Forward group established by Francis Pym in 1985.

Yet the Conservative centre is not only interesting in itself; it can also provide useful insights into the general fortunes of the post-war Party. A centre grouping usually gives essential ballast to any organisation; and, as we shall see, this is particularly true of the Conservative Party. When the Conservative centre is relatively numerous, and its members are broadly happy with policy trends, the Party as a whole is likely to prosper. Largely thanks to the solid centre, it was able to survive even the catastrophe of Anthony Eden's Suez adventure. Equally, the depth of a crisis can often be measured by symptoms of unease within the centre – and when a party is undergoing a painful period of transition its effects will be registered most conclusively in the response of the centre.

The nature and role of the centre

The obvious way to isolate a Conservative centre in the post-war period would be to evaluate the ideological composition of the Party at any given time and discuss those Conservatives whose ideas place them in the middle of a 'left–right' spectrum. This would have to be done on the understanding that we would be aiming at a moving target. We should be prepared for variations in the size and location of the centre over time, accommodating shifts in the Conservative spectrum and changes in the order of political priorities. Thus, for example, Kenneth Clarke could be taken as a reasonable candidate for membership of a 'centre' group of Conservative MPs at the time of his first entry to Parliament at the 1970 general election. He would have to be evicted by 1979, and classified as a member of the near-lunatic leftist fringe in the post-Maastricht period. Yet on domestic subjects Clarke himself certainly did not move to the left; at Health (1988–90) and Education (1990–92) he proved to be an enthusiastic reformer on 'Thatcherite' lines. His changing place in the spectrum reflects the fact that the parliamentary party as a whole shifted more rapidly than he did, but also demonstrates that by the time of Maastricht attitudes to Europe rather than domestic policy had become the key ideological litmus test for members of the Party. By then the Party was united on domestic policies: 'left', 'right' and centre all accepted the broad outlines of 'Thatcherism'.

The problem with an approach which concentrates on ideology is that it is likely to result in a one-dimensional picture, providing an inadequate account of change within the post-war Conservative Party. One must also consider the Party's self-image and ethos. Traditionally, although Conservatives agreed that their Party accommodated a wide range of views, they advertised themselves as a centrist body. Labour, they claimed, was sectional, focusing on the perceived interests of the working class. By contrast, Conservatives sought to govern in the interests of the whole nation. Thus, even if outside observers thought that one ideological faction held the upper hand, by some strange alchemy the Party's policies would always turn out to be centrist. As Francis Pym put it in 1985, 'the harmony of the Conservative Party has never been to do with a crude balance of right and left, but with the absorption of a wide range of views and attitudes. The Party has survived because it has always managed to find a central harmony that binds the disparate elements together.'[2] In 1969 Ian Gilmour argued that the Party had been so successful because it 'has nearly always governed itself from the left and the country from the centre'. This made good electoral sense, Gilmour argued, because the majority of the electorate was conservative 'with a small c'.[3]

Another version of this argument had been advanced by Lord Hailsham (at that time Quintin Hogg) after the crushing 1945 election defeat. Hailsham claimed that the Party's 'eternal and indispensable role is to criticise and mould the latest heresy of the moment'. Conservatives had thrown their weight against *laissez-faire* when it was in vogue; on the same principle, they were now opposing the socialism of Attlee's Labour Government. The common theme for Conservatives at all times was a dislike of 'fixed and unalterable theories of the state', whether of left or right. While the ideologues dreamed their dreams, the Party as a whole provided the nation with a reliable centre of gravity. In the Conservative self-image, what Hailsham described as an 'eternal and indispensable role' had more of the character of a duty.[4]

Despite their superficial differences, Pym, Gilmour and Hailsham agree in their main assumptions about the Conservative centre. In some respects it is *passive*: hence, for Gilmour, the Party is best led by a representative of the left, while Hailsham thinks that the initiative will often lie with the left or the right depending on circumstances. Gilmour clearly assumes that the centre will be happy under leftist leadership, because the arrangement gives the best chance of victory to the 'natural party of government'. But at the same time the centre is *dynamic*. On Gilmour's account, the left might provide momentum, but only on the understanding that the centre will apply the brakes if necessary. The existence of a solid centre within the Party is enough to remind leaders that, regardless of their personal views, they must be pragmatic and adaptable. If the leadership of the Party ever breaks loose from its moorings in the political centre it will be rejected by a centrist electorate.

While many members of the centre no doubt lacked something in eloquence or erudition, it would be a mistake to assume that all of them were 'mute inglorious Miltons', or stereotypical Tory backbenchers like *Private Eye*'s Sir Bufton Tufton. A good example of a ministerial centralist was Philip Cunliffe-Lister, 1st Earl Swinton (1884–1972), who was so far from being a dumb dog that he was credited by Harold Macmillan with 'the ablest and most versatile brain in the Conservative Party'.[5] Swinton's ministerial career began (when his surname was Lloyd-Greame) in the Lloyd George coalition. He was far from being the only double-barrelled Tory in that government; among his more obscure and titled colleagues were the bearers of such names as Worthington-Evans, Griffith-Boscawen and Mitchell-Thomson, as well as the better-remembered Sir Arthur Steel-Maitland.[6] Swinton reached the Cabinet in 1922 as President of the Board of Trade, then served in the National Governments at the Colonial Office and the Ministry of Air before being sacked by Chamberlain in 1938. He returned to the Cabinet under Churchill in 1952, at the Commonwealth Relations Office, leaving government for the last time when Anthony Eden took over as Prime Minister in April 1955. But up to the time of his death he continued to offer advice to Conservative leaders, on strategy and frontbench appointments.

In 1947 Swinton gave the Party much of the family estate near Harrogate, to provide a successor to its residential college at Ashridge. Swinton was a generous and wealthy man, and he recognised that ideas were going to be more important in post-war politics than they had been before 1939. But there was still some irony in his donation because his approach to politics could not be taught. As his biographer has written, 'Swinton's conservatism owed little to ideology. While naturally believing in such civic virtues as patriotism and, above all, the ideal of public service, he found the main attraction of politics in "getting things done".'[7] He also judged leaders by their character rather than their ideas, describing Alec Douglas-Home as 'what every man in public life would wish to be' because of his 'honesty, sincerity and integrity'.[8]

Swinton believed that Home's own integrity had made him a good judge of others, and singled out for praise his appointment of William Whitelaw as 'one of the best Chief Whips the Party has ever had'.[9] Whitelaw and Swinton came from similar social backgrounds, and although their inherited privileges made intellectual distinction a luxury rather than a necessity, both were gifted enough to be educated at Winchester rather than a more mundane public school. Whitelaw also admired Home, and grieved at the task of telling him that he ought to stand down from the leadership in 1965. Later Swinton's grandson married one of Whitelaw's daughters, in a north-country social and political alliance on the approved eighteenth-century model.

Throughout his long political career, from his first entry to Parliament in 1955 to his retirement as a Viscount in 1988, it is difficult to find any trace in Whitelaw's utterances of distinct ideological views. But in October 1980 he praised Stanley Baldwin for having 'tried, before acting, to feel the grain of the public will. Better than anyone he understood how to gauge the importance of various currents of popular opinion and how to balance them and to apply them against the traditional attitudes and established practices of his Party and his country.'[10] This, in Whitelaw's view, made Baldwin a man of the Conservative centre – a forerunner of Home.

Both Swinton and Whitelaw saw a connection between the Conservative centre and a particular type of character. This was not necessarily related to high social standing, but clearly it helped if one had entered politics out of a sense of duty rather than a desire for self-promotion. Asked in 1966 whether he thought that politicians should become more 'professional', Swinton replied, 'by professionalism I suppose we mean that a man is skilful at the game, but I hope being a "player" won't stop him being a "gentleman"!'[11] Looking back on his career after his retirement more than 20 years later, Whitelaw noted that landed gentlemen 'provided a backbone. They had no interest in advancement for themselves. They didn't in the main want to be ministers, they wanted to continue their work in their own counties.'[12]

By the time of Swinton's death both he and Whitelaw had begun to express quiet unease about the general decline of the parliamentary 'gentleman'. As Leader of the Commons in 1971 Whitelaw noted that MPs were 'in general younger, worked harder, were at Westminster for longer and had far more resources than their predecessors'. He gamely added that 'these developments, which are anyway inevitable, are good for both Parliament and the country'.[13] But these new MPs could not contribute so much to the government of their counties, even if they had the will to do so. By implication, younger Conservative MPs could not 'provide a backbone'; and in the absence of a solid phalanx of old-style MPs, new recruits would no longer be socialised into an approximation of the role. Swinton was referring to the same development when he told James Margach that 'the House of Commons appears to me to have become a much more intolerant and noisy Assembly'.[14] It was typical of both Swinton and Whitelaw that they should agree in opposing the fashionable view that the Commons could be improved by reforming the committee system. In 1966 Swinton thought that this was already 'as satisfactory and efficient as you are likely to get', and when Whitelaw was given ministerial responsibility for reform four years later he ensured that the changes were minimal.[15]

The squeezing of the centre

In February 1975 Whitelaw stood against Margaret Thatcher in the second ballot for the leadership of his party. Back in 1963 not everyone was convinced by Home's apparent reluctance to succeed Macmillan; but there was no mistaking Whitelaw's unhappiness. Had the old 'magic circle' been in operation as a way of choosing Conservative leaders his feelings might have been different. As it was, he was faced with the distasteful task of attracting votes from his parliamentary colleagues, with three major disadvantages. First, he was regarded as the faithful lieutenant of Edward Heath, who had been unseated by Thatcher in the first round of voting. Second, he had limited attractions for MPs who were anxious to take on Labour in a 'battle of ideas'; all he had to offer at a time of crisis was the Baldwinesque idea of national unity, which had not served the Party well in the two general elections of 1974. Finally, although he had no difficulty in assembling a campaign team, it naturally included the remaining Conservative MPs who were much like himself. Overall the Thatcher camp had a much keener appetite for the fray.

Mrs Thatcher's victory has been dubbed a 'Peasants' Revolt' – a *coup d'état* by the Party's right wing. Recent research has suggested that the result was a better reflection of the existing ideological composition of the Party than commentators originally thought.[16] But from the perspective of the Party's ethos the old tag still has some insights to offer. As Swinton and Whitelaw detected, the change long predated 1975.

Although research has been conducted into the changing social composition of the Conservative Party,[17] there is a danger that even the most meticulous study will yield only a partial picture. It has to be seen in the wider context of social change, which means that a certain kind of background can no longer be regarded as a guarantee of outlook or conduct. Students of the Party now tend to downplay the impact of the post-war Maxwell-Fyfe reforms, which deterred constituencies from selecting the candidates with the deepest pockets. But there was bound to be some effect on the Party's ethos, eroding the traditional bias of selection committees towards substantial local figures from long-established families. As early as 1953, the observant Angus Maude claimed that the Party had undergone 'a silent revolution between 1945 and 1950'.[18] The transition could not have been so sudden, given the security of tenure for MPs in the safest constituencies. But it was widely regarded as inevitable. While recognising the time-lag, one hostile observer wrote in 1967 that 'even in the absence of other change, the MP of the seventies will be a different person from the MP of the fifties, and still more of the thirties, when such anachronistic worthies as the aptly named Sir Waldron Smithers were still able to be returned time after time to pursue their comic travesty of the role of a British legislator'.[19] Ironically, the late Sir Waldron (1880–1954) had become a figure of fun because of his lonely stance against state intervention as much as his social background. By the 1970s this fossilised relic of the past looked more like a trailblazer of the Conservative future.

In 1973 Julian Critchley argued that it was a mistake to think of the Conservatives as 'the pragmatic party that avoids ideology, defers to its leaders, and attaches overriding importance to the preservation of party unity'. That might have been true once. 'But contemporary politics is about economic management, and Conservative economic policies have changed in recent years both in style and content.' Because of the new dominance of economics, the Tories had become 'a coalition in perpetual conflict'. He distinguished four groups: 'the moderates, upon whom the [Heath] Government relies for support, and from whom, in the main, the Government itself is recruited; the apolitical and the eccentric, the traditional right, and the "radical" or Powellite right'.[20]

Critchley was a partisan, rather than a detached observer. His identification of individual 'moderates' would not have won universal assent. For example, he argued that 'save for Mr John Biffen, the Bow Group are all moderates'. Having chaired the Group in 1966–67, Critchley had good personal reasons for placing its parliamentary old boys among the ranks of the solid citizens with excellent prospects of promotion. While he concentrated on the moderates of his own generation, he also included older MPs like Sir Gilbert Longden (a founder-member of One Nation) and William Deedes.[21]

In hindsight, a list of 'moderates' which includes both Nicholas Scott and Norman Lamont provokes a raised eyebrow; in the 1990s they were identified with the extremes of left and right respectively. But for the present purpose the most interesting of Critchley's categories is the second. He was too prudent to name any examples of 'the apolitical and the eccentric' Conservative members; and if he was pushed he would probably have named Whitelaw among the moderates along with his good friend Bill Deedes. But that would have been misleading. On the key issue of economics it would be more appropriate to consign Whitelaw to the 'apolitical' section than to incorporate him alongside any Bow Group intellectuals.[22] The same would be true of Swinton, Home and other party stalwarts whom we have identified with the Conservative 'centre'. It was a dizzying decline for Home; Prime Minister in one decade, then apolitical, eccentric and irrelevant in the next.[23]

The real (if unwitting) significance of Critchley's testimony is that by the early 1970s the traditional Tory centre was being squeezed. Far from providing the Party with its essential ballast, it was all at sea in the brave new world of economic ideas, still using matchsticks as its ready reckoner when the Bow Group tyros were cutting through swathes of socioeconomic statistics. But Critchley was right in his suggestion that the fortunes of the Heath Government depended crucially on his 'moderates', and in particular the younger members of that group. Their style of politics – described by most contemporaries as 'technocratic' rather than 'moderate' – was highly congenial to Heath himself. They constituted the Party's response to the mood of 'modernisation' which had helped to sweep Home out of Downing Street in 1964. None of the MPs mentioned by Critchley as young moderates were in the Commons when Heath supplanted Home as party leader in the following year.

But that precipitate decision cheered them as much as it troubled the remaining Conservative centre.

The crisis of the centre

The argument so far has suggested two distinct notions of the Conservative centre. The first was based on the body of public-spirited gentlemen who sought a parliamentary seat without hoping for office. These individuals were pragmatists who regarded the Conservative Party as the natural agent of sound government at the national level, just as they were the right people to fill positions of local responsibility. They were alarmed by rigid ideas of any kind; socialism might have upset them more than *laissez-faire*, but the main reason for this was the fact that the Labour Party presented the main electoral threat to the natural order of things in the post-war period. *Laissez-faire*, they believed, had been consigned to an obscure grave with Sir Waldron Smithers.

The second understanding of the Conservative centre began to crystallise in the early 1970s, though the relevant changes began much earlier. The decline of the gentleman-Tory triggered a corresponding change in the Party's ethos. It was now more realistic to define the centre in purely ideological terms, with economics providing the main battle-lines. But even in 1973, there were good reasons for thinking that this new 'centre' would not hold for long. Most of Critchley's 'moderates' may have been supporters of the post-war consensus; but they were interested in ideas in a way which was alien to previous representatives of the Conservative centre. In Hailsham's words, by disposition they were receptive to 'fixed and unalterable theories of the state'. At the same time, as professional politicians their careers depended on electoral success. Their personal loyalties were likely to fluctuate with the opinion polls.

Although the ethos of the new centre was very different from that of its predecessor, when Critchley wrote his article in 1973 there were two good reasons for people like Whitelaw, Gilmour and Pym to hope that 'moderation' would prevail against the less palatable alternatives. First, they could argue that although the Party was certainly trying to govern itself from the left, its appeal to the country was still recognisably 'centrist'. Industrial strife, and the conflict in Northern Ireland, were unmistakable symptoms of strain, reinforced by Labour's adoption in 1973 of the most radical programme for government in its history. But Conservative 'moderates' could argue that this played into their Party's hands, because of a second factor. There was no reason to suppose that the electorate as a whole would respond to any party which embraced 'fixed and unalterable theories of the state'. Indeed, unruly behaviour by some members of the British body politic might have the effect of confirming others in their 'conservatism with a small c'. If the Conservative centre abandoned Heath the only realistic alternative was a rightwards lurch towards 'Powellism', which would alienate the majority of voters.

The last few months of 1973 saw the removal of one remaining prop for the Conservative centre. The oil crisis, and the decision of the National Union of Mineworkers to exploit it by embarking on opportunistic industrial action, provoked a crisis for 'moderates' of all parties. For Conservatives, the problem was particularly acute. The 'natural party of government' was in office, but it seemed that Britain was becoming ungovernable. Some advisers close to Heath argued that an explicit call for national unity was the only way to save the situation. Against his instincts – and the promptings of 'old centrists' like Whitelaw and Pym – Heath was persuaded to call an election in February 1974. His defeat was narrow, but in the circumstances it was a decisive verdict against Conservative rule. A second poll in October delivered the same message.

The electoral evidence showed that Gilmour's recipe for Conservative success no longer satisfied the public taste. Reviewed in the wake of their failure, Heath's enforced initiatives such as controls on prices and incomes and an active industrial strategy looked anything but 'centrist'. To many Conservative activists it now seemed that the old compromise had failed, and that their party had been governing the country in accordance with its own 'semi-socialist' ideas.

The events of the early 1970s would have presented a serious challenge for any governing party. But for the Conservatives the problem was particularly acute. Extrapolating from Critchley's analysis, one can argue that these were years of transition for the Party. The old centre, inspired by the ethos of public service rather than any ideology, was being replaced as the main support for the Party leadership by a group dominated by 'technocratic' moderates. Despite their dedication and intelligence, this group lacked the qualities which had previously provided the Party with its 'backbone'. In troubled times they tended to find their refuge not in judgement and experience, but in ideas. By the beginning of 1974 the limitations of their thinking, in the face of unprecedented problems, were apparent to most observers.

The centre under Thatcher

Whatever the precise reasons for Mrs Thatcher's victory in the February 1975 leadership election, it was possible for her backers to provide an ideological gloss on the course of events which kicked away the last prop from the 'moderate' position. At the first party conference after Heath's dismissal, Thatcher's ally Sir Keith Joseph claimed that the Party had mistaken its audience. The 'middle ground' it sought no longer had anything to do with the real preferences of voters; rather, it represented a watered-down version of whatever Labour happened to be offering. In practice, the perceived 'middle ground' was constantly moving to the left as Labour embraced ever more extreme versions of socialism. Conservatives should reverse this trend, and seek 'common ground' between itself and an electorate which it had abandoned.[24]

Joseph had once been a member of One Nation, and as a baronet he had superficial 'centrist' credentials which (as for so many Tories of his generation) had been reinforced by his wartime experiences. But although he had entered politics out of a sense of public duty, at no time in his career did his outlook resemble that of the old centre. He was a tortured, complex soul – a missionary, who believed that Britain's problems could be solved if only government action could be informed by the right ideas. Lord Hailsham stayed in the Thatcher Cabinet with Joseph until 1986 – indeed, he outlasted him. But on the basis of *The Case for Conservatism*, Keith Joseph was the stuff of nightmares. In a private conversation in 1977, Hailsham agreed with his 'centrist' colleague Lord Carrington that Joseph was 'dotty'.[25]

This exchange between Hailsham and Carrington provides an excellent insight into the dilemma of the residual Conservative centre after Thatcher's victory. When told that he had lost the 1975 leadership election, Whitelaw had responded, 'the party needs Margaret and it needs change'. Later he made a formal pledge of loyalty. But his true feelings were divulged in his replies to centrists who had been dismayed by the turn of events. To his former colleague Robert Carr he confided his view that Thatcher and her supporters 'have no idea at all about running a party ... I suppose rather ironically I am there to save them!'[26]

Whitelaw was not exaggerating his abilities. As Heath's Chief Whip from 1965 to 1970 he had indeed helped to 'run the Party'. But in the crucial period between April 1972 and December 1973 Heath had been forced to manage the ship without him, since he was the only minister who seemed equal to the task of containing the problem of Northern Ireland. Even without this exhausting distraction, Whitelaw would have struggled to 'save' the Party after February 1975. Pinioned in the (meaningless) position of deputy leader, and lacking real firepower in a much-changed party (apart from the nuclear weapon of resignation), Whitelaw could do nothing to restrain Thatcher's radical instincts. In their conversation of

1977, Carrington asked Hailsham 'what are we going to do after she gets in if she gets in?' Hailsham could only reply that 'all we can do is to see she is surrounded by adequate advisers'.[27] Hailsham's old idea that the Conservative Party should provide the country with its centre of gravity now hinged on the possibility that the elected leader might listen to the voice of the 'old centre'; and his evident concern reflected an awareness that this voice had dropped away to a whisper.[28]

Thatcher did indeed 'get in'; and although the Conservative victory in 1979 could be explained in a variety of ways it was difficult for sceptics within the Party to argue against her conviction that she had discovered 'common ground' with the voters. Her internal opponents could still hope for a sobering result when she stood for re-election; but they could hardly pray for a defeat once Labour had adopted a reinvigorated 'socialist' programme after its exercise in hand-to-mouth government under Wilson and Callaghan, and the Liberal/SDP alliance seemed too insubstantial to carry the weight of centrist sentiment. As it was, the Falklands War destroyed any possibility that the 1983 election would prove to be a chastening experience for the Prime Minister.

One centrist casualty of the 1983 general election was the Foreign Secretary Francis Pym, who was dismissed in the subsequent reshuffle. In 1985 Pym wrote that 'At the moment, the only options for a Conservative Member of Parliament are to be praised as an echo, to be castigated as a rebel, or to say nothing.'[29] The former Chief Whip was a most reluctant rebel; but he had been 'castigated' in Downing Street briefings even before he had expressed public dissent. Although he disagreed with the Prime Minister over the correct diplomatic approach to the Falklands crisis, the comparative brutality of his dismissal surely has a deeper significance.

As a 'gentleman' of the old centrist school, Pym's chances of ever leading the Conservative Party should have been finished by 1975. But his prospects actually improved during his spell as Defence Secretary under the new dispensation, so that by October 1980 even a cynical observer like Alan Clark began sounding him out as a potential replacement for Thatcher. Clark believed that Pym's resistance to defence cuts could unite behind him 'the old Heathite gang, those who are resentful of cuts in public spending, *plus* the Union Jack Right who will go to the stake on defence and law-and-order issues'.[30] That was scarcely a traditional 'centrist' coalition; but Downing Street seemed to share Clark's view that it might be too potent a combination. In the following year, Pym's Cabinet allies Gilmour and Lord Soames were dismissed, and James Prior was demoted from Employment to Northern Ireland. Thus, although in 1983 Pym was not quite the last man standing from the old centrist body, he was certainly the only one left with the remotest chance of leading a successful counter-*coup*. Although his appointment to succeed Lord Carrington (another departed ally) at the Foreign Office had been a promotion, Mrs Thatcher was only looking for an opportunity to send him packing.

Pym's book, *The Politics of Consent*, was thus an appeal from the old to the new centre. It was bound to be unavailing, because the new centre was so very different from the old one. Driven by ideas rather than ethos, under Thatcher it had moved to a place in the ideological spectrum which was far to the right of the old 'moderate' group identified by Critchley under Heath. By this time Critchley himself was beyond the pale, having made witty remarks about the 'great she-elephant' in Downing Street. The other 'moderates' mentioned by Critchley in 1973 had endured mixed fortunes. As professional politicians, rather than landed gentlemen, they had been faced with the alternatives of redundancy or compliance. Barney Hayhoe and Timothy Raison survived as junior ministers into the second Thatcher Government. John Gummer had become a diligent ministerial servant, and Norman Lamont had started his ascent to the Chancellorship. Ironically, John Biffen – regarded by Critchley in 1973 as the only right-wing recruit from the Bow Group – suddenly exhumed the old 'centrist' appeal for a 'balanced ticket' before the 1987 general election. For his pains, he was dismissed as brusquely as Pym had been.

In 1990 Philip Norton produced a typology of Conservative MPs which estimated that 217 – 58 per cent of the total – should be regarded either as 'party loyalists' or 'Thatcher loyalists'.[31] As so often, the more detailed research focused on the more committed ideological groupings. Julian Critchley could not have been surprised to see himself named by Norton among the 'wets' of the extreme left, alongside Timothy Raison, Sir Peter Tapsell and Nicholas Scott who had also featured on his 1973 list of 'moderates'. When Heath was Prime Minister, Critchley had thought that his group made up 'the bulk of the party'. On Norton's calculations, less than two decades later it could muster only 27 representatives (and two of these were considered to be doubtful).[32] Sir Barney Hayhoe had dwindled into 'dampness'. But the remainder of the 1973 'moderates' had made their peace with the existing regime, and would be 'Thatcher loyalists' for as long as this remained a paying position.

Norton concluded that the 'party faithful' was still in good shape at the beginning of Thatcher's third term, providing the overwhelming majority of new recruits at the 1987 general election. The 1990 leadership election can be interpreted as the culmination of a process in which 'party loyalists' were gradually detached from 'Thatcher loyalists'; the Prime

Minister's failure to win outright on the first ballot could be attributed to a substantial body of MPs who were able to put aside their gratitude to a three-time election winner in the long-term interest of the Party. Yet it would still be pertinent to ask whether the 'party faithful' of 1990 can be equated with the old centre. Calculations about the chances of retaining a seat at the forthcoming election obviously swayed the decision of many MPs. It would be naive to suggest that this factor had played no part in the downfall of Heath in 1975, or even that of Home a decade earlier. But there is good reason to suppose that in 1990 self-preservation was more important than it had ever been before. That motivation was even more potent at local level, where the old networks of family connection had been superseded by an appointed 'quangocracy', whose tenure apparently depended on the perpetuation of Conservative rule. Thus the Party decided to eject Thatcher on the impeccable Thatcherite principle of individual self-interest.

If the old centre had still wielded its former influence, the Conservatives might have avoided this ugly spectacle by persuading the Prime Minister to stand down after ten years in office. But once Thatcher had been deposed, there was a chance of a new beginning. As the obvious vehicle for the votes of Thatcher *dis*loyalists, Michael Heseltine was likely to be too divisive for comfort. Douglas Hurd had impressive credentials, but was hamstrung by a social background which made him look out of place in the new, 'classless' party. John Major had no worries on that score. Whatever had happened to the old Conservative ethos during the Thatcher years, Major seemed like the perfect rallying post for a new ideological centre. He was almost a parody of centrality, with the knack of giving everyone he met the impression of secret sympathy with their views. He had also won Thatcher's endorsement, but critics of the former regime could be reassured by his refusal to act as her 'poodle' in his brief spell as Chancellor of the Exchequer.

When Major was challenged for the leadership by John Redwood in 1995, pragmatic MPs, like Ian Lang and Gillian Shephard, were prominent in his campaign. But the very fact that Major was challenged – and had to fight so hard to cling on – underlined the weakness of the new Conservative centre. Major clearly wanted to govern the Party and the country from the centre. But in practice he was unable to impose his authority on either, despite his contribution to the 1992 electoral victory. He was the prisoner of parliamentary arithmetic; but the indiscipline that reigned throughout his second term was unprecedented in Conservative history. By the time of the Redwood challenge the issue of Europe had redesigned the ideological battle-lines, and fuelled emotions that swept aside any cautionary counsels from the new 'centre'. Redwood's slogan, 'No Change, No Chance', was nicely calculated to appeal to the large number of self-interested MPs who were fearful for their own seats, instead of focusing on the long-term fortunes of their party.

William Hague's victory in the 1997 leadership election owed much to the fact that senior figures like Michael Portillo and Malcolm Rifkind had lost their seats. Even so, it says much for the state of the Conservative 'centre' after Labour's landslide that the Party had to skip two generations before finding a suitable compromise candidate for the leadership. At first, the 'centrists' who had clustered around Major were strongly represented on Hague's front bench. One by one they were pensioned off by a leader who thought that they were associated with the failures of the recent past. Although Hague did attract loyalty in some quarters, his loyalists never commanded respect. By 2001, the new centre which had tried to coalesce behind Major was in total disarray, and the party looked unelectable.

Conclusion: the Conservative centre today

It was suggested above that a significant centre grouping is essential to any successful political party, and that for historical reasons this has been truer of the Conservatives than of any major rival. The fact that the Conservatives had become 'an ideological party' (in Andrew Gamble's phrase)[33] by 1996 did not rule out the possibility that a solid centre might still be found among the various factions. But the general election of the following year showed that John Major's Conservatives were both ideological and unsuccessful. Indeed, before long commentators were wondering whether the 'natural party of government' could survive as a serious force in British politics.[34]

The case of Kenneth Clarke would be sufficient to demonstrate that the ideological centre of the Conservative Party should be sought a long way to the right of the moderates of 1973. But it is pertinent to ask whether the present-day Conservatives have a discernable 'centre' of any kind. Those who wish to gravitate towards the centre of any 'ideological' political party have to fear two developments – polarisation, and uniformity. On the first scenario, party members are forced to take sides. Centrists start to be seen as inveterate fence-sitters, to be shot at by all other participants. But when a party stops tolerating a broad spectrum of opinion promotion (or even the continued countenance of a constituency party) depends on the acceptance of a particular viewpoint. The ground begins to crumble beneath the centre.

The ideological history of the Conservative Party since 1975 is best viewed as a progression from polarisation to uniformity. The first divisive issue was economic policy, which split the Party between 'wets' and 'dries'. The comprehensive victory of the Thatcherite 'dries' has been marked by the disappearance of alternative economic views. No one in the Party is an open-minded pragmatist on this issue; they only disagree about the best rate of progress towards the single goal of a low-tax economy with a 'flexible' labour market. In short, there is no longer any spectrum of opinion in which a new centre could hold the balance.

Since 1990, the same process has been at work over Europe. For most of the 1990s the Party was polarised between 'Eurofanatics' and 'Eurosceptics' of varying hues. In 2004 the pro-European pole is still on the map; but it has dwindled to a tiny speck. The initiative is firmly in the hands of those who seek withdrawal from the EU. Some observers might have interpreted the change of leadership from Iain Duncan Smith to Michael Howard as a shift back towards the centre ground on Europe. But that would only illustrate the difficulty of discerning a central grouping of any kind in today's Party. Howard was not among the Cabinet 'bastards' identified by John Major during the darkest days of his premiership; but he consistently threw his weight against Major's centrist compromise. By the time of the election Major was pleading that his critics should allow him to negotiate on behalf of the country, 'not in the convenient party political interests of the Conservative Party'. In retirement, Critchley found it hard to recall any previous Tory leader 'who has acknowledged with such candour that the interests of the Conservative Party and the nation are readily distinguishable'.[35] The old centre would have viewed such an admission as a sign that the party was over.

One or two Conservatives in senior positions fight on under the old flag of public service. Michael Ancram and Nicholas Soames would not have been out of place in the party led by Winston Churchill. In the 2001 leadership election Ancram was the only one of five candidates who possessed both 'old' and 'new' centrist credentials. He mustered only 21 votes, finishing in a tie for bottom place. At least in one respect his fate was kinder than Hurd's in 1997; his chances from the outset were so slim that no one needed to discredit him through his aristocratic origins. Still, it is a tribute to the power of the old ethos that these latter-day representatives have proved so tenacious as they slip inexorably into the 'bed-blocker' category.

With the settlement of the economic controversy, and rapid strides towards uniform Euroscepticism, new poles have emerged on other issues. The years of Hague and Duncan Smith were marked by conflict between the 'mods', who want greater social tolerance, and the authoritarian 'rockers'. Controversy died down after the advent of Michael Howard, who combined the track record of a rocker with the chastened demeanour of a moderate moderniser. But the latent feelings persisted; and it seems inappropriate to speak of a centrist group in a polarised party during a temporary truce.

All the dynamic forces within the Party, in or outside Westminster, point to the persistence of a rightwards ratchet which has been in operation for three decades. Keith Joseph may or may not have been right in 1975, when he argued that the Party had been shaping its policies in response to Labour rather than the public. But his theory certainly applies to the situation since 1994, when Conservatives started talking about 'putting clear blue water' between themselves and the Blair-led Opposition. This cry goes down particularly well in the constituency parties which still enjoy so much autonomy in the choice of future candidates – and, under the ill-conceived new rules, have the final say in choosing the leader.

It is tempting to attribute the present plight of the Conservative Party to its failure to reconstitute a substantial and coherent central grouping which enjoys influence and respect. But the relationship between cause and effect is more complex. We have seen that Margaret Thatcher launched a deliberate assault on the centre, and to that extent the Party's condition is a visitation of poetic justice on current members who still idolise the fallen leader. But she was knocking at an open door – or rather, smashing up a building which had already lost its foundations. If post-war social change has been the main solvent of the Conservative centre, Willie Whitelaw may well have been right in identifying a certain inevitability about the whole protracted process.

Notes

1. Julian Critchley, in J. Critchley and M. Halcrow, *Collapse of Stout Party: The Decline and Fall of the Tories* (London: Victor Gollancz, 1997), p.286.
2. F. Pym, *The Politics of Consent* (London: Sphere Books, 1985), p.192.
3. I. Gilmour, *The Body Politic* (London: Hutchinson, 1971 edition), p.90.
4. Q. Hogg, *The Case for Conservatism* (Harmondsworth: Penguin, 1947), p.14.
5. J.A. Cross, *Lord Swinton* (Oxford: Clarendon Press, 1982), p.293.
6. As Ewen Green has emphasised, Steel-Maitland was an original Conservative thinker. See 'An Intellectual in Conservative Politics: The Case of Arthur Steel-Maitland', in E.H.H. Green, *Ideologies of Class: Conservative Political Ideas in the Twentieth Century* (Oxford: Oxford University Press, 2002), pp.72–113.
7. Cross, *Lord Swinton*, p.293.
8. Lord Swinton, *Sixty Years of Power* (London: Hutchinson, 1966), p.201, p.200.

9. Ibid., p.200.
10. Quoted in M. Garnett and I. Aitken, *Splendid! Splendid! The Authorised Biography of Willie Whitelaw* (London: Jonathan Cape, 2002), p.263.
11. Swinton, *Sixty Years of Power*, p.248.
12. Quoted in Garnett and Aitken, *Splendid!*, p.9.
13. Quoted in ibid., p.100.
14. Swinton, *Sixty Years of Power*, p.246.
15. Ibid., p.249.
16. P. Cowley and M. Bailey, 'Peasants' Uprising or Religious War? Re-examining the 1975 Conservative Leadership Contest', *British Journal of Political Science*, September 1999.
17. See, for example, D. Butler and M. Pinto-Duschinsky, 'The Conservative Elite, 1918–78: Does Unrepresentativeness Matter?', in Z. Layton-Henry (ed.) *Conservative Party Politics* (London: Macmillan, 1980), pp.186–209, and D. Baker and I. Fountain, 'Eton Gent or Essex Man? The Conservative Parliamentary Elite', in S. Ludlam and M. Smith (eds), *Contemporary British Conservatism* (London: Macmillan, 1996), pp.86–97.
18. A. Maude, 'The Conservative Party and the Changing Social Structure', *Political Quarterly*, XXIV:2 (April–June 1953), p.144.
19. M. Nicholson, *The System: The Misgovernment of Modern Britain* (London: Hodder and Stoughton, 1967), p.138.
20. J. Critchley, 'Strains and Stresses in the Conservative Party', *Political Quarterly*, 44:4 (October–December 1973), p.401.
21. Ibid., p.404.
22. In an article for the same journal back in 1961 Critchley had reported that 'a certain Brigadier was heard to say that if he ever met a member of the Bow Group he would strangle him'. Whatever his own views, the Brigadier was expressing a dislike of intellectuals which was common among members of the old Conservative centre; see J. Critchley, 'The Intellectuals', *Political Quarterly*, 32:3 (July–September 1961), p.271.
23. Of course Critchley was writing while Home was Foreign Secretary in the Heath Government.
24. 'The Quest for Common Ground', in K. Joseph, *Stranded in the Middle Ground? Reflections on Circumstances and Politics* (London: Centre for Policy Studies, 1976), pp.19–34.
25. G. Lewis, *Lord Hailsham: A Life* (London: Jonathan Cape, 1997), p.326.
26. Garnett and Aitken, *Splendid!*, p.216, p.218.
27. Lewis, *Hailsham*, p.326.
28. Hailsham attacked the idea of 'elective dictatorship' in his Dimbleby lecture of 1976. He was less vocal on this theme after Mrs Thatcher became Prime Minister. The kindest explanation is that his notion of 'balance' was best suited to the Conservative Party when it was in Opposition.
29. Pym, *Politics of Consent*, p.x.
30. A. Clark, *Diaries: Into Politics* (London: Weidenfeld and Nicolson, 2000), p.176, p.174.
31. P. Norton, '"The Lady's not for Turning". But What About the Rest of the Conservative Party?', *Parliamentary Affairs*, 1990.
32. Critchley, 'Strains and Stresses', p.404. Of course one might argue that Critchley, Raison, Scott and Tapsell might have shifted violently to the left

since their old days of 'moderation' – perhaps out of disappointment at their treatment at Thatcher's hands. But it seems improbable that these very different individuals would all have reacted in the same way.

33. A. Gamble, 'An Ideological Party', in Ludlam and Smith, *Contemporary British Conservatism*, pp.19–36.
34. See, for example, I. Gilmour and M. Garnett, *Whatever Happened to the Tories? The Conservative Party since 1945* (London: Fourth Estate, 1997), p.385.
35. Critchley and Halcrow, *Collapse of Stout Party*, p.154.

4
One Nation[1]
David Seawright

Introduction

In the last Conservative leadership election 'run-off' in 2001, before Michael Howard 'emerged' as the new leader in 2003, both Iain Duncan Smith (IDS) and Ken Clarke made claims on the One Nation tradition.[2] This immediately raises the question of how Conservatives who appear so diametrically opposed, on both issues of state intervention and on European integration,[3] could both possibly issue an appeal which extolled the virtues of One Nation Conservatism. This chapter addresses such a conundrum by first analysing the use of One Nation as a central Party myth and secondly, by examining the composition and the legacy of the One Nation dining group of Conservative MPs formed in 1950. Finally, it focuses on and challenges a certain portrayal of One Nation as a group exclusively on the left of the Party, as in any effective exposure of the great myths of British politics it is important to demonstrate just how distorted and pervasive such a view has become.

Students of Conservative Party politics are no doubt well aware of Lord Kilmuir's (David Maxwell-Fyfe) dictum of loyalty being the 'secret weapon' of the Conservative Party.[4] Students and commentators alike should make themselves aware of R.J. White's maxim that 'parties are forever in need of refreshment at the springs of doctrine'.[5] Focusing on the One Nation group of Conservative MPs as a microcosm of Conservative Party politics allows us not only the opportunity to rule out the assertion that loyalty was ever the secret weapon of the Party but to identify the real secret weapon in the manner in which the Party refreshes itself at such springs of doctrine. We shall see that the Conservative Party is more of a doctrinal party than is commonly thought and through examining the composition and actions of the One Nation group we see how a 'creative tension' over doctrine leads the Party to perpetually consider that very refreshment of which White spoke. Thus an examination of the One Nation group is an invaluable exercise in any analysis of the political thought of the post-war Conservative Party, but we begin by a brief but necessary summary on the origins of the 'One Nation myth' itself.

Mythical origins: Disraeli on England

Conservatives have a certain predilection for establishing for themselves a line of party ancestry; hardly surprising, one might think, in a party which eulogises a 'contract' between the living, the dead and those yet to be born. One of the foremost of those ancestral lines is that of Disraeli: 'it has been the habit of Conservatives to go to Disraeli as to a sacred flame'.[6] And Disraeli is commonly held to be the source of the One Nation theme.[7] He incorporated the rhetorical flourishes of the Young England movement into his romantic novels in the first half of the nineteenth century and later in his famous Manchester and Crystal Palace speeches of April and June 1872 respectively. In these works Disraeli outlined his trio of objectives which would enable the Party to transcend the divisive sectional interests in society by appealing to the electorate as *the* Party of the nation. 'Gentlemen, the Tory party, unless it is a national party, is nothing. It is not a confederacy of nobles, it is not a democratic multitude; it is a party formed from all the numerous classes in the realm – classes alike and equal before the law, but whose different conditions and different aims give vigour and variety to our national life.'[8]

In a conjunction between the defence of established institutions and a eulogy to the British Empire, Disraeli espoused as his third great objective the elevation of the condition of the people. 'It must be obvious to all who consider the condition of the multitude with a desire to improve and elevate it, that no important step can be gained unless you can effect some reduction of their hours of labour and humanise their toil.'[9] But, crucially, Disraeli offers an immediate qualifying sentence: '[t]he great problem is to be able to achieve such results without violating those principles of economic truth upon which the prosperity of States depends'.[10] In these two sentences then we find an encapsulation and an anticipation of the later post-war debates concerning affordable social services. These were of course predicated upon a much wider parallel debate within the Party between the protagonists of the extended state and the limited state on the best way to actually achieve the goal of elevating the condition of the people.

But economic reality was never allowed to get in the way of the rhetorical benefits of myth and for Southgate, Disraeli in his 1845 novel *Sybil*, subtitled *The Two Nations*, 'coined a phrase that will live for ever and was immediately arresting' when describing the early nineteenth-century relations between the rich and the poor: 'two nations; between whom there is no intercourse and no sympathy ...'.[11] The solution of course lay with 'the Young England conviction that there could be an alliance between the "nobs and snobs"'.[12] This symbolic union takes place in *Sybil* in the marriage of the aristocratic young hero with the beautiful but penniless heroine.[13] In reality then Disraeli never used the term 'One Nation' (however much he echoed the romantic sentiments of Young England). Furthermore, Smith stresses that the 'gulf between the "two nations" was not bridged' when Disraeli was in power in 1874 or later in the *Tory Democracy* of Lord Randolph Churchill, 'pursuing supposedly the Disraelian tradition ... [in reality] a collection of postures and slogans, rather than policy ...'.[14] The first Conservative to exploit the mythical term in any explicit and systematic way was Stanley Baldwin when appealing for unity, as opposed to the sectional interests of Labour, in the intemperate political climate of the 1920s and 1930s. Baldwin in this period, as well as Chamberlain, advocated a course of action which utilised policies of the extended state to ameliorate the lot of the worker and to have as a goal 'the sense that we stand for the union of those two nations of which Disraeli spoke two generations ago; union among our own people to make one nation of our own people at home which, if secured, nothing else matters in the world'.[15]

This was the 'ancestral mythology' which the One Nation group of MPs utilised in their first pamphlet in 1950 when they traced a lineage from Disraeli through to Winston Churchill of Conservatives who displayed a concern with a one nation approach to social problems.[16] However, just four years later in 1954 one member was of the opinion that the group's 'hereditary line' should reach back even further than Peel, let alone Disraeli, all the way to Lord Liverpool, the arch mediocrity himself found in *Coningsby*.[17] In a letter from Jack Simon to Angus Maude, Simon offers an extract from the House of Lords to advance the case for Liverpool being included in the 1954 booklet:[18]

On 23rd November, 1819, in the House of Lords, Lord Liverpool said: 'the legislature of no other country whatever has shown so vigilant and constant a solicitude for the welfare of the poorer classes; no other has so generally abstained from interference with the details and operations of trade; and it is almost equally demonstrable that the pre-eminent prosperity of our trading classes of every kind has been caused, or at least very quickly aided and promoted, by that judicious abstinence'.[19]

This note to Maude neatly illustrates for us the underlying tension within the One Nation group itself, and not only within the Conservative Party *per se*, over the amount of governmental intervention or judicious abstinence needed to address that solicitude for the welfare of the poorer classes. Below we see such 'tension' embodied in the actual membership of the One Nation group of MPs.

The myth incarnate

The power of such a conceptual myth is matched by the mythical legacy of the group of MPs who combined in 1950 and became known collectively as One Nation. Indeed, as late as 1996, the group, while irritated at the quite puerile 'definitions' of One Nation Conservatism from political enemies and ill-intentioned friends alike, were cognisant of its 'powerful brand-name attractions which PR-conscious politicians want to grab'.[20] But such 'definitions' of One Nation Conservatism are in reality fuelled by the 'ideological divergence' in the group's membership. From its outset in 1950 the group's membership has exhibited the full range of the Conservative ideological continuum. As we shall see, the views of the free market, limited state Conservatives were espoused just as much, or even more so, as the views of Conservatives adhering to dirigiste policies of an extended state. Table 4.1 lists the membership of One Nation from its inception in 1950 to 2003, and reveals this divergence in ideological make-up. A cursory glance finds Angus Maude and Enoch Powell in contrast to Cuthbert Alport and Iain Macleod, Keith Joseph in comparison with Ian Gilmour, or Ken Clarke relative to David Willetts. Intuitively, one may think that such divergence could only constrain debate, limit forthright views and lead to equivocation, but we shall also see that although there may have been times when the 'public face' of the 'Nation' was so curtailed, in the sense of publications, this was not the case in private where group deliberations were to facilitate the candid debate so necessary for our doctrinal refreshment.

The actual formation of the One Nation group was partly fortuitous in that two of the three founding members, Cuthbert Alport and Angus Maude, met by chance at a 'brains trust' before entering Parliament in the new intake of Conservative MPs in 1950. Having met and dined together early in the Parliament of 1950–51, they agreed on the idea of forming a

Table 4.1 Members of the One Nation group, 1950–2003

Year		Year		Year	
1950*	Alport, Cuthbert (Cub)	1976	Brittan, Leon	1992	Ottaway, Richard
1950*	Carr, Robert	1976	Butler, Adam	1992	Robinson, Mark
1950*	Fort, Richard	1976	Clarke, Kenneth	1992	Shaw, Giles
1950*	Heath, Edward	1976	Edwards, Nicholas	1992	Smith, Tim
1950*	Longden, Gilbert	1976	Fowler, Norman	1992	Stewart, Ian
1950*	Macleod, Iain	1976	Hurd, Douglas	1992	Taylor, Ian
1950*	Maude, Angus	1976	Raison, Timothy	1993	Bowis, John
1950*	Powell, Enoch	1976	Rees, Peter	1993	Coombs, Anthony
1950*	Rodgers, John	1976	Walder, David	1993	Faber, David
1951	Vaughan-Morgan, John	1984	Benyon, William	1993	Hague, William
1951	Maudling, Reginald	1984	Blaker, Peter	1993	Jackson, Robert
1952	Ormsby-Gore, David	1984	Bulmer, Esmond	1993	Jopling, Michael
1953	Lambton, Viscount	1984	Carlisle, Kenneth	1993	Malone, Gerald
1953	Simon, Jocelyn (Jack)	1984	Cranbourne, Vicount	1993	Milligan, Stephen
1956	Balniel, Lord	1984	Forman, Nigel	1993	Paice, James
1956	Fletcher-Cooke, Charles	1984	Freeman, Roger	1994	Garnier, Edward
1956	Harrison, Brian	1984	Harlech, Lord	1994	Howarth, Alan
1956	Joseph, Keith	1984	Heathcoat-Amory, David	1994	Sainsbury, Tim
1957	Ramsden, James	1984	Hirst, Michael	1994	Spring, Richard
1957	Rippon, Geoffrey	1984	Hordern, Peter	1994	Wells, Bowen
1958	Deedes, William (Bill)	1984	Lyell, Nicholas	1994	Willetts, David
1958	Low, Toby	1984	Needham, Richard	1994	Yeo, Tim
1958	Hill, John	1984	Pollock, Alex	1995	Fowler, Norman
1963	Hobson, John	1984	Pym, Francis	1995	Hendry, Charles
1964	Channon, Paul	1984	Rathbone, Tim	1995	Hunt, David
1964	Chataway, Christopher	1984	Renton, Timothy	1995	Lait, Jacqui
1964	Gilmour, Ian	1984	Rhodes James, Robert	1995	Lloyd, Peter
1964	Goodhart, Philip	1984	Rhys-Williams, Brandon	1995	Trend, Michael
1964	Longbottom, Charles	1984	Rowe, Andrew	1997	Boswell, Timothy
1964	Ridley, Nicholas	1984	Ryder, Richard	1997	Bottomley, Virginia
1964	Royle, Anthony	1984	Soames, Nicholas	1997	Dorrell, Stephen
1964	Worsley, Marcus	1984	Spicer, Michael	1997	Goodlad, Alistair
1965	Alison, Michael	1984	Temple-Morris, Peter	1997	Hogg, Douglas
1965	Howe, Geoffrey	1984	Walden, George	1997	Maples, John
1966	Howell, David	1984	Watson, John	1997	Shephard, Gillian
1968	Carlisle, Mark	1987	Heseltine, Michael	1997	Winterton, Nicholas
1968	Smith, John	1992	Ancram, Michael	1998	Green, Damian
1969	Biffen, John	1992	Arbuthnot, James	1998	Letwin, Oliver
1970	Macmillan, Maurice	1992	Bonsor, Nicholas	1998	Maude, Francis
1970	Nott, John	1992	Burt, Alistair	1998	Norman, Archie
1970	St John Stevas, Norman	1992	Critchley, Julian	1998	Spelman, Caroline
1971	Baker, Kenneth	1992	Fishburn, Dudley	1998	Tyrie, Andrew
1971	Kimball, Marcus	1992	Hayhoe, Barney	1998	Young, George
1971	Mills, Stratton	1992	Hughes, Robert	1999	Simpson, Keith
		1992	Lee, John	2002	Lidington, David
		1992	Lester, Jim	2002	McLoughlin, Patrick
		1992	King, Tom	2003	Baron, John
		1992	Mans, Keith	2003	Cameron, David
		1992	Mitchell, Andrew		
		1992	Norris, Stephen		

*Original signatory to the 1950 One Nation pamphlet.

Source: Compiled from various sources.[21]

group as both shared the opinion that the severe lack of detail in the frontbench speeches on social policy had to be addressed and such a group could help fill that particular lacuna. They then approached Gilbert Longden whom Alport knew from before the war from the candidate courses run at the Ashridge Conservative College. Richard Fort, Robert Carr and then John Rodgers were recruited next. Rodgers then recruited Edward Heath but later the other group members were to be disappointed to find that Heath's Balliol scholarship was an 'organ scholarship' and he played little if any part in the 'intellectual discussion' of the group. These seven then invited Iain Macleod to join them, and it was Macleod who proposed the inclusion of Enoch Powell in the group to form the original nine members of One Nation. At their first meeting at the Political and Economic Planning (PEP) offices at 16 Queen Anne's Gate, Macleod informed the group that he had been asked to write a pamphlet on the social services for the Conservative Political Centre (CPC) and it was agreed on Macleod's suggestion that this should become a joint production of the group and that it would be published before the 1950 party conference as requested by the CPC.[22]

As Macleod was to be the original author of the CPC pamphlet he was selected as an editor with Angus Maude, but it was Maude who, as the only journalist in the group, was responsible for 're-writing, editing and press preparation work' during the long summer recess of 1950.[23] Chapters were drafted by individual members and the group would meet weekly to discuss their content before Maude eventually applied the polish to the final product. Indeed, it was from this process of meetings that the group agreed to continue dining weekly to become the most auspicious, well known and abiding of the many Conservative dining groups since the war. Although chapters of the *One Nation* book were drafted by certain individual members, there was collective responsibility for Maude's product and this collective imprimatur of a pamphlet became a long-standing tradition of the group. Maude recounts that '[t]he group failed for a long time to agree on a title for the pamphlet. In the end, not long before publication, Maude produced the title *One Nation*, agreed it on the telephone with Macleod and sent it to the printer. This name stuck to the group for good.'[24] An article in the *Daily Telegraph* of August 1950 reinforces this last-minute sense of fate: 'next month a group of Conservative MPs, all of them elected for the first time last February, will publish their views on social policy. Their pamphlet will take as its title – "the Strong and the Weak" – from a speech made last year by Mr Eden.'[25] One can only muse on the longevity of such a group assuming the moniker of 'the strong and the weak'.[26]

At a dinner on 15 November 1951 the group resolved that no member of the government could remain as a member of the 'Nation' as this would compromise the independence of the group. As Edward Heath had now become a government whip, it was decided that 'Mr Heath [be] informed accordingly'.[27] It has been the convention ever since that a member will leave the Nation on accepting governmental office and can re-attend only if that member returns to the back benches or if the Party itself loses office. While emphasising the importance of conviviality and the assumption of friendship as important elements in the Nation's membership, Lord David Howell[28] also stressed that policy would raise its head in serious ways at dinner, in particular when the party is out of office as Opposition is a much livelier affair when the ex-ministers are all back in attendance.[29] With such a notable list of distinguished Conservatives as that shown in Table 4.1, it is hardly surprising to find that members did leave to begin their ascent on the greasy pole, some with more notable success than others. Thus, periodically the One Nation group required a search for new blood and retrospectively we can see from the table of members how successful such transfusions have been, but there were indeed times when members questioned not only the names of potential recruits but the position and viability of the group itself. Thus, before an expected government reshuffle in 1956, Longden, writing to the group on behalf of himself and Maude 'as the two remaining founder-members of the One Nation Group', enquired as to whether the group should continue. In stressing an affirmative answer for themselves, they added: 'we feel that any impact we may have had on the fortunes of the party has been due to our two books; our election as officers of most of the Party Committees; our P.P.S.-Ships; and our corporate action on several critical occasions'.[30]

Notwithstanding these 'critical corporate actions' and their impact on Party fortunes, we should note that such distinguished Conservative names as those found in Table 4.1 do not by themselves demonstrate a causal connection between One Nation and any direct influence on party policy. Seldon accepted that the group 'may have had some influence on opinion in the country in these early years, but it had virtually none on policy'.[31] Indeed, Lord Howell intimated that the whips who were informed of the One Nation discussions 'might or might not take the slightest notice of what we were saying'.[32] However, in the following section which examines the collective views of One Nation we see that not only can a case be made for some direct influence on policy initiatives, but, more importantly, a greater case can be made for an influence on the political climate which by extension influences the Party's doctrinal profile. In short, the 'Nation' by these individual and collective endeavours encouraged the Party's necessary visits to our 'springs of doctrine'.

The pamphlets: 'letting the dog see the rabbit'

The group's most public 'corporate action' was through the publication of their pamphlets. In all, there were just eight of these published by the CPC, from the first in 1950 to the last one in 1996,[33] and it is important to remember that 'no one chapter' was to be identified with any 'one individual' in the group. 'All [were] collective compromises – though no principles had to be jettisoned in arriving at them.'[34] The first and most famous of course was *One Nation*, the eponymous booklet responsible for the rekindling of such ancestral mythology. For Longden, no principles may have been jettisoned, but it is evident from its inception that the group were all too well aware of the tension in balancing the need for policies to elevate the condition of the people while mindful of Disraeli's caveat that such policy cannot violate 'those principles of economic truth upon which the prosperity of States depends'. This is important, as later we shall see that the image of One Nation, both in 'mythical' and group terms, was portrayed exclusively as belonging to just one of the traditional elements in Conservatism, the one associated with state interventionism. In fact, the first chapter of the 1950 booklet is entitled 'The Conflict of Ideas' and does in part appear to bask in the praise of the *Manchester Guardian* for the Party's progressive approach to social policy as evidenced in the 1950 manifesto: 'the Conservatives have never in their history produced so enlightened a statement on social policy – from full employment to education and the social services'.[35] And chapter two of the booklet is a veritable delineation of those Tories who had 'intervened' to ameliorate the condition of the workers; resulting in the support for the social service state of the early twentieth century and the acceptance by the Party in mid century of the welfare state. Indeed, in early 1951 at their second dinner the group agreed that the object in meeting R.A. Butler that evening should be to emphasise that nothing in One Nation was affected by the prospect of rearmament and to stress the danger of 'certain elements in the party urging necessity to slash housing and other social services'.[36]

But, we should note that the other traditional elements of the Conservative position, on private wealth, on individual responsibility and initiative, were also stressed along with the promotion of a competitive market system as the best possible way of producing the necessary resources needed for the elevation of the condition of the people. The booklet is careful to incorporate Disraeli's warning on 'economic truth'. The obverse component found in the 'conflict of ideas' was very much the 'fundamental disagreement between Conservatives and Socialists on the questions of social policy':

> Socialists believe that the state should provide an average standard. We believe that it should provide a minimum standard, above which people should be free to rise as far as their industry, their thrift, their ability or genius may take them ... Socialists believe that private charity has little place in a public service. We do not agree. We believe, in Mr Eden's words, in the 'strong helping the weak,' rather than in the weakening of the strong ... Our economic position does not, and will not for many years, allow us ... to implement in full the social legislation that has been passed since 1944. Therefore, Conservative policy insists on administrative efficiency in the social services, and on the clear recognition of priorities.[37]

Such prioritising between the social services led the group to identify education as second in importance only to housing as these two social services would determine the health, prosperity and morale of the British people. The 1944 Butler Education Act was praised very highly as another Conservative achievement in social policy; indeed, the group actually viewed education as a bulwark of defence against communism in the ongoing Cold War.[38] In chapter five of *One Nation*, housing is viewed as crucial in respect to many aspects of national life, and social collectivist explanations are utilised in identifying bad housing with the rise in broken homes, retarded education and the increasing numbers in borstals and approved schools. But the chapter becomes a eulogy to private enterprise and the need to remove the state and the local authorities from the backs of the private builders. The building industry was to be given an open field with full competition between purchasers and in price of materials which would stimulate the necessary successful investment and enterprise. 'Government assistance is not only unnecessary, but positively harmful.' The solution was in incentives for the private builder: 'our task is to bring back the mass-production element into the house-building industry, which can be done only by enabling it largely to work on its own authority for a prospective demand – by "letting the dog see the rabbit"'.[39] Interestingly, Alport, writing in the early 1980s, identified the speech by Duncan Sandys, Shadow Minister responsible for housing in 1950, as part of the yawning gap in expertise in Conservative policy which led directly to the creation of the One Nation group. Although, he states in retrospect: 'it was not a bad speech and would certainly have appealed to the "market forces private enterprise, laissez-faire" Conservative Party of the present day'.[40] The evidence presented in the *One Nation* pamphlet suggests that it would have appealed to such Conservatives then as now. In terms of influence, Angus Maude claims that the 1950 booklet was 'indirectly responsible (with the fillip of Harmar Nicholls' démarche at the Conference) for the famous "300,000 Houses" policy, apart from its influence on Tory policy for the other social services.'[41] It is important to note, then as now, that *One Nation* was viewed as an influential pamphlet and a review of it was broadcast at the time in many languages on the BBC's European Service: General News Talk by E.W. Ashcroft.[42] So this famous One Nation document espoused Conservative free enterprise ideas as much as acceptance of safety nets for the unfortunate in society. Indeed, in conclusion to the 1950 pamphlet the group offers the caveat that

> it [the state] must not so tax industry that it cannot replace its own capital, with the result that its prices become uncompetitive in world markets. It must not burden the individual so that he loses his initiative and enterprise, or is driven to emigrate ... [The] long-term aim is to encourage, through the financial system, those qualities in which Conservatives particularly believe – energy, initiative, thrift, and individual responsibility.[43]

If a case can be made for free market Conservatism being extant in the 1950 *One Nation* publication then we may describe it as positively thriving by the time of the publication of *Change is Our Ally* in 1954. In the concluding chapter of this 1954 pamphlet, 'Opinion and Change', the group adumbrates their position that during 'the last forty years', but in particular throughout the 1930s when Conservative policy of 'rationalisation' was in many respects similar to that of Labour's *nationalisation* policy, political thought and practice had swung away from *laissez-faire* to the opposite extreme of centralised planning and control. If greater wealth was to be achieved then the pendulum had to swing back towards a more competitive system.[44] Contemporary comments illustrate just how much this document was viewed as a return to the principles of free market economics and the criticism of past practice by both parties. 'Their book is a riot of idol smashing. They lay violent hands on all party idols – not only socialist idols like nationalisation but Tory idols like tariffs and farmers – and they pitch the lot in to the dustbin.'[45]

And Ian Mikardo in the *Tribune* of 28 May 1954 facetiously talks of Mr Maude's and Mr Powell's pregnancy and the infant produced by it:

> a booklet called Change Is Our Ally, edited by the two of them, but bearing the sign-manual of no fewer than ten Tory MPs who call themselves the 'One Nation Group'. It shows us exactly what a fundamental counter-revolution the Tories will carry out in the life of this country if the Labour Party and the electorate are silly enough to let them get away with it.[46]

This criticism of the Conservative policy of the 1930s as dirigiste rationalisation and the idea of a radical counter-revolution is reminiscent of the 1970s neo-liberals' critique on the failure of the Party to address the 'ratchet of socialism'. Indeed, such parallels with Conservative Party doctrinal debates of the 1970s are clear in the correspondence between R.A. Butler and Angus Maude, which neatly illustrates the similar tension over questions concerning the trajectory of doctrine in the 1950s. The *Daily Telegraph* in 1954 had noticed the 'one small but significant point of difference'. R.A. Butler had failed to supply a forward in 1954 as he had done for *One Nation* in 1950, but the *Telegraph* ascribed this to the fact that he was now Chancellor of the Exchequer without the freedom of manoeuvre found in Opposition. Although the paper did point out that 'it is also true that "Change Is Our Ally" has – certainly in respect of one Conservative Minister – a very much sharper cutting edge'.[47] The galley proofs of the pamphlet had been sent to Butler with the request for him to write a forward. But on 1 May 1954, Michael Fraser of the Conservative Research Department sent a memo to Butler intimating that he and David Dear had looked at the booklet and he was now getting James Douglas to have a look at it in detail. Fraser takes issue with the pamphlet's assertion that interwar rationalisation was simply nationalisation writ small. Fraser then offers two reasons why Butler should not be connected with the ideas presented in the booklet. The first is that as Chancellor he should not be associated with any controversial publications touching on economic and industrial policy. But of greater import is the second reason outlined by Fraser: 'because the first part of this document, which is an historical analysis of the inter war years, the war economy and the socialist period, contains much criticism of the policies of the pre-war and wartime Governments of which you yourself were a member ...'. Fraser then offers the advice that Butler uses only the first argument in replying to Mr Maude.[48] This Butler does on 3 May 1954 and Maude replies on 13 May 1954 intimating that he fully understands the reasons for this. On 20 May 1954 Maude sends the finished booklet to Butler, 'with the compliments of the authors', but Butler scrolls across it in red ink, 'Fundamentally insincere'. But on 21 May 1954 he then thanks Maude 'for so kindly letting me have a copy of "Change Is Our Ally"'.[49] Such correspondence of the early 1950s suggests a greater doctrinal tension within the Party than is commonly thought; if nothing else, it throws into sharp relief the ostensible picture of unquestioning loyalty. The *Financial Times*, 21 May 1954, observed that such views represented 'a considerable change in Conservative thinking, a change which had already been observable in policy, but of which this is the first coherent and thorough statement'. One other published comment is of note here. In the *Glasgow Herald*, 12 July 1954, we find a Prospective Unionist Candidate who describes the pamphlet as 'the most important [Conservative] report of them all' produced in the past year. The author is fulsome in his praise for the pamphlet although he does suggest that there will be Conservatives 'who will resist many of the specific proposals as outright Liberal heresies'. The author was Ralph Harris, soon to be the co-founder of the Institute of Economic Affairs (IEA) in 1957.[50]

Of the other pamphlets, *The Responsible Society*, published in 1959 as the CPC's 200th publication, adopted a less strident but similar line to that taken in the 1954 pamphlet. In fact, *The Times*, 24 March 1959, interpreted it thus: 'the writers see the past eight years of Conservative Government as a period during which some progress has been made in halting and indeed reversing the trend towards State domination and giving the individual back some share of initiative'. At a special CPC dinner to launch the publication, Gilbert Longden, as the oldest surviving member, summarised the group's views of the 1950s as condemning indiscriminate state largesse in 1950, encouraging economic change to a freer economy as a prerequisite to enabling any expansion of the social services in 1954, and in 1959 as a 'movement away from State domination, and towards a greater share of individual initiative, as one of the "most beneficial results of Tory rule"'.[51] This interpretation chimes uncannily with the David Willetts' view of the periods when the Party promoted judicious abstinence of state activity as opposed to adoption of policies associated with an extended state.[52] With this in mind, the group's short pamphlet, in the year after Mrs Thatcher became leader, espoused those very interventionist policies of a more active state. This 1976 booklet on relations in the workplace was replete with notions of corporatist arrangements for *One Nation at Work*. The state would compel the establishment of employee councils in works employing over 500 employees[53] and the solutions offered echoed not only co-determination as found in Germany but the compulsive legislation of the Heath Government's Acts of 1972, 1973 and 1974 which forced consultation on employers.[54] In 1984, Philip Goodhart, while reflecting the concern felt in the group over the level of unemployment in society, pointed out that

> individual members of the One Nation Group have advanced a number of widely different arguments as to how the economy should be managed. This pamphlet does not seek to choose between these individual arguments, but it puts forward a number of ideas for coping with the impact of unemployment, which we believe are wholly consistent with the Government's economic strategy.[55]

The tradition of collective compromise, without the jettisoning of ideological principles, does appear to be alive and well in the 1984 booklet. Indeed, Lord Howell believes that an old-fashioned metaphor of 'harness' better describes the intra-party politics of the Conservative Party than the term 'ideology' ever did. For him there were four horses – the tendencies – which were harnessed to the Conservative coach: one of social conscience; one of free markets; the populist or 'poujadist' element, and a fourth one from the knights of the shires.[56] The trick for the Conservative Party was keeping them in harness: 'if they are not managed they dissolve into cliques and cabals and if they are managed it creates a very good and effective atmosphere'. The One Nation group then can be seen as instrumental in the Party's 'management' of that 'effective atmosphere' and Lord Howell's concern as Chairman of the Group in the 1990s was in making an effective contribution to keeping these 'horses in harness'.[57] Lord Howell drafted the *One Nation 2000* and the *One Nation: At the Heart of the Future* pamphlets in 1992 and 1996 respectively. In 1992 the emphasis was placed on the unchanged goal of the group 'to create a Britain in which growing prosperity of the fortunate is reflected in the better welfare of the disadvantaged; in which the benefits of enterprise are the benefit of all ...'.[58] In the 1996 pamphlet, the 'essence of One Nation Conservatism' was outlined in conceptual as well as traditional terms. Very simply, the family was the building block which binds society together and social cohesion could never be imposed from above:

> from this, and not from the state, comes the responsibility, the civic commitment and the common pride and purpose which gives a nation binding strength ... It explains why attempts either to link One Nation

to some trendy interventionist vision, or, *per contra*, to brand One Nation Tories as a bunch of wets who want a federal Europe, are so contemptible.[59]

The important role played by Lord Howell in the formation of Conservative policy over three decades enhances the critique below of such 'skilled propaganda from ill-intentioned friends'.

A great moving left show: one Europe or no nation?

In a four-page leaflet produced in 1962, entitled 'One Nation', Iain Macleod linked the approach of One Nation closely to the work of Lord Hailsham and the Tory Reform Group to R.A. Butler and to the work over the years of the Prime Minister, Harold Macmillan.[60] A minute in 1951 indicates that the group did dine with the members of the 'Tory Reform [Committee]' but there was never any formal connection let alone a conflation of views.[61] Over the years there was always cross-membership of other dining groups on both the left and the right of the Party, and even today there is joint membership of the 'Nation' with such groups on the left as the Lollards and Nick's Diner, as with the No Turning Back group or the Conservative Way Forward on the right. There was also close ties with the Bow Group, right from its inception at the Bow Constitutional Club in January 1951; with a cross-fertilisation of ideas thereafter.[62] But the extra-parliamentary groups on the left of the party have shown a tendency to construct a form of discourse hegemony when it comes to the use of the 'One Nation' term. For example, the group Pressure for Economic and Social Toryism (PEST) was formed in 1963 by university undergraduates and London journalists and was supported by such Tory luminaries as Edward Boyle and Iain Macleod. It urged the Tory party 'to lead a "One Nation" Britain into an outward-looking Euro-Atlantic partnership and to follow policies at home which will induce economic efficiency and ensure social freedom'.[63] On 20 September 1975 the Tory Reform Group (TRG) was formed by the merger of PEST with the regionally based MACLEOD and STAG groups, and in its new year message of 1976, Bill Shearman stated:

> the Party must continue to represent all sections of the community, must pledge itself to end class conflict and govern again on the basis of Disraeli's 'One Nation' ... The way forward to a genuine renaissance of ideas lies in the traditional Tory concern for the social conditions

of the people and a society based on fairness, where exploitation by one group by another is curtailed by State intervention.[64]

The TRG's president was Nicolas Scott of Nick's Diner fame, but more importantly for us we should note that the vice president was Robert Carr and another guest speaker of note at its inaugural meeting was Ian Gilmour.

This was the background then to the wilful distortion and the hegemonic exploitation of One Nation by the left of the Party. From the late 1970s and throughout the 1980s, with the help of lazy journalism, contemporary commentators utilised One Nation as a coded term to denote opposition to Thatcherism.[65] And the published work of Ian Gilmour in the extended state tradition of the Party was to go a long way to reinforcing such identification. For example, in Ian Gilmour's and Mark Garnett's work only the *One Nation* pamphlet exists; the others, like *Change is Our Ally* in 1954 or *The Responsible Society* of 1959, are conveniently air-brushed from Conservative history.[66] There is no doubt that the neo-liberal rhetoric of the 1970s, which drew parallels with the One Nation group's critique of Butler's achievements in 1954, went further in trying to wholly delegitimise the extended state tradition of the Party. But is the creation of another delegitimisation project, which utilises a selective account to marginalise the free market tradition in the Party (which the One Nation group had dated all the way back to Liverpool), really the answer? It is no different from that dogmatic approach to politics that is so ostensibly abhorred by the 'Gilmourites'. In fact, when one peruses the One Nation minutes, it is quite obvious that in any academic study of Conservative principles it would be quite literally impossible to ignore the free market ideas and the role of 'individual responsibility' and 'competition'. Indeed, on 22 March 1967 we see that there was an overwhelming majority of the 'Nation' against the next phase of the government's prices and incomes policy, 'with only Ian Gilmour in favour'.[67]

And this selectivity extends its tentacles to the issue of Europe. In Gilmour's work One Nation is equated with the ideas of One Europe. But the enthusiasm shown for European integration in the mid 1960s was in order that market disciplines could be enforced at home.[68] And by 1971 it was noted that one visible consequence of the European issue was a schism in the One Nation group of Tory MPs. 'Among the few remaining founder members Enoch Powell and Angus Maude voted against the Market. Gilbert Longden and Sir John Rodgers, also founder members and strong Europeans, voted with the Government.'[69] Moreover, the author of *One Europe*, Nicholas Ridley, could not by any stretch of the imagination be classified as Europhile by the 1980s, and Gilbert Longden, a strong supporter of the Conservative Group for Europe, had by the late 1990s joined the Eurosceptic Bruges Group.[70] Of course, many supporters of further European integration are still to be found in the One Nation group – that is not in doubt; even those like Ken Clarke who support a European constitution and the euro, but it is quite wrong to ignore the fact that there are also strong opponents of Europe in the 'Nation'. David Heathcoat-Amory is one:

> The world has moved on, Europe's moved on and the Party has moved on and I actually think that this excessive belief in the European Union, I call it No Nation Conservatism, is an attempt to submerge us into an integrated Europe, like a lump of sugar dissolving in tea and you end up with no nation at all, nothing to call One Nation, nothing to call any nation at all. That is a big abdication of our duties because one of the things the Conservative Party is, is a constitutional party, in fact we are often called that: you will see it in our clubs which are often called Conservative and Constitutional clubs, that is regard for the British constitution, and bedded in that is a strong belief in self government.[71]

For Baldwin nothing was permanent except the folly of mankind. Conservatives must always be wary of the claims of 'permanence', to which the advocates of *Change is Our Ally* attested. Thus, although some One Nation members strongly support the idea of further European integration, others now view such 'European federalism' as a new grand narrative, a new dogma of social engineering against which the Party has to be constantly vigilant; nothing is permanent even for Conservatives.

Conclusion

Hopefully we have seen that it is a rather puerile exercise to endeavour to delegitimise one of the traditional pillars of Conservatism. Chipping at one may well in the long run threaten the whole edifice. It is quite evident from Table 4.1 that the One Nation group, since its inception in 1950, has incorporated a range of views encompassing the whole gamut of the Conservative continuum.[72] Indeed, the future of the group looks assured if we juxtapose such members as Alistair Burt and Damian Green with others like David Willetts and David Cameron (tipped by some for future stardom). In 2004, we find that the 'emerged' Michael Howard is rather upset over Labour cynically stealing Conservative rhetoric,[73] but help may be at hand from the group as once again important debate on the trajectory of doctrine is a main course on the group's menu, in the shape of 'social justice'. Alistair Burt disclosed that a debate was now taking place on the use and utility of such a term between the members of the group, with concomitant substantive questions being raised concerning the future ideological trajectory of the Party. Although Burt believes it is about the whole concept of 'Easterhouse etc.' (*pace* IDS), and that is where he wants the Conservative Party to go and where for him it needs to go, 'back into the cities, yes, social justice exists and there are Conservative solutions to it'. For Burt, it should be part of the Conservative lexicon, 'the centre ground is what you leave to your opponent and this ground should not be left to Labour',[74] but he accepts that others in the group merely see it as a 'mechanistic term'. Indeed, Alport informs us that Enoch Powell hated the term 'because the phrase seemed to him to be waffley and almost meaningless', and in a similar vein David Willetts classed it as merely 'slippery'.[75] But Willetts now accepts that his position has changed somewhat from that classic Hayekian critique; for him, social justice can now be a good word which captures the idea that the distribution of opportunities in life are not simply determined by the market. He elaborates:

> I think we Conservatives denied that and came a cropper as a result, so social justice is in some sense trying to get some sense of social obligation back in, it needn't be egalitarian necessarily but it is trying to get that idea back in and I was overly dismissive of that strand of thought in my book about it, so it is a philosophical strand that you can find in Conservatism that I rejected too forcefully then, and also, at the lowest level of political tactics, we have watched Labour capture so many words from us like community, rights and responsibilities, and the natural Conservative language of enterprise. So part of the revival of Conservatism is to reclaim our vocabulary and if we can press Labour by saying, hold on, we have a different view of social justice than you have and social justice does not just belong to Labour, I think that is an important political task that we have.[76]

So to reiterate, 'tension' and debate within the One Nation group again facilitates that necessary quest for refreshment at the springs of doctrine. Powell in 1952 was well aware of how apparent contradictions which baffle Conservatives are really the historic dilemmas of Toryism; contradictions which have resonance for us today. 'In favour of control yet champion competition; conservers of the constitution but are leading exponents of House of Lords reform; call ourselves the champions of trade unionists but the bosses vote for us; we see ourselves as creators of the social services but depend on votes of those who regard levels of welfare expenditure and taxation as excessive', but he could conclude with the thought: 'Conservatism has neither been defeated nor compromised; it has been transformed. But it could not have performed its own transformation and preserved the nation but for that inner conviction which appeared at first to be in conflict with its doings and sayings in the world about it.'[77] The One Nation group may not 'dance with dogma', but we have seen that it is perfectly at ease with 'dining with doctrine'. The inner conviction of the group has been an important catalyst in the transformation of the political thought of the post-war Conservative Party.

The evidence presented here on the conceptual and empirical use of the 'One Nation' term offers an explanation to the conundrum of why Ken Clarke and Iain Duncan Smith could both claim an affinity with the One Nation ideal. Indeed, Iain Macleod once described his relationship with Enoch Powell thus: 'I am a fellow-traveller, but sometimes I leave Powell's train a few stations down the line, before it reaches, and sometimes crashes into, the buffers.'[78] But, crucially, it may be more important to acknowledge that they both managed to remain on the same train and for so long a journey, in no small measure due to the decisive role of the One Nation group.

Notes

1. I am grateful to the British Academy for the research grant SG 35058 which enabled me to undertake the research for this chapter. I would also like to thank my colleagues Ed Gouge, Stuart McAnulla and Kevin Theakston for commenting on a draft of this work.
2. See for example, *The Times*, 27 August 2001, and the *Daily Telegraph*, 28 August 2001.
3. D. Baker and D. Seawright, *Britain For and Against Europe* (Oxford: Clarendon Press, 1998), and D. Baker, A. Gamble, S. Ludlam and D. Seawright, 'Backbenchers with Attitude: A Seismic Study of the Conservative Party and Dissent on Europe', in S. Bowler, D.M. Farrell and R.S. Katz (eds), *Party Discipline and Parliamentary Government* (Ohio: Ohio University Press, 1999).
4. Earl of Kilmuir, *Political Adventure: The Memoirs of the Earl of Kilmuir* (London: Weidenfeld and Nicolson, 1964), p.324.
5. R.J. White, *The Conservative Tradition* (London: Nicholas Kaye, 1950), p.23.
6. D. Southgate, 'The Defence of Land and Labour', in N. Gash, D. Southgate, D. Dilks and J. Ramsden, *The Conservatives: A History from their Origins to 1965* (London: George Allen and Unwin, 1977), p.125.

7. For example, see S. Fielding, 'A New Politics?' in P. Dunleavy, A. Gamble, R. Heffernan, I. Holliday and G. Peele (eds), *Developments in British Politics 6* (Basingstoke: Palgrave, 2002), p.15.
8. M.A. Kebbel, *Selected Speeches of the Late Right Honourable the Earl of Beaconsfield* (London: Longmans, Green and Co., 1882), p.524.
9. Ibid., p.531.
10. Ibid.
11. Southgate, 'The Defence of Land and Labour', p.123, and B. Disraeli, *Sybil or The Two Nations* (Harmondsworth: Penguin, 1980), p.96.
12. R. Faber, *Young England* (London: Faber and Faber, 1987), p.257.
13. However, the novel ends with what may be termed a 'Cinderella turn' when Sybil is found to be of aristocratic blood, no doubt the source of her noble mien. Interestingly, in Disraeli's previous 1844 novel *Coningsby*, the symbolic union is one between the bourgeois mill owner and the aristocracy (see note 17 below).
14. P. Smith, *Disraelian Conservatism and Social Reform* (London: Routledge and Kegan Paul, 1967), p.323.
15. S. Baldwin, *On England* (Harmondsworth: Penguin, 1926), p.82.
16. I. Macleod and A. Maude (eds), *One Nation: A Tory Approach to Social Problems* (London: Conservative Political Centre, 1950) see note 33 below for full list of One Nation publications.
17. B. Disraeli, *Coningsby, or the New Generation* (London: Everyman's Library, 1967), p.59.
18. E. Powell and A. Maude, *Change is Our Ally: A Tory Approach to Industrial Problems* (London: Conservative Political Centre, 1954); see note 33 below.
19. Conservative Party Archive (CPA): CCO 150/4/2/1, Bodleian Library, Oxford: 'Letter from Jack Simon to Angus Maude 9th April 1954'. I would like to take this opportunity to thank Sheridan Westlake of Conservative Central Office for permission to consult and quote from the CPA at the Bodleian Library Oxford and also to Emily Tarrant, the archivist and Colin Harris and Oliver House for their generous help and guidance in the use of this resource.
20. One Nation Group, *One Nation at the Heart of the Future* (London: Conservative Political Centre, 1996), p.7.
21. *1950–71*: Information gleaned from the papers of Sir Gilbert Longden, London School of Economics and Political Science Library. I am grateful for the kind help from Sue Donnelly, the archivist, and for her permission to consult these papers. And, gleaned also from the papers of Sir John Rodgers, Centre for Kentish Studies, Kent. I would like to thank Sir Piers Rodgers for his permission to view and quote from his late father's papers.

   1971–84: Information from the One Nation booklets: 'One Nation At Work' (1976), 'Jobs Ahead' (1984).

   1992–2003: Information from the One Nation booklets: 'One Nation 2000' (1992) and 'One Nation At the Heart of the Future' (1996), and from the One Nation 'attendance book' 1992–2004. I would like to thank Robert Jackson MP and the current members of One Nation for permission to consult this book.
22. See, for example, Cuthbert Alport, 'The Red Notebook: "Our Nation"' in *Box 44: Notes for a Memoir, etc.* Alport Papers, Albert Sloman Library, University of Essex, undated. I would like to thank Robert Butler the librarian and Nigel Cochrane for their permission to consult these papers and for their help. See

also: *Longden Box List*: Temporary File Number 31, *One Nation, 1950–1990*, document entitled: *The Origin of the One Nation* by Angus Maude, March 1970, Sir Gilbert Longden Papers.

23. *The Origin of the One Nation.*
24. Ibid.
25. Newspaper cutting from the *Daily Telegraph*, 25 August 1950, in *Box 8*, Alport Papers.
26. We should note here that by 1996 Alport believed that Macleod suggested the name and that he, Macleod, was one of the first members to join the group; see 'Forming One Nation', *The Spectator*, 30 March 1996, pp.15–16. But Alport in his 'Red Notebook' file for his future memoirs written in the 1980s (see p.18) clearly accepts Gilbert Longden as the first recruit and states: 'It was Angus Maude who suggested the title "One Nation" for our book which had an immediate and remarkable success' (see p.3), in *Box 44*, Alport papers. The error is reproduced in the work of Iain Gilmour and Mark Garnett, *Whatever Happened to the Tories: The Conservatives since 1945* (London: Fourth Estate, 1998), p.vii.
27. One Nation group minute of 15 November 1951 in One Nation Minutes, in *Box 37: One Nation Papers*, Alport Papers.
28. Lord David Howell was chairman of the group in the 1990s; the practice of having a formal position of chairman was only adopted in the 1960s, until then the form was to 'rotate' the chairman at each dinner.
29. Interview with Lord David Howell at the House of Lords, 23 June 2004.
30. Letter from Longden to the group, 17 January 1956, *Longden Box List*: Temporary File Number 31.
31. A. Seldon, *Churchill's Indian Summer: The Conservative Government, 1951–55* (London: Hodder and Stoughton, 1981), p.58. But see pp.57, 424 and 434 for both the limited and extended state views of the group.
32. Interview with Lord David Howell.
33. *One Nation publications*: I. Macleod and A. Maude (eds), *One Nation: A Tory Approach to Social Problems* (London: Conservative Political Centre, 1950); E. Powell and A. Maude (eds), *Change is Our Ally* (London: Conservative Political Centre, 1954); Lord Balniel, R. Carr, W. Deedes, C. Fletcher-Cooke, R. Fort, B. Harrison, K. Joseph, G. Longden, T. Low, J. Ramsden and G. Rippon, *The Responsible Society* (London: Conservative Political Centre, 1959); N. Ridley (ed.), *One Europe* (London: Conservative Political Centre, 1965); A. Butler, K. Baker, L. Brittan, P. Goodhart and M. Alison (eds), *One Nation at Work: By the One Nation Group of MPs* (London: Conservative Political Centre, 1976); P. Goodhart, *Jobs Ahead* (London: Conservative Political Centre, 1984); One Nation, *One Nation 2000* (London: Conservative Political Centre, 1992); One Nation, *One Nation: At the Heart of the Future* (London: Conservative Political Centre, 1996).
34. Longden in a letter to an old acquaintance on the success of One Nation, 5 February 1951, *Longden Box List*: Temporary File Number 3. The 1984 pamphlet, *Jobs Ahead*, by Philip Goodhart was single authored but again this was given the group's imprimatur.
35. Macleod and Maude, *One Nation*, p.9.
36. Minute of One Nation group, 5 February 1951, in Alport Papers.
37. Macleod and Maude, *One Nation*, p.9.

38. Ibid, p.39. But we find, from a One Nation minute of 29 January 1953, that 'The Education Act, 1944, was deplored' (Alport Papers).
39. Macleod and Maude, *One Nation*, pp.27–38.
40. Alport, 'The Red Notebook', p.2, in *Box 44*, Alport Papers.
41. Harmar Nicholls was MP for Peterborough, 1950–October 1974; see W.J. Biffen, 'Party Conference and Party Policy', *Political Quarterly*, 32 (1962), p.262, for an account of this historical decision of the conference.
42. See *Longden Box List*: Temporary File Number 31.
43. Macleod and Maude, *One Nation*, p.90 and p.93.
44. Powell and Maude, *Change is Our Ally*, pp.96–7.
45. *Daily Mirror*, 21 May 1954.
46. Newspaper cutting in CPA: CCO 150/4/2/1, Bodleian Library.
47. *Daily Telegraph*, 21 May 1954.
48. Memo from Mr Fraser to Mr Butler, 1 May 1954, *RAB H54:32 & RAB H5433*, Butler Papers, Trinity College Cambridge. I would like to thank the Master and Fellows of Trinity College for their permission to consult and quote from these papers.
49. Ibid., *RAB H54:35, 36 and 37*.
50. Thus, arguably the One Nation group played a part in the promotion of such neo-liberal ideas in this period. See also R. Crocket, *Thinking the Unthinkable* (London: Fontana Press, 1995).
51. CPC: 23 March 1959 in *Longden Box List*: Temporary File Number 31. Moreover, Longden was later to associate the *One Nation* work with an anticipation of Thatcherism. 'I hope that I have distilled the thoughts of some Tory backbenchers 35 years ago; and I maintain that they have more affinity with "Thatcherism" than with the views of the "wets" of today' (*Crossbow* (Autumn 1985), pp.22–4).
52. See D. Willetts, *Modern Conservatism* (Harmondsworth: Penguin, 1992).
53. Butler et al., *One Nation at Work*, p.17. Ironically, Margaret Thatcher supplied a forward for this document welcoming the work of the One Nation group of MPs.
54. Ibid., pp.14–16.
55. Goodhart, *Jobs Ahead*, p.5.
56. See 'Varieties of Conservatism', in P. Norton and A. Aughey, *Conservatives and Conservatism* (London: Temple Smith, 1989), pp.53–89.
57. Interview with Lord David Howell.
58. One Nation, *One Nation 2000*, p.5.
59. One Nation, *One Nation: At the Heart of the Future*, p.8.
60. I. Macleod, 'One Nation', pp. 1–2, in *Longden Box List*: Temporary File Number 31, and see Harvester Archives of the British Conservative Party, 1962/107. Here Macleod means the Tory Reform Committee rather than the Tory Reform Group initiated in 1975.
61. One Nation group minute, 28 June 1951, Alport Papers. Indeed, a similar but erroneous extrapolation could be made for an association with Lord Hinchingbrooke (Victor Montagu), who was Chairman of the Tory Reform Committee in 1943 (and was present with Hailsham at this dinner) and who was involved with Angus Maude in the Suez group and was later to become so hostile to European membership as a member of the Monday Club; see

P. Seyd, 'Factionalism within the Conservative Party: The Monday Club', *Government and Opposition*, 7 (1972), pp.464–87.

62. See CPA: CCO3/3/48, Bodleian Library and *Longden Box List*: Temporary File Number 31, for a letter from James Lemkin, 21 March 1957, enclosing copies of Bow Group pamphlets and intimating that: 'the members of the Bow Group last night found the first contact with the One Nation group most valuable'.

63. See CPA: CCO 3/6/138 and CCO 3/7/43, Bodleian Library. But, similar to Hinchingbrooke above, Michael Spicer who was PEST Chairman 1963–67 did not feel constrained to maintain such views, particularly on Europe; see, for example, Baker et al., 'Backbenchers with Attitude'.

64. CPA: CCO 3/7/52, Bodleian Library.

65. For example, see J. Cole, *As it Seemed to Me* (St Ives: Phoenix, 1996), pp.209 and 251. On page 209, he equates One Nation with Gilmour and 'the wets', and on page 251 he identifies Pym as 'One Nation' and makes an explicit contrast with him and John Nott who was more 'Thatcherite than Thatcher', but of course John Nott was a member of One Nation.

66. See Gilmour and Garnett, *Whatever Happened to the Tories*. Unfortunately, such 'Procrustean polemics' merely stretch, push, pull and compress material to 'fit' a particular interpretation of One Nation.

67. For example, see the One Nation minutes, 2 November 1966 and 22 March 1967, in One Nation Minutes, 1965 to 1971, U2332 OP27/8, Sir John Rodgers Papers, Centre for Kentish Studies, Kent.

68. 'What was really meant by this was that people were not prepared to face seeing the petty restrictive practices, the closed shops, the restrictions on trade and competition swept away' (Ridley, *One Europe*, p.9). Lord Howell agreed with this interpretation and added that most Conservatives could not support the present trajectory of the European Union.

69. Peterborough column, in the *Daily Telegraph*, 30 October 1971.

70. See *Longden Box List*: Temporary File Number 22, Conservative Group for Europe, Minutes, 1973–1978, and Temporary File Number 34, Europe and the Bruges Group, 1992–1996.

71. David Heathcoat-Amory, interviewed at the House of Commons, 29 June 2004.

72. Of course, we should note the conspicuous absence of women but this may merely reflect the paucity of women in the parliamentary party itself; see One Nation minute of 24 January 1968 for such a view. Sir John Rodgers Papers, Kent.

73. *Guardian*, 17 November 2004.

74. Alistair Burt, interviewed at the House of Commons, 28 June 2004. See G. Streeter (ed.), *There Is Such a Thing as Society* (London: Politicos, 2002).

75. Alport, 'The Red Notebook', p.16, in *Box 44*, Alport Papers and Willetts, *Modern Conservatism*, p.112.

76. David Willetts, interviewed at the House of Commons, 28 June 2004.

77. Copy of letter from Mr J. Enoch Powell to Mr Angus Maude, 20 October 1952, in *Longden Box List*: Temporary File Number 31.

78. See James Maragach in the *Sunday Times*, 28 April 1968.

Part Two
Themes and Issues

5
The Constitution
Philip Norton

A constitution constitutes 'the set of laws, rules and practices that create the basic institutions of the state, and its component and related parts, and stipulate the powers of those institutions and the relationship between the different institutions and between those institutions and individual'.[1] So defined, all countries have a constitution. The British constitution is often lauded as being 'unwritten'. The description is misleading. Much of it is written. A great deal is embodied in a mass of statute law: the Bill of Rights 1689, the Parliament Act 1911 and the European Communities Act 1972 are all fundamental documents of constitutional law. What distinguishes the British constitution is not that it is unwritten, but rather that it is not codified in a single, higher law document. In this respect, it is distinctive, though not unique. This distinctiveness is important to the Conservative.

For the Conservative, respect for the law and the institutions of the state is intrinsic to the maintenance of a stable polity. Institutions provide structure and continuity. They guarantee the smooth order of society and make possible the freedom for people to pursue a civilised life.[2] Conservatives therefore have a strong attachment to the institutions of the nation – traditionally the Crown, Church and Parliament – as the means of delivering order and stability. Institutions serve not only to channel behaviour in a structured and orderly manner, but also to engage the loyalties of the people, the institutions transcending the particular social or political divisions that may exist within the nation.

For the Conservative, constitutional form is thus crucial to the well-being of the nation. As Conservatives, the natural instinct is to defend established institutions that are the product of prescription and have served the nation well. They have grown into the fabric of the constitution. No institution can be seen as some discrete entity, amenable to abolition or radical surgery without such action having adverse repercussions for the rest of the body politic. The institutions form part of a polity that has evolved over time and which is distinctive to these shores. To abolish them or subject them to regular or harsh surgery is to undermine the stability of that which holds the nation together.

Inherent in this is the realisation that the stability and continued well-being of the nation derives not just from institutions as such but from the relationship between the different institutions and between those institutions and the people. Those relationships have some formal shape through the medium of the law but they are fleshed out by conventions and understandings. Conventions are rules that are not enforced by the courts or by the presiding officer of either House of Parliament, but which are complied with by those affected by them in order to make the system work. They provide for the means of adaptation. Form is maintained but conventions enable it to be adapted to political reality. The Queen retains the legal power to refuse her assent to a bill passed by both Houses of Parliament but by convention does not do so; the last time a monarch vetoed a bill was in 1707. The legal power remains useful as a nuclear option: only to be used in the most dire of emergencies. The convention enables the form to be maintained and for the monarch to transcend political activity and serve as the unifying element within the nation.

Conventions help shape relationships and to fill some gaps. However, the constitution relies to some degree on gaps remaining. It proceeds on the basis of what Michael Foley has characterised as 'condoned obscurities'.[3] The constitution's weakness, he argues, is its realism. Given that constitutions do not necessarily answer all questions of authority and power, then this, Foley argues, also constitutes its strength, 'for it means that British politics have had to acknowledge the incompleteness of the constitution and to work around its formidable gaps. This takes technique, practice, and subtlety.'[4] The silence of the constitution has, from a Conservative perspective, a dual attribute. It avoids the straitjacket of codification which can both constrain government and serve to limit rather than enhance the liberties of the individual. It enables the Tory view of government to be realised – maintaining the strength and autonomy of the Queen's Government – yet at the same time leaving the subjects of the Crown to do whatever they wish so long as it is not proscribed by law.

For the Conservative, the constitution is evolutionary and, like a good chairman, works best when not too obvious. However, the fact that it is evolutionary rather than static means that it admits of the means of change. Conservatives are with Burke in believing that a state without the means of some change is without the means of its own conservation. Change may be necessary in order to maintain or strengthen the existing framework. Conventions provide the means of adaptation but on occasion, when an institution is under threat, there may be a case for something more dramatic and formal. Conservatives are prepared to consider piecemeal change in order to maintain and strengthen existing institutions. A good illustration of this is to be found in the passage of the Life Peerages Act 1958. In constitutional terms, it represented a radical departure from the established basis for membership of the House of Lords. Under the Act, peerages could be created for the lifetime of the holders only and not devolve to their heirs. It enabled people to be brought into the Upper House who otherwise may not have accepted a hereditary title and, in so doing, brought in considerable new blood to the House. The change helped revive an otherwise apparently somnolent chamber. This was the effect intended by the Tory Government of Harold Macmillan and also the reason why the Labour Party opposed the measure. Labour recognised that if it was successful, it may help stall the demands for more radical reform.

Thus, to Conservatives, the constitution is to be defended and protected. It embodies not only essential institutional forms, but also the understandings and, indeed, ambiguities necessary to maintain the essential balance between effectiveness and consent that underpins political stability. 'An organisation that cannot effectively influence the society around it is not', in Richard Rose's words, 'a government.' 'A government that acts without the consent of the governed is not a government as we like to think of it in the western world.'[5] The constitution has delivered continuity with adaptability, enabling the Tory belief in executive authority to cohere with the liberal view of democratic accountability. As David Judge has observed, representative government in the United Kingdom continues to be conceived as a means of legitimating executive power.[6]

The constitution has evolved in such a way as to produce a stable and benign system of government that has certain benefits that are particular to the United Kingdom. The electoral system facilitates the return of a government with an overall parliamentary majority, but does so in a way that ensures the accountability of the government to the people. The desire of the people to have a say in who serves as Members of Parliament proved too powerful to resist in the nineteenth century – although the Tories under Wellington sought to resist it, though later under Disraeli took the lead in accommodating it – but that desire has been adapted to the prevailing executive authority. A government is chosen by the people through the medium of party; the party chosen by the electors at the polls governs until it has to face the electors again. A general election, in Karl Popper's words, constitutes 'judgement day'.[7] The party in power can be swept from office. Recognising that, the party in government is responsive in between elections to shifts in public opinion. The government of the United Kingdom is thus accountable, effective, and responsive.

The accountability of government to the people is exercised within a political structure comprised of several parts operating on a mutually dependent basis and with an understanding of their respective roles. Ministers recognise the need for civil servants to maintain a professional detachment from the partisan activities of their political bosses. Civil servants recognise the political authority of their ministers. Each relies on the other and each operates best by recognising the domain and role of the other. Ministers take decisions but have to justify their actions – and their legislative measures – to Parliament. Both Houses have mechanisms to call government to account. The Opposition recognises that the government is entitled to get its business. The government recognises that the Opposition as well as private members are entitled to be heard.[8] These relationships are variously governed by practice and convention. At the heart of the relationship between government and Parliament are the conventions of individual and collective ministerial responsibility. There is nothing in law that says the prime minister or other ministers have to turn up and answer questions at Question Time but, by convention, they do so. For the entirety of the twentieth century, the relationship between ministers and civil servants was never defined in statute. The position of the most powerful minister, the Prime Minister, was hardly mentioned in law. A combination of institutional structures, conventions and understandings established over time produced what, to Conservatives, has been a perfectly workable system of government for the United Kingdom.

It was not planned as such – a strength in the eyes of Conservatives – but it has emerged and continues to adapt. It may not be the ideal but it is the real and it is worth protecting unless and until something is proven – as opposed simply to being argued – to be better. The level of proof is a high one. Conservatives have a natural aversion to grand theories. Critics who make the case for a new constitution are to be challenged. They fail, as David Willetts has argued, to recognise that the culture and institutions that underpin the existing constitution are more robust than they realise. 'The hold on the popular imagination of the monarchy, the sovereignty of Parliament, even, at times of national crisis or rejoicing, the Church of England is greater than the reformers recognise.'[9] Furthermore, Willetts argues, the institutions work more subtly than the reformers recognise. 'They have seen us through an extraordinary variety of economic and political crises and they have always held.'[10] The fact that other nations have written constitutions is no argument for Britain following suit. What works for them will not necessarily work in a country that has seen no massive constitutional dislocation for more than three centuries: 'to assume that we could somehow replace our constitutional traditions with a new set of arrangements in peacetime without any crisis flies in the face of all the historical evidence'.[11] And, for Conservatives, it is the historical evidence that counts.

The Conservative thus defends the distinctive features of the uncodified constitution, its very ambiguities constituting one of its strengths. Institutions are to be defended – and defended strongly – as part of the essential infrastructure of the polity, so long as they continue to fulfil their purpose. If they falter, then they can be adapted to maintain and bolster their position as an integral part of the relationship at the heart of the British polity.

For most of the twentieth century, Conservatives were comfortable in defending the constitution. When the institutions and the autonomy of the state came under challenge, as in 1926 during the General Strike, the attachment to the constitution was such as to see off the challenge. The constitution proved sturdy not only in time of peace but also in time of war. Government and Parliament continued to function. During the Second World War, Parliament not only met but also managed to extract a notable degree of responsiveness from a powerful executive.[12] MPs discussed the conduct of the war; they continued to raise constituency concerns. Despite damage caused by enemy bombing – the chamber of the Commons was destroyed – Parliament continued to meet. Parliament emerged from the war with its reputation enhanced. In a celebrated 1946 broadcast, American broadcaster Ed Murrow declared:

> I doubt that the most important thing was Dunkirk or even the Battle of Britain, El Alamein or Stalingrad ... Historians may decide that any one of these events was decisive, but I am persuaded that the most important thing that happened in Britain was that this nation chose to win or lose this war under the established rule of parliamentary procedure.[13]

The quarter-century following the Second World War appeared to confirm the Conservatives' high regard for the constitution. It appeared to be effective in providing the framework within which significant social change and relative economic prosperity could be achieved. The period from 1950 to 1964 was perceived at the time, in Bogdanor and Skidelsky's phrase, as an age of affluence.[14] There was a consensus as to Britain's economic and political role. The institutions of the state appeared able to deliver what was expected of them. 'Indeed, one of the most striking characteristic of the 1950s was the absence of any major intellectual challenges to the dominant political assumptions.'[15] Political scientists sought to explain rather than challenge the existing arrangements.

There was not complete silence. Some Conservatives did reflect on the constitution or on the failings of particular parts of our constitutional arrangements. L.S. Amery's 1946 Chichele lectures were published in 1947 as *Thoughts on the Constitution*.[16] He recognised the pressures on the parliamentary system of government, not least from the growth of party, and advanced various proposals for adaptation. In 1949, Conservative MP Christopher Hollis published *Can Parliament Survive?* and in 1950 Lord Cecil of Chelwood called attention in a Lords debate to the growing power of the Cabinet.[17] However, there was little conceptual discussion of the constitution and no challenge to its fundamental tenets and its appropriateness to the United Kingdom.

In a Commons debate in 1981, Home Office minister Timothy Raison recalled that in 1964 he had published a book about politics. 'When I read it not so long ago', he said, 'it struck me that it contained virtually no discussion on constitutional problems ... it was written at a time when, by and large, we did not regard our constitution as something about which we should be having second thoughts.'[18] If the constitution was mentioned, it was more likely to be for the purpose of praise and for possible emulation elsewhere than for critical comment. Students were brought up on Harvey and Bather's *The British Constitution*, in which the authors noted that 'it has not been easy to construct for fifty million people, of varied views and temperaments, a form of government which both follows the stipulated rules and acts with promptness and efficiency'.[19] That the British people had devised a constitution which, if not perfect, at least appears to them to work satisfactorily was not, they said, due to providence but to the vigilance of the people. Government, they declared, was not a science or an art, but a way of living.[20]

It was a way of living that was to be less settled in the 1960s and 1970s. As Raison observed in the 1981 debate, 'over the past decade many issues have come to the fore ... These issues include the future of the other place [the House of Lords], referendums, devolution, the European Community and our accession to it, a Bill of Rights, electoral reform, and what I might call extra-parliamentary forces.'[21] The constitution, or at least particular aspects of it, became the subject of political debate. The debate itself was initially inchoate. Measures of constitutional reform, of the sort mentioned by Raison, were advocated as responses to particular political problems. As Douglas Hurd noted, there was a problem for Conservatives in that, having taken the constitution largely for granted in post-war years, they had largely fallen out of the practice of discussing national institutions and their place in our constitutional arrangements.[22] It was not a problem confined to Conservatives. It was only as the debate progressed that coherent approaches to constitutional change emerged.[23] One of these – the liberal approach – made much of the running in debate in the 1980s and, especially, the 1990s. Its supporters were brought together in the reform movement Charter 88 and made the case for a new constitutional settlement. The constitution was no longer in the settled state that it had been in the quarter-century after 1945.

The last quarter of the twentieth century thus posed a problem for Conservatives. In fact, it posed – or rather exposed – two problems for the Conservative view of the constitution. One is a problem that can be described as an internal dilemma and the other as an external threat. They raise the question as to what stance a future Conservative Government should take on constitutional change.

The internal dilemma

Conservatives face an inherent conflict between continuity and change. How far is change sometimes necessary in order to protect the basic framework of the constitution? For some, a High Tory approach is to be preferred. Change is always seen as likely to lead to worse. There is therefore a reluctance to embrace change, any change. They incline to the view, expressed by Conservative MP John Stokes – a latter-day Lord Hugh Cecil – who in the Commons in 1981 argued that the constitution had grown organically, requiring little if any mechanical tinkering.[24] Others have been willing to accept significant change as a way of bolstering existing institutions or at least staving off change that will be even worse. As Ian Gilmour observed, 'plainly "prescription" does not rule out positive reform'.[25] One Conservative's 'positive reform' may be another's assault on the essentials of the constitution. Some Conservatives prefer to die in the last ditch in defence of existing arrangements; others are willing to embrace or at least acquiesce in change. One illustration of such a clash is that which occurred over the Parliament Bill of 1910–11, a bitter conflict which gave rise to the terminology of 'hedgers' and 'ditchers'.

The Shadow Cabinet decided not to oppose the Parliament Bill after being informed that the King had agreed to create enough new peers to swamp the Upper House. The 'ditchers' organised and fought to the end.[26]

The potential for conflict is not confined to the constitution and indeed there is the potential for conflict between different tenets of Conservative thought.[27] Adherence to national institutions and the relationships between them can, and has, conflicted with pursuit of other goals. This conflict has been realised in the debate over European integration, where the desire to achieve economic growth and international stability has clashed with adherence to the Tory view of executive authority.

Pursuit of European integration has formed the fault-line of Conservative politics at least since 1945 and at times, to follow the analogy, has given rise to a number of earthquakes. In the 1960s, the economic and political certainties of the previous decade gave way to decline, conflict and uncertainty. It was a Conservative Government that first sought membership of the European Community and another Conservative Government that delivered it. The motivation for membership was primarily political but was also linked inextricably to the economic. The point was stressed by Harold Macmillan in writing to President Kennedy: 'if we are to meet the challenge of communism [we must show] ... that our modern society – the new form of capitalism – can run in a way that makes the fullest use of our resources and results in a steady expansion of our economic strength'.[28] It was a point reinforced by Edward Heath: 'the political objectives of the Community have therefore to be achieved by economic means'.[29]

For the Conservative, the potential to lead the European Community was a means of re-establishing Britain's role on the world stage. It was also a means of achieving a free market. There were thus powerful imperatives for the United Kingdom to become part, belatedly, of the European Community. Pursuing these imperatives was, though, at the expense of adherence to the nation's established constitutional arrangements. Membership added a new judicial dimension to the constitution. Parliament enacted a self-denying ordinance in the form of the European Communities Act 1972, giving the force of law not only to existing but also to all future Community law. As a consequence of membership, any conflict between European and UK law was to be resolved by the courts, with precedence given to the former. Various policy competences were transferred to the institutions of the EC. These competences were increased with succeeding treaties and the institutions of the Community strengthened. The Council of Ministers was strengthened at the expense of national institutions by the extension of qualified majority voting under the Single European Act, ratified in 1987, and the European Parliament strengthened by the introduction and extension of the co-decision procedure, making it more of a partner with the Council in approving legislation.[30]

At the time of membership, there was little reflection on or understanding of the implications for the nation's constitutional arrangements. The government, in a White Paper, declared that there was 'no question of any erosion of essential parliamentary sovereignty'.[31] From a purely formal view, this was correct in that Parliament retained the power to repeal the 1972 Act. In every other respect, it was contestable. The nature of the constitution up to the time of EC membership had 'ensured that the judicial contribution to our constitutional thought and culture has been minimal'.[32] Now, the judiciary was empowered to make a substantial contribution. It could develop a European jurisprudence and could strike down a provision of British law as being incompatible with European law. The significance of this was realised in the 1990s in a number of important court cases.[33] On 4 March 1994, the House of Lords in *R. v Secretary of State for Employment, ex p. the Equal Opportunities Commission* struck down certain provisions of the 1978 Employment Protection (Consolidation) Act as incompatible with EC law.[34] The following day, *The Times* declared that 'Britain may now have, for the first time in its history, a constitutional court.'

Parliament was thus limited, by its own actions, by membership of the EC. Despite the government's assertion, the consequences were apparent at the time of membership. 'The relegation of the Westminster Parliament', declared Uwe Kitzinger in 1973, 'in matters where the Community has competence was not so much an unfortunate accidental disadvantage as inherent in the essence of the Community as such, and thus part and parcel of the aim of entry.'[35] In the laconic observation of David Coombes, 'where Community business is concerned, Parliament has to accept certain special limitations'.[36] Those limitations ran counter to the core constitutional tenet of parliamentary supremacy: the outputs of Parliament were no longer binding and now could be set aside by a body other than Parliament itself.

The limitation on sovereignty extended beyond the doctrine of parliamentary sovereignty to that of national sovereignty. Her Majesty's Government no longer enjoyed autonomy in determining policy in certain specified sectors. The domain of the EC expanded with successive treaties. Even if the claim advanced by successive governments that the UK had a greater say through the pooling of sovereignty is accepted, the embrace of a pooling in perpetuity ran counter to Conservative perceptions of Britain's role in the world. Tensions remained in relation to its attachment to both the Commonwealth and the United States. Britain could lead through running an Empire, but as a consequence of membership of the EC, 'the British Parliament will be reduced', declared Neil Marten in 1970, 'to the status of a County Council as we know it. And that ... is for ever.'[37]

Membership of the EC, now the European Union, thus invited a conflict within Conservative ranks. The conflict is particularly stark for neo-liberals. By virtue of their adherence to the market, they favour free trade. The EC offers the means for removing trade barriers and achieving free trade within an ever-growing community. Yet it is neo-liberals who tend to be most virulently opposed to European integration and, indeed, were generally opposed to membership. Though some have reconciled the conflict by perceiving the EU as 'fortress Europe' and an obstacle to global free trade, others have sought alternative trading blocks to counter EU influence and in so doing confirmed the inherent conflict between economic goals and attachment to the established constitution.

Membership of the EU is also seen as a threat to the legitimacy of the nation's constitutional arrangements. The fundamental underpinnings of the constitution derive from popular acceptance. If the institutions of the EU fail to engage the people in the way that national institutions do, then the legitimacy of the constitution is undermined. There is little evidence of popular engagement with the European Union. Most electors stay at home during elections to the European Parliament. As the powers of the European Parliament have grown, popular support and interest have not; if anything, the reverse. There is a perceived 'democratic deficit' in the EU with a notable degree of detachment between leaders and citizens. Popular disengagement undermines the basis of the constitution. The institutions of the EU are *sui generis*, bearing no relationship to what people understand and feel comfortable with and the potential for an EU constitution introduces a concept that is alien to the British political culture.

European integration, however, has not been the only cause of conflict. Another conflict was apparent under the Thatcher Government in its pursuit of a free market. Achieving a free market required a strong state in order to achieve the conditions for its realisation.[38] For critics of the government, including some within its own ranks, it was pushing its powers too far and undermining the traditional balances within the system.[39] It was also undermining the One Nation emphasis on maintaining the unity and social fabric of the nation, pursuing policies that were divisive. The 1980s witnessed serious divisions within

Conservative ranks. However, there was a defence of government from the Tory view of the constitution. The government was not only utilising those powers which inhered in government, available to be used when necessary, but were being employed on a temporary basis in order to restore the autonomy of government that had been eroded in the period of the post-war consensus. For some, Margaret Thatcher was a threat to the nation's constitutional arrangements. To others, she was working to bolster them. Under her premiership, the basic institutions of the state remained intact; the relationships at the heart of the constitution underwent some but relatively little change. She did not so much transform the constitution as use the powers it conferred. In so doing, she demonstrated an inherent problem that is most usually identified by Conservatives as an external threat.

The external threat

There is, then, the potential for conflict when Conservatives are in office, but the greatest threat is not from Conservatives fighting one another when in office, but from other parties when in power. However, the very nature of the constitution renders it vulnerable. The strength of the constitution is also its Achilles' heel. The problem has been well summarised by Vernon Bogdanor. 'The existence of a constitution', he wrote, 'implies a set of rules determining political behaviour; but the peculiarity of the British constitution is that it lacks an umpire. It is the players themselves, the government of the day, who interpret the way in which the rules are to be applied.'[40] Indeed, it is the government that can not only interpret the rules but, as long as it has a parliamentary majority, change them. The very flexibility of the constitution is both its strength and its weakness. There is no entrenchment that definitively limits government. Government has to work within the parliamentary process but through that process can change the constitution.

To the Conservative, there is therefore a potential threat when those not wedded to constitutional norms are returned to office. Ian Gilmour identified a number of threats to Britain's free institutions. One, he said, was government elected by universal suffrage. 'Or rather it comes when the government that is elected is a Labour Government. Conservative Governments have many faults, but they do not pose a threat to freedom or to the constitution.'[41] Early Labour Governments – those of MacDonald, Attlee and Wilson in his first term – remained within the British constitutional tradition. 'It is only since 1970 that the Labour Party has become a threat to the constitution, both in Opposition and in Government.'[42] For Gilmour, the threat came from Labour's shift to the left. Since the 1990s, the threat has come from the Party's shift to the right or rather the shift to a set of leaders with no grounding in the norms and understandings that underpin the constitution.

In the 1974–79 Parliament, a government returned with a minute majority (that later disappeared) on the basis of less than 40 per cent of the votes cast in the general election, sought to achieve passage of major and contested legislative measures. In the period of Labour government since 1997, with a large parliamentary majority in successive Parliaments, the threat has been more severe. The Labour Government has achieved passage of a raft of measures of constitutional change, including devolution, the Human Rights Act, reform of the House of Lords and the greater use of referendums. It has also challenged or undermined the fundamental relationships at the heart of the constitution. The government entered office not understanding government. The relationship between civil servants and ministers has undergone major change, necessitating a commitment to a Civil Service Act to delineate the relationship. The Prime Minister has sought to distance himself from his own Cabinet as well as from Parliament. There has been a fragmentation within government; the glue that has held the different parts of government together has started to dissolve.[43]

The extent of change under Labour has been summarised by Robert Stevens. Previous major constitutional changes, he noted, were often independent acts rather than part of a dramatic period of constitutional change. The period from 1970 to 2000, he argued, was different, offering a practical and psychological transformation comparable with the revolutionary period from 1640 to 1720.[44] The reforms lack coherence in terms of any clear view of constitutional change.[45] Ministers have no clear conception of the constitution and, hence, of the constitution they wish to see in place for the United Kingdom. As one Whitehall insider told Peter Hennessy: 'most of the senior ministers involved in constitutional reform either don't believe in it, aren't interested in it, or don't understand it'.[46]

The constitution, as Amery recognised, is more than majority rule. 'The idea that a majority, just because it is a majority, is entitled to pass without full discussion what legislation it pleases ... is wholly alien to the spirit of our Constitution.'[47] However, ministers since 1997 have equated government with majority rule. Given that the constitution has been protected by convention and understandings, the lack of understanding has robbed it of one of its most important underpinnings.

In this, there is a fundamental dilemma for the Conservative. There is unity in opposing a government intent on destroying the norms of the constitution. There is a problem, however, in deciding how to curb such abuse. McAuslan and McEldowney, writing in the period of the Thatcher Government, contended that once the barnacles encrusted on the ship of state had been removed, it stood revealed for what it has always been: 'a vehicle for swift and effective action'.[48] Given the Conservatives' adherence to that constitution, should not the use made of it by a government be accepted? Or should institutional constraints be worked into our constitutional arrangements? In other words, should Conservatives seek to protect the constitution by themselves accepting the need for reform? This therefore brings us full circle, back to the internal dilemma.

During the period of the Labour Government from 1974 to 1979, a number of Conservatives advocated constitutional reform in order to limit the excesses of government. For Lord Hailsham, who coined the phrase 'elective dictatorship', the answer was to be found in a written constitution. 'The time has come', he declared in the 1976 Dimbleby Lecture, 'to take stock and to recognise how far this nation, supposedly dedicated to freedom under law, has moved towards a totalitarianism which can only be altered by a systematic and radical overhaul of our constitution.'[49] He envisaged a bicameral legislature, with both houses elected, an entrenched Bill of Rights, and devolved government. He dressed this up in Conservative terms – 'my object is continuity and evolution, not change for its own sake'[50] – but what he was advocating was to form the basis of the most radical approach to constitutional change, that of the liberal approach, a decade later. In essence, to save the constitution it had to be replaced with what he effectively conceded was a new constitution. Some were prepared to contemplate such an approach.[51] Others were less radical but nonetheless advocated changes that would have the effect of undermining or destroying the attributes of the constitution. For Ian Gilmour, if Labour shifted further to the left, then salvation lay in electoral reform.[52] Dr Rhodes Boyson advocated an entrenched Bill of Rights and referendums.[53] Sir Keith Joseph made the case for a Bill of Rights in order to place a constitutional limit on taxation.[54]

The return of a Conservative Government in 1979 largely stilled the debate in Conservative ranks. In 1992, Lord Hailsham published a volume, *On the Constitution*, which read as if he had no recollection of his 1976 lecture. The constitution, he conceded, was under strain, but 'patent medicines do not work'.[55] He was no longer advocating the very medicine he had prescribed. He was not the only Conservative to respond to the reform agenda advocated by Charter 88. Once it became apparent that proponents of a new constitutional settlement were not going to go away, Conservatives – led by John Major, John Patten and Douglas Hurd – weighed in to make the case for the existing constitution.[56]

However, the basic dilemma returned with the Labour Government of 1997. The dilemma was not so much immediate as prospective. The Labour government was wreaking havoc with the nation's constitution, borne not out of malice but political imperatives and ignorance. The immediate response of the Conservative Party was instinctive: to defend the existing constitution and hence to oppose the changes brought forward by the government. That was not the problem. The dilemma was not that of deciding how the Conservative Opposition should respond but rather determining what a future Conservative Government should do.

At the end of the twentieth century, the Conservative Party faced a constitutional landscape that was not the one it had tended and defended in government. A prospective Conservative Government thus faces three options. They are the reactionary, conservative and radical and they encapsulate the dilemma facing any Conservative in the face of radical surgery to the constitution.

Reactionary

The reactionary option entails returning the constitution to the position it was in when the Conservatives were last in office. This is a desirable approach in respect of restoring the relationships, and bolstering the trust, that underpins the constitution. However, it is more problematic in terms of structures. Once changes have taken place, they are difficult to reverse, especially with the passage of time. The Scottish Parliament is now a highly institutionalised body, occupying a dedicated building, its creation having been sanctioned by a referendum of the people in Scotland. The relations between the devolved bodies and the centre have developed without engendering great tensions within the system.[57] Once an institution is in place, helping shape behaviour and forming part of a network of stable relationships, then there becomes, for the Conservative, a problem in justifying abolition or radical surgery. The problem was recognised by William Hague when leader of the Party. In a speech to the Centre for Policy Studies in 1998, he conceded that devolution was an established fact and that the Conservative Party would work within the new framework rather than seek to dismantle it.[58] Some nonetheless advocate a reactionary approach. In this there is nothing new. In 1978, Rhodes Boyson advocated making all life peers hereditary peers.[59] In

2004, Lord Pearson of Rannoch introduced a bill (unsuccessfully) to abolish the Scottish Parliament.

Conservative

This option entails conserving that which exists at the time that the party returns to office. Much depends on how different the constitution is seen to be from that which existed before 1997. Has the Labour Government vandalised the constitution to the extent that it is no longer recognisable and hence in need of restorative surgery? Or will the constitution still retain its basic features? According to the Labour Lord Chancellor, Lord Falconer, the result of the changes since 1997 is to add to the existing constitutional arrangements rather that constituting a new constitutional framework for the United Kingdom.[60] It is a view shared by Nevil Johnson. In terms of the normative content of the customary constitution, he argues, the reforms have served to render its contours more blurred than before, but the reforms themselves are essentially pragmatic experiments to suit political needs. One could seek to justify the changes in theoretical terms as facilitating the better management of the state as an enterprise association; in practical terms, Johnson notes, 'the reforms have the overall effect of maintaining unimpaired the capacity of a British government, working to some extent through the familiar institutions of the customary constitution, to exercise the maximum discretion in the pursuit of whatever happens to be its political objectives and interests'.[61] What would be being conserved by a future Conservative administration would thus be a modified form of the Westminster, or customary, constitution, retaining its essential attributes.

The Conservative leadership has not only accepted already some of the changes implemented by a Labour Government, such as devolution, but also embraced the use of referendums for seeking the assent of the people to particular measures of public policy. Though the Conservative Party has previously toyed with the use of referendums – the Party in 1910 committed itself to their use to resolve major constitutional issues – their employment has been challenged for undermining the parliamentary process.[62] Absent a clear dividing line between what is and what is not subject to referendum, they undermine a core institution of the British polity. However, insofar as their use becomes regularised, they then become part of the practice to be conserved.

Radical

The previous option is the one that is most obviously compatible with a Conservative view of the constitution, but it fails to address the inherent tension within the nation's constitutional arrangements. For what is being conserved is a system that permits its use for unacceptable ends and for its own demise. The essential message on which Margaret Thatcher and Ian Gilmour could make common ground was in asserting that the constitution was safe under the Conservatives but not under Labour. However, in order to make it safe entails in large measure destroying it. The grounds for a radical approach – essentially crafting a new constitutional settlement – are that the existing constitution is no longer up to the task of protecting the rights of the individual and that there is no longer the attachment to the old forms and traditions that underpinned the constitution. 'If weaknesses such as these are to be taken seriously', writes Johnson, 'it becomes necessary to consider whether there is an alternative approach to constitutional renewal, and in particular to the achievement of changes that might begin to tackle the challenge of devising counterweights to set against the claims of the "elective dictatorship" or "mandated majority rule".'[63] As he recognises, going down this path entails accepting the need to accept some codification of the constitution.

Protecting the constitution from an over-mighty government would thus involve the sort of changes that Hailsham advanced three decades before, in effect destroying the existing constitution. There are some who wish to pursue such a path, looking – as a number did during the last period of Labour government – to the United States, and seeking a more formalised separation of powers. They share the envy expressed by Rhodes Boyson in 1978 of the checks and balances of the American constitution.[64] However, this – as Roger Scruton has observed – is to accept that constitutions can be 'made' rather than recognising, as the Conservative does, that the constitution is the inherited principle of the life of the state.[65] There is also the complication that to achieve a radical alternative would necessitate a change in social and political attitudes that, as Johnson indicates, has not yet taken place. There may have been some decline in deference and support for existing norms of the constitution, but they have not been supplanted by attitudes that would sustain a new constitution for the United Kingdom.

The actions of a Labour Government have encouraged some Conservatives, as we have seen, to toy with some proposals that would constitute radical departures from existing norms and structures. Their programmes have not been embraced, though at times the party has toyed with particular radical departures. In opposition after 1997, the leadership embraced for political reasons the policy of a predominantly or wholly elected second chamber, a policy that would have the same effect as electoral reform in destroying the accountability at the heart of existing arrangements.[66] It was a policy that exemplified the internal dilemma for the Party. When the House of Commons voted on various options for reform of the House of Lords in February 2003, more Conservative MPs voted against the official policy than voted for it.[67]

Conclusion

For the Conservative, there will always be an inherent conflict over how far to go in order to preserve the forms and attributes of the constitution. To what extent is change necessary in order to conserve? Under the constitution that the Conservative embraces, there will always be the potential threat from those prepared to use it to subvert it and limit the liberties of the individual. Protecting it from such threats is likely to destroy the very thing that the Conservative seeks to preserve. And even then, there is no guarantee that the alternatives will deliver the protection that is expected of them. As Johnson concedes, neighbouring societies with codified constitutions have witnessed the passing away of the values of liberal constitutionalism.[68] For the Conservative, the task is not to destroy and look for alternatives but rather to think of ways to bolster and reinforce. That comes not just through institutions but, essentially, through the relationships between institutions and the individual. The task is a human one of making sure that the institutions are fit for purpose. What is needed is not blueprints but human endeavour.

Notes

1. Select Committee on the Constitution, House of Lords, *Reviewing the Constitution: Terms of Reference and Method of Working*, 1st Report, Session 2001–02, HL Paper 11, p.9.
2. P. Norton and A. Aughey, *Conservatives and Conservatism* (London: Temple Smith, 1981), p.26.
3. M. Foley, *The Silence of Constitutions* (London: Routledge, 1989), p.114.
4. Ibid., p.97.
5. R. Rose, 'Ungovernability: Is There Fire behind the Smoke?', *Political Studies*, 27 (1979), p.353.
6. D. Judge, 'Whatever Happened to Parliamentary Democracy in the United Kingdom?', *Parliamentary Affairs*, 57 (2004), pp.696–7.
7. K. Popper, 'The open society and its enemies revisited', *The Economist*, 23 April 1988.
8. P. Norton, 'Playing by the Rules: The Constraining Hand of Parliamentary Procedure', *Journal of Legislative Studies*, 7:3 (Autumn 2001).
9. D. Willetts, *Modern Conservatism* (London: Penguin Books, 1992), p.154.
10. Ibid., p.155.

11. Ibid.
12. See P. Norton, 'Winning the War but Losing the Peace: The British House of Commons during the Second World War', *Journal of Legislative Studies*, 4 (1998), pp.33–51.
13. Quoted in ibid., p.46.
14. V. Bogdanor and R. Skidelsky (eds), *The Age of Affluence 1951–1964* (London: Macmillan, 1970).
15. V. Bogdanor and R. Skidelsky, 'Introduction', in Bogdanor and Skidelsky, *The Age of Affluence*, p.11.
16. L.S. Amery, *Thoughts on the Constitution* (Oxford: Oxford University Press, 1947; 2nd edition 1953).
17. Hansard Society, *Parliamentary Reform 1933–60* (London: Cassell, 1967, 2nd revised edition), p.133.
18. *House of Commons Official Report (Hansard)*, sixth series, Vol. 2, col. 1260. The book was *Why Conservative?* (Harmondsworth: Penguin, 1964).
19. J. Harvey and L. Bather, *The British Constitution* (London: Macmillan, 1968, 2nd edition), p.13.
20. Ibid., p.13.
21. *House of Commons Official Report (Hansard)*, sixth series, Vol. 2, col. 1260.
22. D. Hurd, *Conservatism in the 1990s* (London: Conservative Political Centre, 1991), p.6.
23. P. Norton, *The Constitution in Flux* (Oxford: Martin Robertson, 1982) and P. Norton, 'The Constitution: Approaches to Reform', *Politics Review*, 3 (1993), pp.2–5.
24. *House of Commons Official Report (Hansard)*, sixth series, Vol. 2, col. 1213–19.
25. I. Gilmour, *Inside Right: A Study of Conservatism* (London: Hutchinson, 1977), p.212.
26. See D.G. Phillips, 'Lord Willoughby de Broke: Radicalism and Conservatism', in J.A. Thompson and A. Mejia (eds), *Edwardian Conservatism: Five Studies in Adaptation* (London: Croom Helm, 1988), pp.79–85.
27. This was apparent in the 1980s over economic policy with the conflict between economic neo-liberals ('dries') and One Nation Tories ('wets'). See Norton and Aughey, *Conservatives and Conservatism*.
28. H. Macmillan, *Pointing the Way* (London: Macmillan, 1971), p.310.
29. E. Heath, *Our Community* (London: Conservative Political Centre, 1977), p.4.
30. See M. Shephard, 'The European Parliament: Crawling, Walking and Running', in P. Norton (ed.), *Parliaments and Governments in Western Europe* (London: Frank Cass, 1998), pp.167–89.
31. *UK and European Communities*, Cmnd 4715 (London: Her Majesty's Stationery Office, 1971), para. 29.
32. P. Birkinshaw, *European Public Law* (London: Butterworths, 2003), p.159.
33. See B. Fitzpatrick, 'A Dualist House of Lords in a Sea of Monist Community Law', in B. Dickson and P. Carmichael (eds), *The House of Lords: Its Parliamentary and Judicial Roles* (Oxford: Hart Publishing, 1999), pp.171–95.
34. P. Maxwell, 'The House of Lords as a Constitutional Court – The Implications of EX PARTE EOC', in Dickson and Carmichael, *The House of Lords*, pp.197–211.

35. U. Kitzinger, *Diplomacy and Persuasion* (London: Thames and Hudson, 1973), p.32.
36. D. Coombes, 'Parliament and the European Communities', in S.A. Walkland and M. Ryle (eds), *The Commons in the Seventies* (London: Fontana, 1977), p.214.
37. Quoted in Norton, *The Constitution in Flux*, p.166.
38. A. Gamble, *The Free Economy and the Strong State* (London: Macmillan, 1988; 2nd edition 1994).
39. See P. McAuslan and J. McEldowney, 'Legitimacy and the Constitution: The Dissonance between Theory and Practice', in P. McAuslan and J. McEldowney (eds), *Law, Legitimacy and the Constitution* (London: Sweet and Maxwell, 1985), pp.37–8.
40. V. Bogdanor, 'The Constitution', in A. Seldon (ed.), *The Thatcher Effect* (Oxford: Oxford University Press, 1989), p.139.
41. Gilmour, *Inside Right*, p.200.
42. Ibid., p.200.
43. P. Norton, 'Governing Alone', *Parliamentary Affairs*, 56 (2003), pp.543–59.
44. R. Stevens, *The English Judges* (Oxford: Hart Publishing, 2002), p.xiii.
45. See Norton, 'Governing Alone', pp.546–7.
46. P. Hennessy, *The Prime Minister* (London: Allen Lane, 2000), p.510.
47. Amery, *Thoughts on the Constitution*, p.46.
48. McAuslan and McEldowney, 'Legitimacy and the Constitution', p.37.
49. Lord Hailsham, *Elective Dictatorship* (London: BBC, 1976), p.3.
50. Ibid., p.17.
51. See E. Barendt, 'Constitutional Reforms', in Lord Blake and J. Patten (eds), *The Conservative Opportunity* (London: Macmillan, 1976), pp.27–41.
52. Gilmour, *Inside Right*, p.227.
53. R. Boyson, *Centre Forward: A Radical Conservative Programme* (London: Temple Smith, 1978), pp.156–66.
54. K. Joseph, *Freedom Under the Law* (London: Conservative Political Centre, 1975), pp.11–12.
55. Lord Hailsham, *On the Constitution* (London: HarperCollins, 1992), p.105.
56. See, for example, J. Patten, *Political Culture, Conservatism and Rolling Constitutional Change* (London: Conservative Political Centre, 1991); Hurd, *Conservatism in the 1990s*; J. Major, *Scotland in the United Kingdom* (London: Conservative Political Centre, 1992); and B. Mawhinney, *Safeguarding our Constitution* (London: Conservative Political Centre, 1996). See also J. Patten, *Things to Come* (London: Sinclair-Stevenson, 1995), ch.3.
57. See Select Committee on the Constitution, House of Lords, *Devolution: Inter-Institutional Relations in the United Kingdom*, 2nd Report, Session 2002–03, HL Paper 28 (London: The Stationery Office, 2003).
58. William Hague, speech to the Centre for Policy Studies, 24 February 1998.
59. Boyson, *Centre Forward*, p.165.
60. Lord Falconer of Thoroton, Lord Chancellor, evidence; Select Committee on the Constitution, House of Lords, *Meeting with the Lord Chancellor*, 10th Report, Session 2002–03, HL Paper 180 (London: The Stationery Office, 2003), Q55.
61. N. Johnson, *Reshaping the British Constitution* (Basingstoke: Palgrave Macmillan, 2004), p.309.

62. See Norton, *The Constitution in Flux*, p.222.
63. Johnson, *Reshaping the British Constitution*, p.314.
64. Boyson, *Centre Forward*, p.159.
65. R. Scruton, *The Meaning of Conservatism* (London: Macmillan, 1984, 2nd edition), p.46.
66. P. Norton, 'Achieving Accountability', *The House Magazine*, 28 (17 March 2003), pp.34 and 36.
67. See P. Norton, 'Reforming the House of Lords: A View from the Parapets', *Representation*, 40 (2004), pp.185–98.
68. Johnson, *Reshaping the British Constitution*, p.312.

6
Europe
Andrew Geddes

Introduction

There seems no longer to be a compelling Conservative narrative about the state, nation and Britain's place in the world that includes the European Union (EU) as currently constituted. Diminished and marginalised are those strands of Conservative thought that marry traditional perspectives on the family and social order with progressive values on economic intervention and social welfare combined with some commitment to transnational co-operation. Accentuated are those strands that emphasise the threat to the state, the nation and self-government (or more particularly the Conservative governing project as it developed after 1979) posed by European integration, which coalesced into a potent Eurosceptic critique from the late 1980s onwards.

Much attention has been directed towards the effects on the Conservative Party's electoral fortunes of divisions over Europe in the latter years of the Thatcher premiership and throughout John Major's Downing Street tenancy.[1] These tend to leave open the question of the influence of ideas about Europe and Britain's place in the world on Conservative decline and the prospects for Conservative renewal. Could ideas have causal effects on the Conservative Party's fortunes independent of institutional settings? Delineating the impact of ideas is a difficult task. Politicians may say that beliefs inspired their actions because they then appear principled, but beliefs may merely provide *ex post* rationalisation. It may also be that ideas are mere turbulence provoking a bumpy ride, but far less important than the day-to-day grind of politics. Alternatively, ideas may be of fundamental importance in shaping the boundaries of the Conservative governing project and politics of nationhood and, through these, recasting ideas about Europe in ways that were to provoke real tensions between the Conservative Party and the EU as currently constituted.

This chapter is also an argument about slippery and sometimes elusive 'ideas of Europe' and about the decline of Conservatism as a governing practice, to which the issues of European economic and political integration are inextricably linked. The essence of Conservatism for Lynch had been a pragmatic rejection of 'activist or ideological politics based on end state goals, being instead a form of limited politics shaped by philosophical scepticism and a concern with specific circumstances'.[2] Gamble locates a strategic context to which the politics of support and the politics of power are integral.[3] Pragmatism was seen as an essential component of success during the 'Conservative century'.[4] There are reasons, however, for supposing that more grandiose visions – and sometimes misrepresentations – of 'the European project' might not rest easily with the self-consciously pragmatic, sceptical and anti-rationalist foundations of Conservative thought. Indeed, European integration was to induce bitter divisions within the Party that could not be resolved by normal techniques of Party management because for some they became ideological.

The power of ideas

What role did ideas about Europe within the political thought of the Conservative Party play in this state of affairs? Ideas about Europe, or to be more specific, ideas about the nation, the state and sovereign authority mattered intensely and were particularly evident in the period between Margaret Thatcher's Bruges speech of 1988 and the June 1995 leadership challenge to John Major, after which the Conservative Government entered a period of stasis prior to their ejection from office in 1997. During this period government policy towards the EU remained fairly consistent with what had gone before. What changed were the tone and rhetoric with the emergence of a Eurosceptic critique. Ideas and the use made of them mattered.

When thinking about Europe in the political thought of the Conservative Party we need also to consider the form and character of European integration, which is clearly not a mere foreign policy issue 'external' to the UK. It is a unique form of supranational governance of which the UK has been a leading, albeit often awkward, member for more than 30 years.[5] Supranationalism means the creation of institutions 'above' the nation state with the power to make and enforce laws that bind participating states.[6] There has been a complex, multi-levelling of European politics that is not easily captured by two-level game analogies that focus only on interactions between the national and EU levels.[7] As Wallace puts it: 'to a remarkable degree the processes of government in Europe overlap and interlock: among different states, between different levels of governance below and above the old locus of sovereignty in the nation state'.[8] We need to understand how, why and in what ways the EU challenges a vocabulary of political analysis focused on the territorial state. But to do this requires recognition too that European integration is linked to more general changes in British government and politics over the last 25 years or so and to 'changed patterns of governance' that were, to a considerable extent, induced by the Conservative Party in office between 1979 and 1997. Power has moved 'up' to Brussels, 'out' to agencies and private sector organisations and (albeit since 1997) 'down' to sub-national government, particularly in Scotland and Wales. The vocabulary of political analysis has altered with far less focus on government as formal structure centred on Westminster and Whitehall and more attention paid to governance as an activity that goes beyond the state to include a range of private and public actors. Europe is a component of these changes and of an attendant changed vocabulary of politics, but not the sole manifestation of such changed patterns of governance.

There is some scepticism that ideas have any real effects at all: 'ideas, and doctrinal consistency, are for amateurs. Serious politicians as professional players, must relegate them to their memoirs.' Thus wrote Bulpitt in a volume dedicated – rather ironically – to the 'ideas that shaped post-war Britain'.[9] Attention, it seems, should be directed towards 'the governing project' and to the historical patterning of political action. Ideas can play little independent role in all of this. Where they do enter the analysis it is as exogenous factors 'that, like any *deus ex machina* ... work their magic by entering the drama, causing trouble and leaving'.[10] But can ideas have causal or independent effects? Weber famously argued that 'world images' created by material interests and ideas 'have, like switchmen, determined the tracks long which action has been pursued by the dynamic of interest'.[11] Put another way, the battle over ideas plays an important part in configuring political discourse and establishing political boundaries. For example, it will be argued later that while Margaret Thatcher's 1988 Bruges speech did not change the substance of Conservative Government policy towards the EU, it did reconfigure Conservative political discourse on Europe and legitimated Eurosceptic opinion, and that this is important. Ideas can 'lend representative legitimacy to some social interests more than others, delineate the accepted boundaries of state action, associate contemporary political developments with particular interpretations of national history and define the context in which many issues will be understood'.[12]

This chapter discusses the influence of a set of ideas about the state, the nation, sovereign authority and Britain's place in the world that came to exercise powerful influence over Conservative thinking on Europe. This is not to say that these ideas were consistent or uncontested, but that they do help explain a Conservative critique of European integration that was to have important implications for both the Conservative politics of nationhood and the 'governing project' because Europe was represented as a threat to both.[13]

Statecraft and the governing project

Statecraft is concerned with the ability to make and enforce collective decisions and sustain a political community in the face of enduring differences.[14] Statecraft as usually understood is affixed to a territorial state, which Weber saw as the endpoint of political action and governing because 'in the end, the modern state controls the total means of political organisation, which actually come together under a single head'.[15] For Bendix, however, the territorial state was not an endpoint, but rather a staging post 'to new and yet unrealised or unrecognised institutional patterns in the future'.[16] European integration could thus be a pathway to lead European states and their peoples out of the era of the nation state.[17] The effect could then be the 'unbundling' of territoriality into functional regimes replacing 'the reification of state borders'.[18] Such functional imperatives were most clear in the work of David Mitrany who sought a 'working peace system' to replace the violent excesses of the nation state.[19] Such visions have, however, encountered the continued resonance of the territorial state 'as communities of people who have learned to communicate with and understand each other, beyond the mere interchange of goods and services'.[20] Territorial states founded on ties of solidarity that are to some extent distinct and differentiated from outsiders can create feelings of historical continuity and connect individuals to a particular geographical place and legitimate self-governance.[21]

The territorial state in Europe has not been 'unbundled', or at least not yet. This is because a strong intergovernmental impetus has provided a powerful corrective to functional 'logics' of integration. The EU is a hybrid form of international organisation combining elements of intergovernmentalism expressed through the role of member states in the Council of Ministers and the European Council and supranationalism expressed by the role of the Commission, the European Parliament and the European Court of Justice.[22] This hybrid system defies easy categorisation and requires that attention be paid to the nature of the component entities, their constitution, the strength of identities, and then, the nature of the new unit and the organisation of relations and interactions within it.[23] The EU remains significantly the creature of the member states where larger member states are prime movers with the Franco-German relationship often seen as the key axis around which power in the EU revolves (which has been one reason why some Eurosceptics have seen the EU as irredeemable).

There is a strand of liberal intergovernmental thinking on European integration that would tend not to posit the EU as a particular threat to the territorial state because the EU has created new forums within which member states can achieve their objectives and may actually have strengthened rather than weakened participating states.[24] In the words of Moravcsik, the EU has evolved into 'a stable form of pragmatic co-operation tailored to the enduring, increasingly convergent interests of European firms, governments and citizens'.[25] This tends not to be the prevailing Conservative Eurosceptic view with the EU seen, for example, as a Franco-German plot with UK interests necessarily marginalised or a device to secure Socialist re-regulation of the UK economy.[26]

It is certainly the case that the nature of the game has changed since the mid 1980s with EU responsibilities increased since Margaret Thatcher agreed to the Single European Act (SEA) in 1986. Since the SEA, the Maastricht Treaty (1992), the Amsterdam Treaty (1997), the Nice Treaty (2000) and the draft constitutional treaty signed in November 2004, the EU now impinges far more directly on 'high politics' that are closely linked to national sovereignty.[27] Treaty reform signifies a change too in the vocabulary of political analysis, which brings us to a discussion of the EU concepts jungle and those attempts within Conservative thought to make sense of the relationship between a politics of nationhood, the Conservative governing project as it developed in the 1980s and the EU as a unique form of supranational governance.

The concepts jungle

If we are to think about Europe within the political thought of the Conservative Party then necessarily we engage in discussion of state, nation and sovereign authority, or more precisely the role of the state, the idea of the nation and the substance of sovereignty. The philosophical origins of the Conservative politics of nationhood and the organisation of political life can be traced to David Hume and the delineation of core conservative themes of community, organic development, tradition, authority, hierarchy and anti-rationalism. For Edmund Burke a nation 'is the choice not of one day or one set of people, not a tumultuary and giddy choice, it is a deliberate election of ages and generation'. From the time of Disraeli the Conservatives dominated the politics of nationhood. According to Blake,[28] Disraeli made the Conservatives the national party with a patriotic discourse focused on monarchy, Empire and 'One Nation' envisaged as a national community in which people were bound together by recriprocal obligations plus patriotic respect for the constitution, Church and social hierarchy.'[29] This does not necessarily give some ethnic or racial marker to nationhood – although more cultural strands of Conservative thinking on state and nation have been evident that do, such as Powellism in the 1960s and 1970s.

The Conservative politics of nationhood has contained both civic and cultural/ethnic elements. As such they can be seen to lie somewhere between a French republican politics of nationhood within which, according to Ernest Renan's classic formulation, the Church, army and education were important agents of national socialisation and German *volkisch* ideas of a nation in search of a state 'conceived not as the bearer of universal political values, but as an organic cultural, linguistic or cultural community – as an irreducibly particular *Volksgemeinschaft*' with nationhood as an ethnic cultural rather than political fact.[30]

Within the civic strand of Conservatism emphasis has been placed on allegiance to history, institutions and a political culture fostering common values. Lynch sees this as deriving from parliamentary sovereignty, a Whig history of progress and exceptionalism combined with values and interests of an Anglicised elite.[31] Expressions of civic conservatism are most clear in the work of Michael Oakeshott, Friedrich von Hayek and Shirley Robin Letwin. More cultural accounts can be found in the work of Roger Scruton and John Casey and were articulated by Powell and his English nationalism (and to a lesser extent by Thatcher). Powell saw the Conservatives as a nationalist rather than a national party committed to a strong nation state and neo-liberal economics. Powellite nationalism was, according to Lynch, weakened because it was essentially an oppositional strategy 'driven by ideology and removed from and unsuited to the demands on party statecraft imposed by the realities of government'.[32] These limits and differences between Powell and Thatcher became clear when Powell expressed strong opposition to the Anglo-Irish agreement and the Single European Act.

With these civic and ethnic strands within the Conservative politics of nationhood could space be found for European integration? In the 1950s there was little interest in or enthusiasm for European integration because of the competing influences of the Empire/Commonwealth and the special relationship with the US.[33] These were seen as the route to international influence and the maintenance of great power status. Ideas of Europe were marginal. Britain was 'with' but not 'of' Europe, as Churchill put it. There was too a fear that Britain could become just another European country. When accession was sought in 1961–63, 1967 and, successfully, after 1970 culminating with accession on 1 January 1973, Europe was an 'external Zimmer frame'[34] that lent legitimacy to national modernisation strategies. The problems from the 1980s and particularly following the Single European Act of 1986 were that European integration in the form of social, economic, monetary, fiscal and regional policies was seen to impinge too directly on the Thatcherite modernisation strategy and executive autonomy to pursue this.

Here we must consider the question of sovereignty, particularly in its substantive form linked to statecraft, although we find some disdain for political ideas and their influence in the reported remark by one of Margaret Thatcher's Conservative Party colleagues who remarked that 'she [Thatcher] stood out on the grounds of sovereignty, a concept she had read about somewhere but could never tell you where'.[35] Sovereignty in its absolute form was defined by Hinsley as 'the idea that there is final and absolute political authority in the political community ... and no final and absolute political authority exists elsewhere'.[36] Sovereignty associated with the territorial state provides a means of ordering of what is internal to states where a monopoly of the legitimate use of violence is maintained and what is external to them where interdependence is a necessary feature of a political universe of sovereign states.[37] It is not particularly helpful to imagine that there was an old era of sovereignty and a 'modern' era of interdependence. As Waltz puts it, 'sovereign states have rarely led free and easy lives'.[38] Interdependence has long been a fact of life for a nation with an imperial and trading history such as Britain; it wasn't invented on 1 January 1973 when Britain joined the EC.

European integration does, however, change relations between member states because the EU alone as an international organisation possesses the power to turn treaties between states into laws that bind those states. An anarchical European order thus becomes more ordered and hierarchical. Caporaso[39] outlines various forms of state within the EU and argues that the traditional Westphalian model of state authority has been joined by more regulatory and postmodern forms of state-like organisation. Regulatory forms of state centre on countering 'international externalities' that hinder trade and thus with enforcing the European single market so that an EU-wide level playing field can be created. EU institutions concentrate on regulation of the market rather than with the redistributive (welfare provision) and substantive (fiscal, monetary and economic policies) concerns of the member states. The European Commission and the Court of Justice devote themselves to eliminating international externalities in the form of unfair national rules that can frustrate competition.[40] This vision accords quite closely with the preferences of British governments and would be the most likely Conservative vision of the EU. Problems with this form of state are that the appeal of this 'Anglo-American' approach does not stretch too far across the EU while a problem with regulatory structures and agencies at EU level is that they are difficult to hold to account and can be captured.

Postmodern forms of state present plural and diverse views of Europe's future with fundamental shifts in thinking about sovereignty in directions that are more 'abstract, disjointed, increasingly fragmented, not based on stable and coherent coalitions of issues or constituencies, and lacking in clear public space within which competitive visions of the good life and pursuit of self-interested legislation are discussed and debated'.[41] The postmodern state possesses a weak core that is not certain to grow with EU activity found at many locations within a 'multi-locational' polity.

Eurosceptic rhetoric with its focus on the traditional locations of political authority in Westminster and Whitehall has not adapted easily to changes in forms of state organisation, which is ironic when it is considered that Thatcherite attempts to roll back the state and induce changed patterns of governance have contributed in no small manner to the reconfiguration of state authority.

As a representation of the debate about sovereignty within the Conservative Party, Lynch makes a useful distinction between state sovereignty manifested at the external frontiers of the territorial state; constitutional sovereignty expressed through Parliament (and usually masking executive predominance); and popular sovereignty reliant on the will of the political community.[42] This threefold breakdown is helpful because it allows us to see the ways in which sovereignty has many faces and has also been used to support and oppose European integration.

For supporters of European integration, sovereignty is not some precious jewel to be preserved. Rather it is a practical device that can be deployed in the most effective way to attain state objectives. In some situations this may be through the 'pooling' of sovereignty. For Sir Geoffrey Howe, 'sovereignty is not some pre-defined absolute, but a flexible, adaptable, organic notion that evolves and adjusts with circumstances'.

From a Eurosceptic perspective sovereignty is absolute and can be neither pooled nor shared.[43] The Thatcherite view as it evolved after the 1988 Bruges speech was focused on state authority and individual liberty with a Europe of sovereign states the only version compatible with British nationalism. Despite some hopes that the single European market could represent a chance to 'Thatcherise' the EU, at heart, Thatcherism was 'non-exportable' and 'British by essence not accident'.[44] This suggests a fundamental incompatibility between the governing project as developed during Margaret Thatcher's period in office and European integration as it developed since the 1980s.

Ideas were to become central to debates about Europe within the Conservative Party. Ideas are, of course, not neutral and can mean different things to different people at different points in time. The chapter's next section explores Conservative attitudes to Europe, with a particular attention paid to the period following the 1988 Bruges speech. It is argued that while the substance of government policy did not change, the boundaries of Conservative political discourse about Europe were reconfigured in ways that brought Euroscepticism to the heart of the Party. Ideas did matter. Particularly, ideas about state, nation and sovereign authority have had important effects on the Conservative politics of nationhood and the Thatcherite variant of the Conservative governing project. Eurosceptics largely won the battle of ideas within the Conservative Party between 1988 and 1997, but at the cost of divisions that consigned the Party to Opposition.

The Conservatives and Europe

The governments of Harold Macmillan and Edward Heath sought EC membership as part of a national modernisation strategy. For Macmillan the EC represented a powerful economic bloc with important political implications on Britain's doorstep from which Britain could not afford to be excluded. For Heath, a commitment to European integration was a long-standing component of his political credo and had been the subject of his maiden speech to the House of Commons in 1951 extolling the virtues of European Coal and Steel Community membership for Britain. Heath was also a political leader shaped by his experience of war and, in this sense, shared much with other European leaders who saw European integration as an essential element of peace in Europe.[45]

Lord distinguishes between 'transformationalists' such as Heath with a pragmatic emphasis on pooled sovereignty but a preference for intergovernmentalism and the defence of 'essential national sovereignty' (as the 1971 White Paper on EC membership intriguingly put it) with 'traditionalists' such as Enoch Powell who saw national sovereignty as absolute and sought to defend it.[46]

This debate between transformationalists and traditionalists needs to be placed in its wider context. The 'choice for Europe' did not represent a positive embrace of the European ideal or signify any great enthusiasm for federal visions of a united Europe. If anything, the choice was born from a lack of alternatives as the vision of a Commonwealth as a world power bloc with Britain at the helm receded, the special relationship no longer seemed quite so special (and the US was pushing the UK towards the EC anyway) and a general perception of decline induced a national identity crisis. Britain, as Dean Acheson famously put it in 1962,

> has lost an Empire and has not yet found a role. The attempt to play a separate power role – that is, a role apart from Europe, a role based on a 'special relationship' with the United States, a role based on being the head of a 'Commonwealth' which has no political structure, or strength and enjoys a fragile and precarious economic relationship by means of the sterling area and preferences in the British market – this role is about to be played out ... Her Majesty's government is now attempting, wisely in my opinion, to re-enter Europe, from which it was banished at the time of the Plantagenets, and the battle seems about as hard fought as those of an earlier day.[47]

The approach of British governments (Conservative and Labour) to European integration has contained three main elements: intergovernmentalism and a self-consciously pragmatic distrust of grand projects; Atlanticism; and a preference for free trade combined with market liberalisation. A 'coolness about the European project' and the intention to dissect it to its fundamentals seem very Thatcherite attributes, but they were views ascribed to her predecessor in 10 Downing Street, James Callaghan.[48] At the time, of course, the Conservative Party led by Margaret Thatcher were the party of Europe, albeit on pragmatic pro-business grounds. In office, Thatcher continued a pursuit of a budget rebate, which was finally secured at the Fontainebleau summit meeting of EC leaders in June 1984. The resolution of the British budget dispute – or 'Bloody British Question' as Roy Jenkins put it in his memoirs of his time as Commission President, allowed member states to focus on the bigger picture and think about the shape, form and content of future integration. It is at this point that we see some confluence between the Thatcherite governing project and European integration. The Conservative Government was prepared to support the Single European Act because of an apparent commitment to market liberalisation on a pan-EC scale. To secure these objectives, the Conservative Government was also prepared to allow more qualified majority voting (and hence the effective disappearance of the national veto) in some areas of decision making.

For the British government, the SEA was an end in itself. For other member states, the SEA was a means to an end: that end being the rejuvenation of the European project and integration in other areas linked to the single market such as social, economic, fiscal, monetary and regional policies. This vision was shared too by new Commission President Jacques Delors. In the language of neo-functional theory, the socioeconomic implications of single market integration could be seen to represent 'spillover effects'. For Hoffmann the weakness of functional theory was that it wrote state interests out of the equation: 'functional integration's gamble could only be won if the method had sufficient potency to promise an excess of gains over losses, and of hopes over frustrations. Theoretically this may be true of economic integration. It is not true of political integration',[49] and thought that shifts into 'high politics' would be derailed by state interests. By the late 1980s, however, there was a core group of member states ready to see much bolder forms of European integration that moved directly into areas of high politics. Hoffmann summed up the dilemma for the British Conservative Government in the face of plans for a significant deepening of political integration: 'Russian roulette is fine only as long as the gun is filled with blanks.' This may have been true for the vision of sovereignty espoused by the UK government, but the notions of sovereign authority held by other EC governments were very different to the extent that ceding of sovereignty on a far grander scale was considered both practicable and desirable. This was not some functional imperative driven by higher forces, this was a choice for Europe made by European governments. It was a choice that the British government could not share because it was perceived as incompatible with the key elements of the Thatcherite governing project. For example, the British government refused to sign the 1989 non-binding Social Charter because for Thatcher it reflected Marxist ideas of class struggle. This reflected too the gulf between Thatcherite Conservatism and the Christian Democrat and Social Democrat governments of other member states that adhered to ideas of social solidarity that had become thoroughly 'wet' in Thatcherite discourse.

It is at this point that we see real tension between the Thatcherite governing project and those sections of the Conservative Party that supported it and European integration. These tensions become clear within a speech delivered at the College of Europe, Bruges, on 20 September 1988. It is worth quoting this speech at some length because it is central to understanding the ways in which Conservative discourse on Europe was reconfigured. The Bruges speech was seminal in that respect. It may have been only a change in tone, but it was highly important for that and its effects were to be felt for years after.

The speech began with some assertions that are not unfamiliar in British relations with European integration. Thatcher argued that

> willing and active co-operation between independent sovereign states is the best way to build a successful European Community. To try to suppress nationhood and concentrate power at the centre of a European conglomerate would be highly damaging and would jeopardise the objectives we seek to achieve. Europe will be stronger precisely because it has France as France, Spain as Spain, Britain as Britain, each with its own customs, traditions and identity. It would be folly to try to fit them into some sort of identikit European personality.

There was nothing in this statement that was inconsistent with the approaches of other British governments towards the EC. She then went on to acknowledge that Europe would be stronger if countries worked together. Here too, there was no inconsistency with the longer-standing intergovernmental preferences of British governments that persist to this day. It was from this point that Thatcher began to develop a distinct Conservative Eurosceptic critique of European integration as it had developed since the SEA.

> Working more closely together does not require power to be centralised in Brussels or decisions to be taken by an appointed bureaucracy. We have not successfully rolled back the frontiers of the state in Britain, only to see them reimposed at a European level, with a European super-state exercising a new dominance from Brussels.

Thatcher saw European integration as a threat to her governing project and began to articulate a view about the state, nation and sovereign authority that were to be core components of the Eurosceptic critique.

This is not to say that Thatcherism was necessarily a coherent governing ideology. For Riddell, Thatcherism was 'an instinct, a series of moral values and an approach to leadership rather than an ideology'.[50] Lynch does not see a coherent national strategy on the issues of sovereignty and European integration, as marked by the willingness to cede substantial amounts of sovereign authority through the SEA.[51] Other studies of Thatcherism are sceptical about the cohesiveness of the project and see radical policies in some areas, implementation gaps in others, and some continuity too.[52] It has also been observed that many Conservative MPs were not Thatcher-ites.[53] The key point here, however, is that the Bruges speech marked the beginning of the end for Margaret Thatcher as Prime Minister because, as Bulpitt put it, Thatcherism 'began as a modernisation strategy sweetened by the language of national greatness. It ended when the language of national greatness had adversely affected the modernisation strategy.'[54] After 1988 the tone of debate about Europe changed in a Eurosceptic direction with five main rhetorical components of this scepticism: the insincerity of other member states that reneged on their commitment to free market principles; the incompatibility between the EU and British legal, political, social and economic institutions; the unacceptable SEA 'spillover' effects in areas such as social, fiscal, economic and monetary policy; the threat to sovereignty posed by autonomous EU institutions such as the Commission and Court of Justice; nationalism, xenophobia and an obsession with the Second World War, with Margaret Thatcher's seminar on German national character a good example of this.[55]

Divisions about Europe within British party politics are far more likely to be found within rather than between the main parties. Labour's divisions were to help impel the Social Democratic Party breakaway in the early 1980s. Divisions on Europe went right to the top of the Con-servative Party and its ruling elite. Discord plagued Thatcher's Cabinet and led to the resignations of Michael Heseltine, Leon Brittan, Nigel Lawson, Geoffrey Howe, Nicholas Ridley and, ultimately, Thatcher herself. Major had to reconcile himself with three 'bastards' inside the Cabinet rather than outside augmenting the ranks of the dispossessed and never possessed.[56]

The significance of the Bruges speech was that it marked a rhetorical shift in the tone and tenor of debate about Europe, reconfigured the boundaries of discourse about Europe within the Conservative Party by legitimising Euroscepticism from the top, and impelled a huge and divisive internal debate within the Party to which ideas about the state, the nation and sovereign authority were crucial. These are all hugely significant when it is recalled that the success of Conservatism was as a pragmatic concern with electoral success and with government rather than ideological principle. Ideology and insurgency were to become key features of Conservative Party politics in the 1990s. Political ideas for better or for worse played a key role in this. Worse still, the language of sovereignty made the gulf between 'poolers' and 'absolutists' too great to bridge by normal methods of Party management. However, this change of tone did not mean a change of policy content. Thatcher may have left office in 1990 and felt free to proclaim that she would not have signed the Maastricht Treaty and to call for a referendum on it; but there are strong consistencies in Major's approach and the actions of the Thatcher Government. For example, Major secured an opt-out from Stage 3 of the plan for European Monetary Union when a single European currency would come into effect. He refused to agree to extended social policy provisions, which meant that the Social Chapter was appended to the Treaty as an agreement between the other eleven member states. Separate intergovernmental 'pillars' were created for Common Foreign and Security Policy and Justice and Home Affairs where the role of supranational institutions would be very marginal. This negotiating stance was compatible with that of other British governments at other negotiations, including governments that Margaret Thatcher led. What had changed were the tone and tenor of debate. Discussion of Europe within the Conservative Party was reconfigured in the wake of the Bruges speech and the bitterness engendered by Thatcher's leaving of office. The effect was that ideas mattered intensely in Conservative political debates about Europe.

These developments do not rest easily with the Conservative Party's traditional emphasis on unity and loyalty. The strength of the Conservative Party during the 'Conservative century' was the avoidance of division. Labour were the Party of factions and the Conservatives the Party of tendencies: 'a tendency is a stable set of attitudes rather than a stable set of participants'. Factions are 'self-consciously organised groups that persistently advance a programme for government and a leader to govern'. For students of the Conservative Party, prior to the 1990s there was 'no Conservative dogma to be preserved from ephemeral and power conscious heretics'.[57] In a similar vein, Norton and Aughey wrote that Conservatism was not monolithic, that it embodied the 'messiness of an operational ideology' that stressed loyalty and unity: 'the Conservatives stress a pragmatism, compromise and the tempering of policy disagreements that has its roots in the fear that confrontation between factions within the privileged groups could of itself undermine the whole structure of the political organisation of society'.[58]

Europe changed the rules and nature of the game. Intense divisions emerged on the question of Europe during the 1990s.[59] These divisions convulsed the parliamentary party and constituted a 'continuous, comprehensive and public penetration' of the governing code.[60] Baker, Gamble and Ludlam argue that the issue was important because it connected domestic and international politics in the same way that had debates about free trade and tariff reform.[61] As such they also exacerbated a basic tension within the Party and the British political tradition more generally between intervention and the free market.[62] Europe, however, cut across this division because the potential for the use of sovereign authority in pursuit of free market or interventionist objectives had changed.

The strategic context for the Eurosceptics was also transformed by the relatively small majority of 21 seats in the House of Commons that Major won at the 1992 general election, which was then further reduced as a result of by-elections and defections. There was far greater scope for Eurosceptic rebellion to have effects because of this precarious majority.[63] However, Eurosceptic scheming and concessions to their position were counteracted by a powerful body of pro-EU thought represented at the Cabinet table by ministers such as Kenneth Clarke and Michael Heseltine.

Pilkington identifies a continuum within the Conservative Party stretching from Euroenthusiasts to Europrogressives to Eurosceptics and Europhobes.[64] The enthusiast and progressive wing were, though, to find themselves increasingly marginalised as opinion within the parliamentary party became more Eurosceptic and then, after 1997, was hardened by a decisively more sceptical intake.[65] There was not just one strand of Eurosceptic thought within the Conservative Party. As we have already seen, there are various interpretations of the themes central to debate about Europe – the state, the nation and sovereign authority. Conservative MP and leading sceptic Michael Spicer distinguished between die-hards and anti-marketeers such as Teddy Taylor who had opposed the 'Common Market' in the 1970s and the SEA in the 1980s with equal vigour to their opposition to Maastricht. To this, according to Spicer, can be added the neo-liberals who saw creeping re-regulation from the EU as a threat to the socioeconomic policies introduced since 1979 which, in their view, had seen a rolling back of the state.[66] A third strand of opposition was the constitutionalists such as Bill Cash MP who were particularly focused on the threat they saw to parliamentary sovereignty and self-government. Finally, there were patriots and nationalists such as Tony Marlow MP who saw the EU as a foreign threat to national identity.

The period between 1988 and 1995 saw these strands coalesce into an effective critique of European integration within the Conservative Party bolstered by strong financial backing from outside Parliament and support from national newspapers such as the *Telegraph* and *The Times*. The Conservative Party became more divided, more ideological and almost completely focused on European integration, at the expense of engaging with the concerns of the electorate, among which Europe did not rank very highly. The debate became ideological and reflected the shift in the Conservative governing project induced by Thatcher in office since 1979 and her attempt both in office and after her departure to elucidate a critique of the European Union. There had already been a diminution of that strand of Conservative thinking that emphasised progressive values on economic intervention and social welfare, coupled with support for transnational co-operation. Instead, a set of ideas about the nation, the state and sovereign authority became common currency within the Conservative Party that questioned Britain's future within the EU. The result today is a Party that espouses a fundamental re-evaluation of the relationship with the EU based on a renegotiation of the Treaties. If that were to fail – and it would require tremendous good will from other member states to succeed – then any future Conservative-led Britain would presumably develop a more formalised semi-detached relationship with the EU. This requires that some attention be paid to developing an 'alternative political economy' capable of imagining Britain outside the EU either through closer links with the US or through a remodelling of the UK on the lines of smaller European states such as Norway and Switzerland.[67] The fact that the Conservatives have had to give thought to an alternative political economy is evidence of the changes in the boundaries of political discourse that occurred since the 1980s that have shifted the accepted boundaries of state action and have associated contemporary political developments with particular interpretations of national history, and through that have defined the context in which European integration and the underlying issues of nation, state and sovereign authority are understood within the Party.

Conclusion

The narratives that political parties tell to themselves and to the electorate are important. They can energise and mobilise the believers and reach out to a broader mass of supporters. The Conservative century was founded on a compelling Conservative narrative that built a powerful cross-class coalition. The Conservative narrative about Europe has been and still is essentially a story about the nation, the state, sovereign authority and Britain's place in the world. European integration was compatible with national modernisation in the 1960s, at the time of accession and until the SEA. After the SEA, the EC was seen to impose itself on core elements of the Thatcherite governing project and the ability of British governments to achieve their objective. This could be and was portrayed by some as a threat to parliamentary sovereignty, but is in reality a threat to executive power and autonomy, which is the fact that lies behind the quaint and outdated notion of a sovereign Parliament. The ways in which European integration was seen to impinge on core elements of the Thatcherite governing project gave rise to a potent Eurosceptic critique that contained a variety of components and was not necessarily either consistent or coherent, but was to have important effects on the Conservative Party between 1988 and 1997. During this period ideas mattered and they mattered intensely. It was not so much the content of policy that changed between 1988 and 1997. Rather, the tone and rhetoric of debate and the use of underlying concepts changed. This shows that ideas are not neutral. They are used in different ways at different points in times by different people. This chapter has argued that the ways in which they are used matters. More than that, it mattered intensely for the Conservative Party and shows how, why, when and for what reasons ideas about Europe were central to a realignment of Conservative thinking about Europe that has had dramatic effects on the Party's fortune and the narrative it seeks to construct as it attempts to reach out to the wider electorate beyond the believers.

Notes

1. J. Turner, *The Tories and Europe* (Manchester: Manchester University Press, 2000); A. Forster, *Euroscepticism in Contemporary British Politics* (London: Routledge, 2002); A. Geddes, *The European Union and British Politics* (Basingstoke: Palgrave Macmillan, 2004).
2. P. Lynch, *The Politics of Nationhood: Sovereignty, Britishness and Conservative Politics* (Basingstoke: Macmillan, 1999).
3. A. Gamble, *The Conservative Nation* (London: Routledge and Kegan Paul, 1974).
4. A. Seldon and S. Ball (eds), *Conservative Century: The Conservative Party Since 1900* (Oxford: Oxford University Press, 1994).
5. S. George, *An Awkward Partner: Britain in the European Community* (Oxford: Oxford University Press, 1998, 3rd edition); Geddes, *The European Union and British Politics*; I. Bache and A. Jordan (eds), *The Europeanisation of British Politics* (Basingstoke: Palgrave Macmillan, 2005).

6. F. Capotori, 'Supranational Organizations', in R. Bernhardt (ed.), *Encyclopaedia of Public International Law* (Rotterdam: Elsevier, 1983).
7. R. Putnam, 'Diplomacy and Domestic Politics: The Logic of Two-Level Games', *International Organization*, 42 (summer 1984).
8. W. Wallace, 'The Sharing of Sovereignty: The European Paradox', *Political Studies*, 47:3 (1999), p.503.
9. J. Bulpitt, 'The European Question: Rules, National Modernisation and the Ambiguities of *Primat der Innenpolitik*', in D. Marquand and A. Seldon (eds), *The Ideas that Shaped Post-War Britain* (London: Fontana, 1996), p.252.
10. M. Blyth, '"Any More Bright Ideas?" The Ideational Turn of Comparative Political Economy', *Comparative Politics*, 29:2 (1997).
11. Cited in W.R. Brubaker, *Citizenship and Nationhood in France and Germany* (Cambridge, Mass.: Harvard University Press, 1992), p.17.
12. P. Hall, 'Policy Paradigms, Social Learning and the State', *Comparative Politics*, 25:2 (1993), p.289.
13. M. Holmes, *European Integration: Scope and Limits* (Basingstoke: Palgrave Macmillan, 2001).
14. P. Selznick, *The Moral Commonwealth* (Berkeley: University of California Press, 1992).
15. In H.H. Gerth and C. Wright Mills, *From Max Weber: Essays in Sociology* (London: Routledge, 1991).
16. R. Bendix, 'Introduction', in R. Bendix (ed.), *State and Society* (Boston: Little Brown, 1968).
17. K. Deutsch, *The Analysis of International Relations* (Englewood Cliffs, NJ: Prentice Hall, 1968).
18. J. Ruggie, 'Territoriality and Beyond: Problematising Modernity in International Relations', *International Organization*, 47 (1993).
19. D. Mitrany, *A Working Peace System* (Oxford: Oxford University Press, 1943).
20. J. Olsen, 'Survey Article: Unity, Diversity and Democratic Institutions: Lessons from the European Union', *Journal of Political Philosophy*, 12:4 (2004), pp.471–2.
21. D. Miller, *Citizenship and National Identity* (Cambridge: Polity Press, 2000).
22. S. Hix, *The Political System of the European Union* (Basingstoke: Palgrave Macmillan, 2nd edition, 2005).
23. Olsen, 'Survey Article'.
24. A. Milward, *The European Rescue of the Nation State* (London: Routledge, 2nd edition, 2000); A. Moravcsik, *Why the European Community Strengthens the State: Domestic Politics and International Co-operation*, Harvard University Center for European Studies Working Paper Series No. 52 (1994).
25. A. Moravcsik, *The Choice for Europe: Social Purpose and State Power from Messina to Maastricht* (London: UCL Press, 1998), p.176.
26. Bulpitt, 'The European Question'; T. Gorman, *The Bastards: Dirty Tricks and the Challenge to Europe* (London: Pan Books, 1993).
27. S. Hoffmann, 'Obstinate or Obsolete? The Fate of the Nation State and the Case of Western Europe', *Daedalus*, 95 (1966).
28. R. Blake, *The Conservative Party from Peel to Thatcher* (London: Fontana, 1985).
29. Lynch, *The Politics of Nationhood*, p.10.
30. Brubaker, *Citizenship and Nationhood in France and Germany*, p.1.

31. Lynch, *The Politics of Nationhood*.
32. Ibid., p.46.
33. H. Young, *This Blessed Plot: Britain and Europe from Churchill to Blair* (London: Papermac, 1999); J. Young, *Britain and European Unity 1945–1992* (Basingstoke: Macmillan, 1993); Geddes, *The European Union and British Politics*.
34. Bulpitt, 'The European Question'.
35. Lynch, *The Politics of Nationhood*, p.81.
36. F.H. Hinsley, *Sovereignty* (London: Watts, 1966), p.2.
37. A. Giddens, *A Contemporary Critique of Historical Materialism*, Vol. 2: *The Nation-State and Violence* (Cambridge: Polity, 1985).
38. K. Waltz, *Theory of International Politics* (New York: McGraw-Hill, 1979), pp.95–6.
39. J. Caporaso, 'The EU and Forms of State: Westphalian, Regulatory or Post-modern?', *Journal of Common Market Studies*, 34:1 (1996).
40. G. Majone, *Regulating Europe* (London: Routledge, 1996).
41. Caporaso, 'The EU and Forms of State', p.45.
42. Lynch, *The Politics of Nationhood*.
43. N. Malcolm, 'Sense on Sovereignty', in M. Holmes (ed.), *The Eurosceptical Reader* (Basingstoke: Macmillan, 1996).
44. S.R. Letwin, *The Anatomy of Thatcherism* (New Brunswick, NJ: Transaction Publishers, 1993).
45. E. Heath, *The Course of My Life: My Autobiography* (London: Hodder and Stoughton, 1998).
46. C. Lord, *British Entry to the European Community Under the Heath Government of 1970–74* (Aldershot: Dartmouth, 1993).
47. Cited in J. Dumbrell, *A Special Relationship: Anglo-American Relations in the Cold War and After* (Basingstoke: Palgrave Macmillan, 2001).
48. K. Morgan, *Callaghan: A Life* (Oxford: Oxford University Press, 1997), pp.412–13.
49. Hoffmann, 'Obstinate or Obsolete?', p.882.
50. P. Riddell, *The Thatcher Government* (Oxford: Robertson, 1983).
51. Lynch, *The Politics of Nationhood*.
52. D. Marsh, 'Explaining Thatcherite Policies: Beyond Uni-dimensional Explanations', *Political Studies*, 43:4 (1995); D. Marsh and R. Rhodes, *Implementing Thatcherism* (Oxford: Oxford University Press, 1992).
53. P. Norton, 'The Lady's Not for Turning, but What About the Rest? Margaret Thatcher and the Conservative Party 1979–89', *Parliamentary Affairs*, 43:2 (1990).
54. Bulpitt, 'The European Question', p.240.
55. G. Urban, *Diplomacy and Disillusion at the Court of Margaret Thatcher: An Insider's View* (London: I.B. Tauris, 1996).
56. J. Major, *John Major: The Autobiography* (London: HarperCollins, 1999).
57. W.J. Biffen, 'Party Conference and Party Policy', *Political Quarterly*, 32:3 (1961), p.259.
58. P. Norton and A. Aughey, *Conservatism and Conservatives* (London: Temple Smith, 1981), pp.50–1.
59. Forster, *Euroscepticism*.
60. Bulpitt, 'The European Question'.
61. D. Baker, A. Gamble and S. Ludlam, '1846 ... 1906 ... 1996? Conservative Splits and European Integration', *Political Quarterly*, 64:4 (1993).

62. W.H. Greenleaf, 'The Character of Modern British Conservatism', in R. Benewick, N. Berki and B. Parekh (eds), *Knowledge and Belief in Politics: The Problem of Ideology* (London: Allen and Unwin, 1973).
63. M. Aspinwall, 'Structuring Europe: Powersharing Institutions and British Preferences on European Integration', *Political Studies*, 48:3 (2000).
64. C. Pilkington, *Britain in the European Union Today* (Manchester: Manchester University Press, 2001).
65. A. Geddes, 'Europe: Major's Nemesis', in A. Geddes and J. Tonge (eds), *Labour's Landslide: The 1997 British General Election* (Manchester: Manchester University Press, 1997).
66. Although see M. Moran, *The British Regulatory State: High Modernism and Hyper-Innovation* (Oxford: Oxford University Press, 2003).
67. J. Bercow, 'Aiming for the Heart of Europe: A Misguided Venture', in M. Holmes (ed.), *The Eurosceptical Reader 2* (Basingstoke: Palgrave Macmillan, 2001).

7
Economic Statecraft

Andrew Taylor

Quandaries, institutional stability and statecraft

The Conservative Party's ideological flexibility and lust for office are customarily cited as the main reasons for its ability to evolve and prosper.[1] 'Any political party', *The Times* argued, 'which is to have a hope of recovering must reach out to voters ... Wise Conservatives deal with the world as it is, not as it should be or once was. They respect the changing landscape and are sensitive to its contours.'[2] Adaptation is an intensely political, not technical, process and is seldom smooth or unproblematic because adaptation challenges the extant definition of what Conservatism is. Parties exist in a system of rules producing stability (or inertia) which inhibits adaptation.[3] Adaptations are more radical than the policy or tactical shifts of electoral politics, they occur at a deeper level and in response to influences broader than those in the electoral cycle. Adaptation requires the Party to reinterpret policies and style, modulating these with perceived changes in the Party's milieu, thereby redefining Conservatism. Successful adaptation delivers power. If not, a further adaptation occurs. After 1945 the Party undertook two successful adaptations: to the post-war settlement and to markets, currently the Party is groping to find another successful adaptation.

Schofield has captured this process through the interplay of 'Architects of Order' and 'Prophets of Chaos'.[4] At any given time a liberal-democratic capitalist society will have a set of rules, ideas and a language which constitutes 'received wisdom', this determines what is politically acceptable and feasible. This amalgam comprises the constitution which provides stability and predictability and is the result of Architects of Order adding to, or adjusting, the constitution in response to crises. The underlying belief in capitalist liberal democracy coupled with any adjustments, constitute society's core belief within the heart of the constitution. Within the heart, however, exist alternative potential core beliefs, therefore the dominant core belief is contingent. Those who challenge the currently dominant core belief are the Prophets of Chaos. Criticism has little effect until a situation develops – a quandary – which casts doubt on the core belief's ability to resolve this quandary. Constitutions are humanly devised and exist in a dynamic environment. Inevitably there will be mistakes in governance and circumstances change, opening a gap between reality and the prescriptions associated with the core belief. When a quandary exists, 'received wisdom', the foundation of present belief and action, weakens but the prior constitution and core belief retain substantial residual power. Nevertheless, ideas and policies previously thought unthinkable become part of 'the set of collective actions that may be "rationally" entertained [because] as core beliefs fragment at the onset of a quandary, the heart of the constitution expands to include behaviour that was previously inconceivable'.[5] The greater the dissonance between prescription and reality, the more the core belief is undermined, so giving credence to the Prophets of Chaos' criticisms creating a space for political entrepreneurs advocating a new core belief. This may culminate in a belief cascade, producing a metamorphosis of the core belief and constitution: Prophets of Chaos become Architects of Order.[6]

How a quandary is resolved cannot be predicted because of competing potential core beliefs. Which becomes the new core is determined by politics. The policies of a Conservative Government elected in 1945, for example, would have flowed from the Coalition's: 'the Beveridge business would have been carried out ... presumably we should not have gone in for all these silly nationalisation schemes'.[7] The modern Conservative Party emerged between 1918 and 1924 when politics came to be dominated by relative decline and mass democracy. Conservative politics was moulded by three threats: the USSR and communism, the Labour's Party's socialism, and trade union power. These were constants in Conservative politics but changing circumstances produced different responses. By the mid 1990s the Soviet threat had evaporated, Labour had relaunched, and the unions had been crushed. Thatcherism represents the destruction of the historic Conservative Party and posed a question none of her predecessors needed to ask and which John Major, William Hague and Iain Duncan Smith were unable to answer: what was the Conservative Party for? They failed to find an adaptation appropriate to the post-Thatcher world. Whether Michael Howard will be any more successful is an open question.

The post-war settlement was an institution: 'the rules of the game in a society ... the humanly devised constraints that shape human interactions ... structure incentives in human exchange, whether political, social or economic'.[8] The post-war settlement was a matter of tendencies not rigidities but at its core lay the 1944 White Paper, *Full Employment* (Cmnd. 6527).[9] Ambiguities and unresolved questions, exogenous events and structural weaknesses, destabilised the post-war settlement and created space for alternatives. The weaknesses of the post-war settlement were known, as was the need to address structural economic weakness, but the political imperative behind the post-war settlement proved irresistible.[10] The failure of the Macmillan, Wilson, Heath and Wilson–Callaghan Governments to revive the post-war settlement prefigured the changes of the 1980s. Continuation depended on participants accepting unemployment, the quandary that underpinned its original negotiation, remained the overriding concern. This brings us to statecraft. Statecraft is

> the art of winning elections and achieving some necessary degree of governing competence in office. It is not synonymous with, though it may be related to, pragmatism or expediency. It is concerned primarily to resolve the electoral and governing problems facing a party at any particular time. As a result it is concerned as much with the 'how' as the 'what' of politics.[11]

The Conservative Party's fixed purpose is to win office, govern satisfactorily and retain office, but the method(s) and appeal(s) vary according to circumstance and past practice. Statecraft has four dimensions: party management, a winning electoral strategy, political argument and governing competence, but a winning electoral strategy is the primary objective. Effective statecraft also requires a convincing narrative of what Conservatism is.[12] The central bind of post-war British politics and Conservative statecraft was how to combine full employment and low inflation.

The *deliberate* creation of unemployment to curb inflation risked conflict with the unions and working class. Privately, civil servants and ministers were impressed by the union leaderships' moderation, but nonetheless regretted that full employment distorted the balance of power between bargainers.[13] The post-war settlement was folded into the Party's longstanding concern; 'the political objective of the Government was, and must remain, establishment of the Conservative Party, in the eyes of public opinion, as a national party which was concerned to represent the interests of all sections of the community'.[14]

Between 1945 and 1975, Conservative politics were about sustaining and renewing the post-war settlement which can be defined as

> a balanced, harmonious set of remedies for outstanding grievances from the inter-war years, and planned with increasing vigour as the great emergency receded, the settlement was modified to take account of a hostile economic post-war climate and then, through the affluent 1950s, maintained with much less difficulty than the authors had imagined would be possible. Questioned by some of the participants even before the good years ended, it was briefly revived at the start of the 1960s.[15]

The post-war settlement used corporate bias involving industry, unions and government to avoid destabilising conflict. Corporate bias meshed with the Party's statecraft, but despite its importance, was contingent. Michael Fraser, a key figure in post-war Conservative politics, wrote that 'in 1945, the spectre of Britain becoming a full-blown socialist state loomed [and] the Conservative Party might become a permanent or semi-permanent minority'. The Party was anti-socialist, terrified of what Labour could do with the wartime state, and Fraser dismissed the consensus politics thesis as 'a load of balls'. Equally, the Conservatives could not ignore the war's legacy.[16]

Architects of order: Harold Macmillan and Conservative statecraft

The quandary of the 1930s was mass unemployment which, many feared, might lead disaffected voters to endorse fascism or communism. Both were antithetical to the political and economic freedoms which lay at the heart of the liberal-capitalist constitution. Keynes' *The General Theory* (1936) agreed with Lenin's *The State and Revolution* (1917) that liberal democracy was 'the best possible shell for capitalism', so the task was to save capitalism from itself. In Britain this quandary was given an added twist by the 'people's war'. The Architects of Order adopted some of Keynes' insights (but not Keynesianism) and other measures such as the welfare state to preserve the status quo.[17]

The post-war settlement was Conservatism's default setting. It was an adaptation of Conservative politics to the core belief of welfare spending, the mixed economy and full employment.[18] This core belief was never hegemonic. Prophets of Chaos maintained from the outset that it contained the seeds of its own, and society's, destruction. Full employment, when combined with the dislocations of war, continued structural weaknesses in the UK economy, the increased power of organised labour, the growth of the state and a political class determined to maintain political stability, would inevitably trigger inflation, declining output and growing unemployment, producing an overloaded political system vulnerable to a governability crisis. If liberal-democratic capitalism was to be preserved this quandary would, sooner or later, have to be addressed; the longer remedial action was postponed, the more radical it would have to be.[19]

The kernel of the problem was that the working class 'have been taught to believe that if the Tories were to come back their wages would be reduced and they would be faced with unemployment'. This fear inhibited the Party, predisposing it to accept Labour's state 'provided that it is in good hands', a policy inspired 'mainly [by] the fear of losing an election'.[20] These considerations were uppermost in Churchill's mind when he told the House of Commons that 'the two sides ... face each other deeply divided by ideological differences ... they are separated by a wider and deeper gulf than I have ever seen before in our island ... We shall certainly not survive by splitting into two nations. Yet that is the road we are travelling now.'[21] Macmillan was 'impressed by the class solidarity of the Labour vote. They grouse, and tell the Gallup poll man that they will never vote Socialist again – but when the election comes, they vote the party ticket.'[22]

Any notion of 'setting the people free' through welfare spending cuts or denationalisation was speedily forgotten or downgraded. Operation Robot, for example, a radical change in fiscal policy, was 'logically unassailable' but was 'open to the very gravest political objections'. It would force the country 'to live within its means' but entailed 'sacrificing the controlled economy and the policy of full employment'. Macmillan criticised those civil servants and politicians who 'have gone once more whoring after the 19th stuff'.[23] In this stalemate there lurked a strategic opportunity for the Conservatives:

the Socialists have fought the election (very astutely) not on Socialism but on Fear. Fear of unemployment; fear of reduced wages; fear of reduced social benefits; fear of war. These four fears have been brilliantly, if unscrupulously, exploited. If, before the next election, none of these fears have proved reasonable, we may be able to force the Opposition to fight on Socialism. Then we can win.[24]

Central is the thesis that, confronted by a choice between stability (supplemented by piecemeal modernisation) and destabilising radical reform, Conservatives would choose the former.

By 1955 inflation was *the* economic problem. 'We are', Macmillan wrote, 'enjoying the greatest boom in history. Stock exchange prices have almost doubled in a year. The rate of unemployment is the lowest since records began. Exports are still increasing. How can 700,000 industrial workers be asked to forgo their share?'[25] Working-class psychology had changed dramatically, 'two decades of full employment and the growth of the Welfare State have largely banished the fear of insecurity'.[26] When Chancellor, Macmillan urged policies on Eden which 'may save the economy from a complete collapse – which may come in a few months. But the plan is *very tough* and will be politically very unpopular. (But the collapse of Sterling and the capitalist system wd be worse!).' Despite the approaching apocalypse Macmillan's last-ditch attempt to save capitalism degenerated into squabbles about milk and bread subsidies, bargaining, a resignation threat, and finally compromise.[27] The primacy of political calculation born of a sense of powerlessness was voiced by the Prime Minister: 'short of taking deflationary measures to a length which is politically intolerable, I do not see how we can hope to limit wage claims'.[28]

Macmillan's successor as Chancellor, Peter Thorneycroft, argued that a new approach to inflation was needed to avert political and economic disaster. Moderate deflation would reduce inflation and a manageable rise in unemployment would discipline bargainers. Macmillan agreed that inflation caused party management problems, undermined the Party's claim to economic competence and that there was too much money in circulation, but there was, Macmillan believed, little room for the scale of cuts Thorneycroft envisaged. Macmillan's ideal was steady disinflation *and* full employment so that 'we shall lose no voters and injure nobody'.[29] When Thorneycroft, Birch and Powell resigned in January 1958, inflation was corroding the post-war settlement, forcing politicians to attempt to reorient on the core belief. Inflation was threatening Conservative statecraft by stoking up resentment in the Party, and threatened a clash with the unions.[30]

'Full employment, an expanding economy,' Macmillan commented, 'stable prices and a strong pound; these were the balls the Chancellor of the Exchequer, like a new Cinquevalli, was expected to keep in the air together.'[31] Macmillan's letter (24 October 1955) to Eden setting out his conditions for accepting the chancellorship urged the need to be 'revolutionary' in economic policy. In papers circulated to colleagues, *Dizzy with Success* and *First Thoughts from a Treasury Window*, he advocated policies he previously dismissed as 'whoring', but as a self-confessed expansionist, Macmillan lapsed into orthodoxy. Inflation was a political management problem, relying on 'steady pressure and pleading', as in the 1956 White Paper, *The Economic Implications of Full Employment* (Cmd. 9725), the toothless Council on Prices, Productivity and Incomes, and the 'you've never had it so good speech' at Bedford (20 July 1957). Deflation was compatible with the post-war settlement and the core belief because it was a short-term response to a temporary disequilibrium, whereas Thorneycroft's 'swingeing cuts in the Welfare State' was a blatant challenge. Thorneycroft, Birch and Powell's stand in 1958 was literally incomprehensible, it 'could not be sustained by reason but required an act of faith', their position was held 'with almost fanatical rigidity'.[32]

Scepticism about the Party's strategy was suppressed by electoral success and mass affluence, but the July 1961 crisis reopened the debates which had lain at the heart of Operation Robot and the 1958 resignations. The government's response was 'modernisation': EEC membership, tripartism to promote economic growth (National Economic Development Council) and restrain inflation (National Incomes Commission), tighter control of public spending, 'commercialised' nationalised industries, and a further reduction in the UK's global role. This putative 'settlement of 1961' did not break with the core belief but aspired to renovate its rules and institutions to preserve the post-war settlement. Like the original, this had fatal flaws built into it. The NEDC, for example, had no planning powers and wages and prices were excluded from its remit. Macmillan's strategy fell apart.[33] In May 1962 Macmillan confessed that inflation and growth were 'intractable, obscure, and baffling problems ... colleagues are all confused' and he sensed a wider change:

> a conjunction of a spiritual vacuum and a vague feeling in the middle class that all they had striven for was turning to Dead Sea fruit. They were becoming aware that power was passing to organised labour, and that the period since 1832, in which the middle classes had dominated government and politics was disappearing.[34]

Variations on this strategy – adjustment through modernisation – were pursued by all governments between 1962 and 1979, but an alternative core belief was emerging. The Institute for Economic Affairs, founded in 1957, sought to alter the ideological climate in favour of low taxes, free markets and a smaller state, and *A Giant's Strength*, published in 1958, advocated a new legal framework for trade unions. In Whitehall and the Conservative Research Department there was a search for alternatives.[35]

Defeat in 1964 and 1966 saw the Conservative Party under its new leader, Edward Heath, undertake a dramatic policy rethink. The changes (union reform, welfare selectivity, tax cuts, tighter spending control, central and local government reform, and privatisation) appeared to herald a direct assault on the post-war settlement as a core belief.[36] Heath did not, however, seek a fracture with either the Conservative or the country's immediate past. His strategy of adjustment through modernisation did not differ from Macmillan's or Wilson's. It is easy to overemphasise the radicalism of the rethink, and the limits of Heath's 'quiet revolution' were revealed during 1971–72 when the attempt to adjust the core belief provoked serious conflict. This coincided with changes in the international environment and with unforeseen exogenous shocks, notably the 1973 oil crisis. The Heath Government seemed to demonstrate the state's vulnerability and that the polity was on the brink of collapse. Between 1970 and 1974 the gap between the core belief's prescription and the new quandary – stagflation – grew. Conservative statecraft collapsed, weakening severely the post-war settlement as a core belief and there existed a truly radical alternative: Enoch Powell's blend of free markets and nationalism.[37] Powell's overt influence was circumscribed by its identification with racism after his 'Rivers of Blood' speech, but he articulated a Conservatism which resonated powerfully inside the Party and overlapped with the CRD and think tanks who were 'thinking the unthinkable'. This nexus of critical ideas received an enormous infusion of energy with Heath's fall.

Prophets of Chaos: Joseph and Thatcher

The Prophets of Chaos interpreted 1974 as a judgement on Conservative competence and uncertainty about what Conservatism represented.[38] Joseph argued: 'We made things worse when, after the war, we chose the path of consensus', and now 'we have reached the end of the road.' The strategic error was that 'we competed with socialists in offering to perform what is in fact beyond the power of government … we strained the economy to the point where jobs, living standards and the savings of millions have been jeopardised'. Corporate bias had enabled sectional interests to undermine governability, the solution was neither an old-style Conservative nor a National Government which 'would destroy the free economy and free society'. A Conservative Party committed to a new core belief would transform the conduct and content of politics: 'we should show a way forward, away from the discredited policies and failed institutions ... we need radical approaches'.[39] Several Shadow Cabinet members

> thought the paper was too critical of the recent past and, in particular, of recent Conservative policy. They emphasised that the Party should not repudiate its previous attempts to reach a national consensus and to hold the middle ground of opinion, as this was the key not only to electoral success, on which all else depended, but also to governing and staying in power. Conservative policy should be evolutionary, and build upon the past, not revolutionary, rejecting the past.[40]

Prophets of Chaos sought a national consensus based on a new core belief. The middle ground was no longer equidistant between left and right, and growing dissatisfaction would increase the numbers willing to endorse the new core belief.[41] Mrs Thatcher expressed it thus:

> one of the reasons for our electoral failure is that people believe too many Conservatives *have* become socialists already. Britain's progress towards socialism has been an alternation of two steps forward with half a step back ... we did not appear to stand for anything distinctive and positive.[42]

Keynes was dead and Labour's leftward shift meant (Joseph's 'ratchet' theory) that the Party 'could not afford to be passive: it needed to provide a positive alternative to socialism. It was the absence of a clear Conservative programme [after] 1962 that gave the initiative to the socialists.'[43]

The Prophets of Chaos had predicted unemployment would rise, and 'the longer there was delay in combating inflation the more unemployment would rise'. Furthermore, 'there could be no discipline or restraint in the public sector without the ultimate sanction of redundancy'.[44] The Macmillan–Heath conceptualisation of unemployment, inflation and union power as political management problems retained support. Reginald Maudling described monetarism as an 'old fashioned "squeeze"', and James Prior, whilst admitting that the Social Contract had failed and agreeing that a 'tight monetary policy is essential', insisted '[w]e need some form of wage restraint'.[45] Unemployment was inevitable because of high inflation. High interest rates and monetary discipline would spur the private sector to greater efficiency; spending cuts and reducing the public sector borrowing requirement would do the same in the state sector, but unemployment would increase. However, if action was not taken, Weimar-style hyperinflation would result.[46] The Economic Reconstruction Group did discuss the feasibility of unemployment as a tool of economic management. Unemployment would be unpopular but 'it was thought possible that unemployment in the 1970s would be (or could be) less unpalatable than unemployment in the past.'[47]

Unemployment, whether as a deliberate policy or the by-product of irrational behaviour, was at the centre of the new core belief. It might, the CRD warned, be 'necessary to attempt a redefinition of what is the highest sustainable level of unemployment', but inflation might 'not be able to work itself through much or, perhaps, at all in a period of such high unemployment as we have entered on'.[48] 'It was now [1978] clear that pay policies should be avoided' and that monetary control was critical 'in reducing inflationary expectations, since excessive pay settlements would result in higher unemployment' so 'negotiators would have to choose between more responsible pay bargaining or increased unemployment. Unless this policy was pursued there would be no ... understanding that increased living standards can only come through increased productivity.'[49] Moderation 'can only be learnt by a slow and painful process of conditioning' lasting as long as bargainers refused to acknowledge the consequences of their actions.[50] Senior Conservatives remained nervous of the costs. The Shadow Cabinet agreed that the Party should 'not give the impression that the net effect of our policies would be to increase unemployment permanently'. Nigel Lawson was concerned that so many frontbench spokesmen believed that 'our economic policies ... would cause increased unemployment'. The truth, he argued, was 'quite the reverse, in fact, given the incentive effect of our income tax proposals'; he concluded, 'I do hope our doubting colleagues can be straightened out before the Campaign!' Discussing the second draft of the unused 1978 manifesto, the Shadow Cabinet decided that 'more prominence would be given to the need for an attack on unemployment, and the main emphasis would be on tax cuts and the creation of wealth'.[51]

The monetarist experiment failed and was abandoned.[52] Failure did not mean it lacked 'positive' consequences. When asked what he thought were the Conservative Government's achievements, Alan Clark could think of only one: 'we really have succeeded in putting a lot of people out of work', but the unions had been 'disciplined by the fear of being put on the dole and this is a considerable, though brutal achievement'.[53] 'Keynesianism' was the problem, not the solution; an interpretation seemingly proved by the political and economic turmoil of the 1970s. The erstwhile Prophets of Chaos became the new Architects of Order. Their solution to the stagflation quandary – a smaller state, lower direct taxes, an assault on union power, law and order, and more and freer markets – constituted the Party's second adaptation. This core belief achieved dominance in the 1980s.[54]

Only the most purblind monetarist believed that controlling the money supply *per se* would transform the UK. Change was neither automatic nor instantaneous; there would be serious transaction costs. This was 'stickiness': the stability (or inertia) inducing properties of rules, institutions, ideas and language in the political process.[55] Under the post-war settlement this scenario was positive because it maximised consent and, in the short to medium term, eased the stress on the political process. Critics countered that these virtues were, in fact, vices; an analysis set out in the *Stepping Stones Report* (1978). Hitherto the government's response had been to bolster its authority and effectiveness via corporate bias, but 1970–74, the Social Contract and the Winter of Discontent showed that this was no longer viable.[56] Stickiness could not be bargained away, it had to be stripped out. Between 1945–51 and 1965–70 statecraft was revised with the post-war settlement as a core belief, but between 1975 and 1979 the Party evolved a new statecraft in a context where the benchmark – the core belief – was unclear. Fiscal crisis and a crisis of political authority created space for alternatives, but the new Conservative statecraft depended on a frontal assault on institutions which stood in the way of the new core belief. Such an attack was unheard of in Conservative history.

Plausible policies are essential in an effective response to a quandary, but the response also requires a convincing narrative.[57] In the 1970s and 1980s the narrative focused on socialism's eradication; the Party's task was now 'to give intellectual content and political direction to these new dissatisfactions with socialism in practice, with its material and moral failures, we must convert disillusion into understanding'.[58] This narrative served the Party well, but after 1987 it weakened, culminating in Mrs Thatcher's ouster. One of Major's tasks was constructing a new narrative, but this was accompanied by a collapse in governing competence after Black Wednesday (16 September 1992) and Party management problems over Europe. The government and Conservatism was caught in a strategic dilemma: 'permanent revolution' or a 'new' Conservatism?[59]

The dilemmas of post-Thatcher Conservatism

Major extended Thatcherism significantly, but he also sought a 'big idea'. The Citizens' Charter and 'Back to Basics', for example, used language derived from the One Nation tradition to advocate free market policies.[60]

'The modern Conservative Party', Major claimed, 'is heir to both the great nineteenth-century political traditions: to the Whigs, in our free market radicalism; to the Tories, in our belief in community and tradition'. This created a paradox: 'we need to change in order to preserve: if we cling to outdated habits, rules and restrictions, we risk the collapse of our economy and society. On the other hand, change is itself destabilising ... by removing just one brick, we may risk bringing the whole house down.' Major's strategy was to locate Thatcherism in the Conservative tradition and continue modernisation, a formulation, Major believed, familiar to Burke, Disraeli and Salisbury.[61] To strike off in a wholly new direction would have been to disavow 'Thatcherism', a project which became more coherent in retrospect, and pressure to pursue it continued despite its electoral unpopularity.[62] In a context of collapsing trust and competence, Major's reconciliation failed. His 1995 resignation, fighting a 'back me or sack me' leadership election, resolved nothing and ended in the devastating defeat of 1997.

A common complaint was that the Party had become obsessed with economics. In 1976 Joseph criticised this attitude as 'helpful to socialism', arguing that patriotism, crime, immigration, social security abuse and home ownership should be central to the Party's appeal.[63] In 1993 Peter Lilley argued that the 1980s had been about reversing economic decline; in the 1990s social and national problems (above all Europe) would take centre-stage.[64] The problem after 1997 was that which faced Major: what were the contours of post-Thatcherite Conservatism?

Previously, Architects of Order could define Conservatism in relation to threats (the USSR, socialism, union power) but by the mid 1990s these threats had disappeared and the free market core belief was unchallenged. Defining the Party on a non-economic agenda proved highly divisive. This was exacerbated by defeat and the apostasy of some former Thatcherites. In the mid 1980s the Conservatives appeared to have evolved a highly effective statecraft which had won power by creating an electoral coalition (the first and second dimensions of statecraft) but failed on the third: insulating 'itself, as far as possible, from both domestic and external pressure'.[65] No institution escaped the thud of the prime ministerial handbag and there was a contradiction between the first and second dimensions, and the third. Conservatives aspire to 'depoliticise' dangerous issues. As problems mounted the Thatcher/Major Governments pursued incompatible strategies: shedding functions (privatisation), intervening to try and control its environment, and searching for self-governing mechanisms (the Exchange Rate Mechanism). This statecraft's limits, exposed by the poll tax, were apparent by 1989. The privatisation/marketisation of the public sector and the creation of the regulatory state rendered the Thatcher/Major Governments as vulnerable as their predecessors, but the source of their vulnerability changed. With the unions broken, turbulence came from the public services of health, education and welfare.

Prophets of Chaos? Lilley and Portillo

Well before the 1997 defeat, Conservatism seemed afflicted by 'revolutionary defeatism': 'dump Major ... purge the rest of the Europhiles, reunite [under] whichever Euroscep hero is in vogue ... then sweep back to power and complete the Thatcherite revolution'.[66] The scale of defeat scuppered this. Hague's first conference speech as leader attempted to reinvent the Party. The Conservatives would become a party 'that cares for the poor, disadvantaged and oppressed, and is more liberal in its attitude both to people who bring up families outside marriage ... a party determined to show it cares'.[67] The inclusive strategy was disliked inside the Party and, most important of all, had no effect on Hague's or the Party's standing. From this developed 'bandwagon' politics.

'The fundamental problem of the Conservative Party', focus group research found, 'is that it doesn't have a strategy – and hasn't had one for at least four years and arguably the best part of a decade.' Defeat was 'wholehearted, premeditated and thorough': in the polls the party flatlined at about 30 per cent, had no clear critique of New Labour, it was not trusted, was believed incompetent and was perceived as nasty. The Party had to demonstrate a willingness to change, and 'the more that Conservatives talk like (and, as a party, look more like) the rest of Britain – in both language and content – the more credible our political message'. Vulnerabilities (for example, public services) had to be addressed, and 'we must define our purpose for the years ahead, fashioning a new narrative', which required new thinking on traditional Conservative issues. The objective was 'a narrative of modern Conservatism ... which is about much more than just economics'; central were '10,000 volt initiatives' to demonstrate change and capture attention. These should be 'bold, decisive and often confrontational'.[68] *Kitchen Table Conservatism* 'will be seen as a shift to the political centre even though many of the individual programmes ... could be considered radical and "right wing"'. Influenced by the Republican Party victory in the 1996 US mid-term elections, it was interpreted erroneously as a return to the baseball cap. *Kitchen Table Conservatism* had been around for some time, but Hague's failure to consult was resented by his colleagues.[69]

Like Joseph in 1974, Lilley and Portillo, hitherto gold-plated Thatcherites, used defeat to rethink Conservatism. What Lilley and Portillo were trying to achieve was presented as a conflict 'between those sensitive to changing times and those inclined to nostalgia ... between those with a gaze fixed on new horizons and those either blinkered or still dreaming'.[70] This is too simplistic. Unlike the 1940s or the 1970s, there was no obvious quandary for the Prophets of Chaos to attack. The core belief in markets was not being challenged; in fact, New Labour's acceptance of markets strengthened the core belief immeasurably and 'the post-1997 Conservatives were remarkably united in their approach to economic questions'.[71] Having no equivalent of stagflation they attacked, or *appeared* to attack, the Party and its recent history and the result was bitter conflict over this legacy. Debates on strategy degenerated into how to present the past and, not surprisingly, generated elemental passions.

In April 1999 Lilley delivered a '10,000 volt' shock. Lilley argued that the Party must broaden its agenda because Conservatism was equated solely with free markets. This 'blighted' the Party's revival and 'unless and until we are prepared to accept there is more to life and more to Conservatism than defending and extending the free market we will always be on the intellectual back foot'. This was a call not to abandon markets but to champion better public services. The nucleus of Lilley's message was to recognise that markets had limits and to 'stop identifying Conservatism with market economics'.[72] Lilley's lecture must be one of the most incendiary in history. The speech was portrayed as 'the most significant break with the past', intended to 'have the same effect on voters as Labour's abandoning its adherence to funding higher public spending from tax rises'.[73] Criticised as an assault on the Party's core (Thatcherite) beliefs, Hague's inclination was to face down the revolt, but the pressure proved too great. The row reinforced Hague's conviction that challenging openly the Party's political culture was dangerous. Lilley was sacked in June.

The destructive power of Lilley's speech was amplified because it coincided with the celebrations for the twentieth anniversary of the 1979 victory. In Lady Thatcher's presence, Hague articulated the difficulty of 'moving on':

we owe it to you to make sure that the Conservative Party once again connects with those values of the British people. We must be true to our inheritance. For tonight, as we celebrate the 20th anniversary of one of our greatest election victories, we do so in the shadow of one of our greatest election defeats. We changed Britain. It would be a tragedy if the one institution in Britain that didn't change was the Conservative Party.

The Conservatives' task, as between 1974 and 1979, was to reconnect via a new mission. This had five elements: (1) a fresh enterprise revolution emphasising deregulation, global free trade and low taxes; (2) increased choice and decentralisation in the public services; (3) to address 'head on' the English question in a devolved polity; (4) 'to be true internationalists; to keep Britain in Europe, but not run by Europe'; and (5) to 'defeat the moral emptiness and media obsession' of New Labour. This agenda would be rooted in 'enduring Conservative principles of independence and responsibility, freedom and community, nationhood and a global role'.[74]

Portillo's analysis began with the proposition that the world had changed irrevocably as a result of Labour's victory. The Conservatives had not been defeated because they had abandoned One Nation politics but because 'the party became associated increasingly with the most disagreeable messages and thoughts'. The Party was 'thought to be uncaring about unemployment, poverty, poor housing, disability and single parenthood ... favoured greed and the unqualified pursuit of the free market'; 'we were thought to be arrogant and out of touch' and 'too elderly, or too vulgar ... unfamiliar and unrepresentative', and sleaze 'disgraced us in the eyes of the public'. This caustic analysis was careful to acknowledge Britain's transformation in the 1980s, a transformation *not* achieved by rampant *laissez-faire*. Policies had to be recast and explained, utilising immutable Conservative principles of choice, aspiration, opportunity and compassion. Portillo sought to reorient the Thatcherite legacy 'to deal with the world as it now is', including 'our attitude to the personal relationships that people chose to enter'. The Party had to use Opposition 'to reflect and listen and ... understand' and 'spread our appeal and attract different sorts of people: different ages, social types, ethnic groups and cultures'.[75]

By the time Portillo re-entered the House of Commons in September 1999, Conservative politics had moved on. His speech to the 2000 party conference, his first in four years, generated an uproar. 'A lot of water', Portillo noted, 'has flowed under the bridge' since 1997, and he depicted his defeat at Enfield, and by implication the Party's, as a favour which enabled him 'to connect with the Britain of today'. The imputation being that the Party had failed to reconnect. There was no repudiation of the 1980s but, Portillo stressed, the world had changed and so must the Conservatives:

'We are a party for people, not against people. We are for all Britons: black Britons, British Asians, white Britons. Britain is a country of rich diversity ... Conservatives don't look for uniformity, but for the qualities that mark people out as individuals and exceptional. We are for people whatever their sexual orientation ... Why should people respect us if we withold respect from them?'

Despite being Shadow Chancellor, Portillo said little about economic policy, but he concluded: 'we will be the party of tax cuts, and welfare reform. Of social justice and full employment.'[76]

Portillo's speech precipitated a major falling-out at a dinner of the Thatcherite No Turning Back group. Eric Forth MP querulously demanded of the speech, 'What was it all about? You should be attacking the Labour Government, not talking about yourself.'[77] The speech exposed further the Party's adaptive problem. The Thatcherites fragmented not over economics but over the Thatcher legacy's evolution. The discord proved that 'we have been unable to concede and move on'.[78] Portillo's re-election complicated Hague's task. 'Touchy-feely' politics failed to improve either his or the Party's poll ratings. The reaction to the Lilley row laid the foundations for Hague's 'lurch to the right' because 'the Party's staunchest supporters were asking what the Conservatives are for'.[79] This question could not go unanswered and led directly to speeches on asylum, law and order and several that censured the liberal establishment, climaxing in an attack on the Macpherson Report. By this approach, Hague believed, 'it was possible to be both a mainstream traditionalist and reach out to new voters'. Hague (dubbed 'Billy Bandwagon') was accused of chasing panaceas.[80] The impression given was of a party lacking a settled strategy, which sharpened the conflict over the remaking of the Conservative image.

Architects of Order? Hague, Duncan Smith and Howard

Before 1979, opinion favoured contraction, and government responded quickly, shifting from direct to indirect taxation, but 'the core services of the welfare state – health, education, housing, and provision for the old, the ill, and the unemployed – are almost universally (usually more than 90 per cent) regarded as government responsibilities'.[81] By the early 1990s a new quandary had emerged: how to fund and satisfy the demand for public services without increases in direct taxation.

Despite the twists and turns in party politics, the continuities of thinking in post-Thatcherite Conservatism are remarkable. Hague argued that Conservatism's backbone was 'individuals and families shaping their own lives within a framework set by strong but limited Government', a relationship embracing personal, market and institutional ties. This was intended as a reproof to the supposed Thatcherite view that there was no such thing as society and their 'unleashing the unbridled forces of the free market'. The challenge 'is to keep open, equitable financing which had been the great twentieth century advance in health and education while at the same time trying to bring back some of our local pride and that rich experimentation and diversity which was such a strength in nineteenth century Britain'. This required a new agenda 'that goes beyond economic policy and addresses such issues as identity, community and nationhood. An agenda that dispels the myth that the Conservatives are only able to speak convincingly about money and how to make it.'[82] This agenda embraced 'traditional' values (such as Clause 28 and the family) and the free market, low-tax agenda. New Labour's state would be rolled back and an enabling state created, permitting the flowering of personal choice.[83] This culminated in *The Common Sense Revolution* whose 'very strong and very familiar themes' (crime, asylum, Europe, tax, bureaucracy) aimed at a 'fundamental shift to a smaller state' formed the basis of the 2001 election campaign. Common sense would enable Conservatives to 'build a kinder, more united Britain by encouraging greater personal responsibility and responsibility for others as the foundation of civil society ... underpinned by a dynamic economy'.[84]

Both Hague and Iain Duncan Smith (IDS) were impressed by George W. Bush's compassionate conservatism which 'recognised the strength and appeal of the basic Conservative message, of cutting taxes, of reducing the size of government, of waging war on crime'. The 'Bush formula' appealed to values despised by the liberal elite and offered 'bold and distinctive social policies that would address ... the quality of life agenda'.[85] Bush won because voters 'trusted him to deliver the changes they thought necessary precisely because they saw someone with principles who wasn't afraid to articulate them'. IDS believed that 'we can learn a great deal from [Bush] mapping out a distinctively conservative agenda that appeals to the common ground ... challenging those popular prejudices about conservatives.'[86]

IDS identified the public services as the Party's main concern and therefore central to its core belief and narrative.[87] 'This', he told Conference, 'is our greatest mission at home over the coming years: to assemble the coalition of charities and churches, the public and private sectors that will deliver results.' The Party would examine foreign models and then formulate a programme. This effort was comparable to 1974–79 when 'we were faced with the task of turning Britain around ... the challenges were mainly economic ... we tamed the power of the unions and unleashed the latent spirit of enterprise within our nation [but] time has moved on.' Education, health and crime were 'real problems', taking precedence over lifestyle issues. Independence, personal freedom, choice and enterprise were fundamental to the continuing efforts to recast Conservatism.[88]

Speaking to Conservative Way Forward, IDS engaged with the Thatcher legacy: 'during the 1980s [the] overriding concern was their standard of living. But today, people are confronted by the declining quality of our public services.' Opposition provided an opportunity to 'ignite a Conservative revolution', but 'with the defeat of old-fashioned socialism, the clash between the main parties lacks the drama of the Cold War years'. Nevertheless, the Party was undergoing 'a process of policy renewal as sweeping and extensive as that of the 1970s'.[89] IDS summarised this approach thus:

> our twin aims in the public services – to reform them in order to improve them, while cutting waste in government – is consistent with our values of careful stewardship of public money. That is why ... the Conservative Party is naturally a lower tax party than Labour ... We will reorient our public services to respond to people not politicians ... we want to turn our schools and hospitals into independent local institutions ... accountable to the people they serve, not to government targets ... We do not believe that the government should be the only source of funding available for public services.

This, IDS argued, continued the old agenda by new means: 'in the 1980s a Conservative government reformed and improved the performance of the economy, keeping taxes low. The challenge for Conservatives today is to show how we can reform and improve the performance of our public services, keeping taxes lower than Labour.'[90]

This climaxed in the Fair Deal strategy. 'We have', IDS argued, 'always been the party of one nation. The social and economic reforms of the 1980s were only possible because we built a coalition across social and economic groups.'[91] Ironically, the most developed presentation came after his resignation. The Fair Deal was 'an agenda as radical and attractive as that drawn up by Keith Joseph at the dawn of the Thatcher era'. What IDS defined as his legacy was based on four principles:

the need for a complete renewal of our public services ... the need
to place social justice, and concern for the plight of the vulnerable,
at the very core of Conservative thinking ... the need for freedom,
the rule of law and a strong competitive economy ... the need for
the state to defend itself and the constitutional arrangements of the
United Kingdom.

One Nation Conservatism opposed 'the liberal left' and the 'nihilistic
individualism of the libertarian right'.[92] As Shadow Chancellor, Michael
Howard endorsed a low-tax economy, but 'the public services must be put
first and that the provision of the resources which are necessary in order
to meet the current crisis may have to take priority over tax cuts'.[93]

The problem was that while Conservative issues rose up the agenda
and New Labour experienced serious difficulties, the Party's standing was
unaffected. This generated the 'lurch to the right' reflex: 'halfway through
the previous parliament, after initially dabbling with an "inclusive"
approach, Mr Hague lost his nerve when the polls refused to budge and
turned to his "core vote" strategy, based on being anti-Europe, anti-asylum
seekers and cutting taxes'.[94] IDS's lurch was the purge of Portillistas from
Central Office and Barry Legg's appointment as chief executive in early
2003. This was one of the most hamfisted episodes in the Party's history,
for which IDS later apologised but which sealed his fate. *A Fair Deal for
Everyone* was designed to appeal to the Party and non-core voters, but its
message failed because of a poor leader/Party image which exacerbated
Party management problems, and in turn these amplified the difficulty
of getting across the Party's response. The inclusive strategy was dead:
it caused too much trouble for no reward. IDS's last conference speech
pushed the right buttons on tax ('We'll be tough on tax and the tough
on the causes of tax'), public sector reform, extending choice and the
single currency. IDS declared:

I believe in hard work, in rewarding people who play by the rules, in
small government. I believe in punishing criminals, in trusting nurses,
teachers, police officers. I believe in a low tax economy. I believe we
all have a special duty of care for the most vulnerable people in our
country – children, pensioners and the poor. And, most of all, I believe
in the sovereign right of the British people to govern themselves.[95]

IDS's 'unite or die' speech outlined the new narrative, stressed the
importance of further modernisation, and emphasised the centrality
of improving public services and reconnection with the electorate.[96]

Unity around a common narrative did not depend upon a 'Clause 4 moment'; both 'mods' and 'rockers' could subscribe to an agenda drawn from but different from Thatcherism. This addressed the larger question facing 'parties in the aftermath of the Thatcher–Blair revolution, [namely] whether the nature of the early-21st century political settlement can be reconciled with the nature of the mid-20th century political settlement that preceded it'.[97]

As Leader, Howard did not depart from the agenda mapped out by IDS. Conservatives had to 'show they understand 21st century Britain' while opposing state control and extending choice and responsibility, lower taxes, personal security and fairness. Conservatives would 'Promise less, deliver more'.[98] Howard's theme at the 2004 party conference was delivery. Ten words – 'school discipline. More police. Cleaner hospitals. Lower taxes. Controlled immigration' – expressed the essence of this 'Credible, Mainstream, Practical, and Accountable' Conservatism.[99] The reformulation of One Nation Conservatism shows that Howard took on board Hague's *mea culpa*: 'I got this Parliament the wrong way round. I should have spent the first year or so shoring up the base Conservative vote and then reached out later on.'[100]

Open coffin Conservatism?

Core beliefs map and conceptualise the world in a communicable way, and as the world changes, the pressure on the core belief to change increases. Thatcherism predominated, but this is not teleological because statecraft is not fixed, nor is the quandary facing politicians unchanging. In 1959, Macmillan's Conservatism seemed as secure as Thatcher's in 1987. Core beliefs are complex group products, used by politicians whose interpretation of reality changes so as to legitimise different policies. Core beliefs consolidate a perspective which hitherto had not been so clearly identified, but the meaning cannot be held constant because of society's diversity and complexity, hence the tendency to fragmentation. The core belief is brittle; it evolves, adapting to a quandary, or breaks.

After 1945 the Conservative Party negotiated successfully two quandaries. The Party adapted its statecraft and core belief, secured extended periods in office but was then defeated. After 1997 this sequence was disrupted. Faced by a new quandary – the problem of financing and delivering public services – the Party evolved neither a convincing narrative nor effective statecraft. The response to the stagflation quandary 'ideologised' the Party and, in attempting to reverse national decline and root out socialism, the Conservatives rendered themselves vulnerable.

This created an image of an uncaring and, after 1992, incompetent party which culminated in electoral defeat.

Where the Party's current situation differs from that of the 1940s and 1970s is that it is locked into a systemic crisis. The market-based core belief offered no solution acceptable to an electorate who saw the Conservatives as nasty and incompetent. The threats which had sustained the Party in the twentieth century no longer applied. Cross-party agreement on economic management left Conservatism bereft of a mobilisational statecraft. Poor leadership and Party image, despite the Blair Government's problems, obscured the Party's emerging response to the quandary, and aspects of this were vulnerable to appropriation by New Labour. Conservatives have been unable to develop an electorally convincing narrative with sufficient credibility to challenge New Labour's administration of the core belief and constitution.

Notes

1. J. Barnes, 'Ideology and Factions', in A. Seldon and S. Ball (eds), *The Conservative Century: The Conservative Party since 1900* (Oxford: Oxford University Press, 1994), pp.315–46.
2. 'Mods and rockers', *The Times*, 6 July 1998.
3. K. Shepsle, 'Institutional Arrangements and Equilibrium in Multidimensional Voting Models', *American Journal of Political Science*, 23 (February 1979), pp.27–59.
4. N. Schofield, 'The Heart of the Atlantic Constitution: International Economic Stability, 1919–1998', *Politics and Society*, 27:2 (June 1999), pp.173–215. 'Architects of Order' refers to the political, bureaucratic and intellectual groups that coalesce in developing a response to a quandary.
5. Schofield, 'The Heart of the Atlantic Constitution', p.181.
6. S. Lohmann, 'The Dynamics of Informational Cascades: The Monday Demonstrations in Leipzig, East Germany, 1989–1991', *World Politics*, 47:1 (October 1994), pp.42–101.
7. Cuthbert Headlam MP, diary 17 August 1947. S. Ball (ed.), *Parliament and Politics in the Age of Churchill and Attlee. The Headlam Diaries 1935–51* (Cambridge: Cambridge University Press for the Royal Historical Society, 1999), pp.518–19.
8. D. North, *Institutions, Institutional Change and Economic Performance* (Cambridge: Cambridge University Press, 1990), p.3. Schofield broadens this to include language ('The Heart of the Atlantic Constitution', p.179).
9. P. Addison, *The Road to 1945 British Politics and the Second World War* (London: Jonathan Cape, 1975) and K. Jefferys, *The Churchill Coalition and Wartime Politics 1940–1945* (Manchester: Manchester University Press, 1995).
10. M. Kalecki, 'Political Aspects of Full Employment', *Political Quarterly*, XIV:4 (October–December 1943), pp.322–31, C. Barnett, *The Audit of War. The Illusion and Reality of Britain as a Great Nation* (London: Macmillan, 1986),

and C. Barnett, *The Lost Victory. British Dreams, British Realities 1945–1950* (London: Macmillan, 1995).

11. J. Bulpitt, 'The Discipline of the New Democracy: Mrs Thatcher's Domestic Statecraft', *Political Studies*, XXXIV (1986), pp.19–39 at p.21.

12. M. Bevir and R.A.W. Rhodes, 'Narratives of "Thatcherism"', *West European Politics*, 21:1 (1999), pp.97–119.

13. 'Industrial Relations, 1955'. *PREM 11/921*.

14. CC (57) 60th Conclusions, 1 August 1957, p.5. *CAB 128/31*.

15. K. Middlemas, *Power, Competition and the State. Volume 1, Britain in Search of Balance, 1940–1961* (London: Macmillan, 1986), p.3.

16. M. Fraser, 'British Politics, 1945–1987', in P. Hennessy and A. Seldon (eds), *Ruling Performance. British Governments from Attlee to Thatcher* (Oxford: Blackwell, 1987), pp.309–10, and interview with Lord Fraser of Kilmorack, 18 January 1990.

17. P. Clarke, 'The Keynesian Consensus', in D. Marquand and A. Seldon (eds), *The Ideas that Shaped Post-War Britain* (London: Fontana, 1996), pp.67–87.

18. See J. Ramsden, *A History of the Conservative Party: The Age of Churchill and Eden, 1940–1957* (London: Longman, 1995), ch. 4, for the 'remaking' of Conservatism.

19. Examples of Prophets of Chaos are F.A. von Hayek, *The Road to Serfdom* (London: Routledge and Kegan Paul, 1944), and J. Schumpeter, *Capitalism, Socialism and Democracy* (London: G. Allen and Unwin, 1943).

20. Headlam Diary, 11 September 1947 (p.521), John Maclay to R.A. Butler, 9 June 1949, and Sir Hubert Henderson to Butler, 5 July 1949, *CRD 2/49/11*.

21. *H.C. Debs*, 7 March 1950.

22. P. Catterall (ed), *The Macmillan Diaries: The Cabinet Years 1950–1957* (London: Macmillan, 2003), 21 September 1951 (p.100).

23. E. Shuckburgh (ed.), *Descent to Suez: Diaries 1951–56* (London: Weidenfeld and Nicolson, 1986), mid February (p.37), and Catterall, *Macmillan Diaries*, 1–5 September 1952 (p.184). On Operation Robot, see P. Burnham, 'Britain's External Economic Policy in the Early 1950s: The Historical Significance of Operation Robot', *Twentieth Century British History*, 11:4 (2000), pp.379–408.

24. Catterall, *Macmillan Diaries*, 28 October 1951 (p.113); Ramsden, *The Age of Churchill and Eden*, pp.275–81 and pp.294–305 for electoral politics.

25. Catterall, *Macmillan Diaries*, 7 January 1955 (p.378). Macmillan was referring to a wage settlement in the loss-making nationalised railway industry.

26. W. Strath to R.A. Butler, 29 June 1955. *T 234/91*.

27. Catterall, *Macmillan Diaries*, 19 January 1956 (p.528).

28. A. Eden to H. Macmillan, 11 April 1956. *PREM 11/1402*.

29. 'Wages, Prices and the Pound Sterling'. C.(57) 103, 27 April 1957. *CAB 129/87*, and 'The Economic Situation'. C.(57) 194, 1 September 1957. *CAB 129/88*.

30. E.H.H. Green, 'The Treasury Resignations of 1958: A Reconsideration', *Twentieth Century History*, 11:4 (2000), pp.409–30.

31. H. Macmillan, *Memoirs. Riding the Storm, 1956–59* (London: Macmillan, 1969), p.3.

32. Ibid., p.363 and p.365; J. Ramsden, *A History of the Conservative Party. The Winds of Change: Macmillan to Heath, 1957–1975* (London: Longman, 1996), ch. 1. See also, Green, 'The Treasury Resignations of 1958'.

33. S. Wood, 'Why "Indicative Planning" Failed: British Industry and the Formation of the National Economic Development Council (1960–64)', *Twentieth Century British History*, 11:4 (2000), pp.431–59. Ramsden, *Winds of Change*, ch. 3 ('Modernise with Macmillan').

34. H. Evans, *Downing Street Diary: The Macmillan Years 1957–64* (London: Hodder and Stoughton, 1981), p.196 (14 May 1962).

35. R. Cockett, *Thinking the Unthinkable. Think-Tanks and the Economic Counter-Revolution, 1931–1983* (London: Fontana, 1995), and R. Skidelsky, 'The Fall of Keynesianism', in Marquand and Seldon, *The Ideas That Shaped Post-War Britain*, pp.41–66.

36. On the remaking of policy, see B.J. Evans and A.J. Taylor, *From Salisbury to Major. Continuity and Change in Conservative Politics* (Manchester: Manchester University Press, 1996), pp.141–60; Ramsden, *Winds of Change*, pp.253–60 and pp.297–303.

37. Evans and Taylor, *From Salisbury to Major*, pp.169–70; Ramsden, *Winds of Change*, pp.276–86 and pp.290–7, and I. McLean, *Rational Choice in British Politics. An Analysis of Rhetoric and Manipulation from Peel to Blair* (Oxford: Oxford University Press, 2001), pp.128–40. McLean comments, 'before Powellism came to mean racist nationalism, it meant a passion for deregulation, privatisation, and control of inflation by controlling the money supply' (p.139).

38. Evans and Taylor, *From Salisbury to Major*, pp.183–204; Ramsden, *Winds of Changes*, ch. 6; D. Kavanagh, '1970–74', in A. Seldon (ed.), *How Tory Governments Fall: The Tory Party in Power* (London: Fontana, 1996), pp.359–92, and M. Holmes, *The Failure of the Heath Government* (London: Macmillan, 1997).

39. 'Notes Towards the Definition of Policy'. Sir K. Joseph, 4 April 1975. *Thatcher MSS 2/6/1/56*.

40. Leader's Consultative Committee, 11 April 1975, p.1. *Thatcher MSS*.

41. For a case study of the strengths and weaknesses of this see, B.J. Evans, 'Thatcherism and the British People', in S. Ball and I. Holliday (eds), *Mass Conservatism. The Conservatives and the Public since the 1880s* (London: Frank Cass, 2002), pp.218–41.

42. 'My Kind of Tory Party', *Daily Telegraph*, 30 January 1975; original emphasis.

43. Leader's Consultative Committee, 11 April 1975, p.3. *Thatcher MSS*.

44. Steering Committee, 13 May 1975. *Thatcher MSS 2/6/1/233*, and Leader's Consultative Committee, 14 May 1975. *Thatcher MSS*.

45. 'Some Thoughts on Inflation, Wages and Money'. R. Maudling, 19 May 1975. *Thatcher MSS 2/6/1/233*, and 'Counter Inflation Policy'. J. Prior, 13 May 1975. *Thatcher MSS*.

46. Notes on an all-day discussion on economic policy held at 61 Fentiman Road on Sunday 18 May 1975. *Thatcher MSS 2/6/1/92*.

47. Economic Reconstruction Group, 8 July 1975, p.2. *Thatcher MSS 2/6/1/37*.

48. 'Countering Inflation'. A. Ridley, 15 December 1976. *Thatcher MSS 2/6/1/37*.

49. 'Pay Determination'. 20 March 1978, p.1. *Thatcher MSS 2/6/1/93*, and Minute of the Meeting to Discuss Pay Bargaining, 15 February 1978. *Thatcher MSS 2/6/1/96*.

50. 'Inflation, Pay Determination and the Labour Market'. A. Ridley, 16 March 1978, para. 15, p.11. *Thatcher MSS 2/6/1/96*.
51. N. Lawson to M. Thatcher, 19 July 1978. *Thatcher MSS 2/1/2/12a*, and Leader's Consultative Committee, 10 May 1978, para. 6(v). *Thatcher MSS 2/6/1/162*.
52. D. Smith, *The Rise and Fall of Monetarism: Theory and Politics of an Economic Experiment* (Harmondsworth: Penguin, 1987), and P.M. Jackson, 'Economic Policy', in D. Marsh and R.A.W. Rhodes (eds), *Implementing Thatcherite Policies: Audit of An Era* (Milton Keynes: Open University Press, 1992), pp.11–31.
53. A. Clark, *Diaries: Into Politics* (London: Weidenfeld and Nicolson, 2000), 27 January 1981 (p.202).
54. Schofield, 'The Heart of the Atlantic Constitution', p.175.
55. M. Olson, *The Rise and Decline of Nations* (New Haven: Yale University Press, 1982), p.203.
56. A.J. Taylor, 'The Conservative Party and the Trade Unions', in J. McIlroy, N. Fishman and A. Campbell (eds), *British Trade Unions and Industrial Politics. Volume 2. The High Tide of Trade Unionism, 1964–79* (Aldershot: Ashgate, 1999), pp.151–86, and A.J. Taylor, 'The "Stepping Stones" Programme: Conservative Party Thinking on Trade Unions, 1975–79', *Historical Studies in Industrial Relations*, 11 (Spring 2001), pp.109–33.
57. 'Thoughts on the Coming Battle'. Nigel Lawson to Sir Michael Fraser, 15 October 1973. *Thatcher MSS 2/6/1/146*.
58. 'The New Renaissance'. M. Thatcher, speech to the Zurich Economic Society, 14 March 1977, f.6. *Thatcher MSS*.
59. B.J. Evans, *Thatcherism and British Politics, 1975–1999* (Stroud: Sutton Publishing, 1999), chs 6 and 7, give a clear account of the Major years.
60. 'His or hers?', *The Economist*, 12 October 1991, p.42. On 'Majorism', see, S. Hogg and J. Hill, *Too Close to Call: Power and Politics – John Major in No. 10* (London: Little, Brown, 1995).
61. 'Conservatism in the 1990s: Our Common Purpose'. *Press Release 17/93*, 3 February 1993 (mimeo).
62. N. Tebbit, *Unfinished Business* (London: Weidenfeld and Nicolson, 1991), and *Clear Blue Water. A Compendium of Speeches and Interviews Given by the Right Hon. Michael Portillo MP* (London: Conservative Way Forward, 1994), for example.
63. 'Our Tone of Voice and Our Tasks'. K. Joseph, 7 December 1976. *Thatcher MSS 2/6/1/160*.
64. 'Making the 90s Another Tory Decade'. Speech to Conservative Way Forward, 7 October 1993. (mimeo).
65. Bulpitt, 'The Discipline of the New Democracy', p.27.
66. B. Anderson, 'Major v The Bolsho-Tories', *The Spectator*, 12 October 1996, p.8.
67. *The Times*, 10 October 1997.
68. 'Kitchen Table Conservatives, A Strategy Proposal', internal Conservative Party document, November 1998, p.1, p.4, p.5 and p.7.
69. *The Times*, 8 March 1999.
70. 'Mods and rockers', *The Times*, 6 July 1998.
71. M. Garnett, 'A Question of Definition? Ideology and the Conservative Party, 1997–2001', in M. Garnett and P. Lynch (eds), *The Conservatives in Crisis. The Tories after 1997* (Manchester: Manchester University Press, 2003), p.106.

72. R.A. Butler Memorial Lecture. Rt. Hon. P. Lilley MP, 20 April 1999. *Press Release 0420176*; S. Walters, *Tory Wars. Conservatives in Crisis* (London: Politicos, 2001), pp.116–17.
73. *The Times*, 20 April 1999.
74. Speech Celebrating the 20th Anniversary of the 1979 General Election, 20 April 1999 (mimeo).
75. '*The Ghost of Toryism Past; the Spirit of Conservatism Future*'. M. Portillo. Centre for Policy Studies Autumn Lecture, October 1997 (mimeo).
76. Party Conference Speech, *Press Release*, 3 October 2000.
77. *The Times*, 28 October 2000, and Walters, *Tory Wars*, pp.86–100.
78. *Conceding and Moving On*, internal Conservative Party document, February 1999, p.1.
79. *The Times*, 24 April 1999.
80. Walters, *Tory Wars*, p.105 and p.115.
81. M. Kaase and K. Newton, *Beliefs in Government, Volume Five* (Oxford: Oxford University Press, 1995), p.69 and p.95.
82. 'Freedom and Community'. Speech to Politeia, 27 July 1998 (mimeo).
83. Speech to the Institute for Economic Affairs, 5 December 2000, <www.conservatives.com>. Unless stated otherwise, all speeches cited hereafter are from this website.
84. 'A Common Sense Conservative Vision for the Future', 25 January, and 'Renewing Civil Society', 7 February 2001.
85. 'The Forces of Conservatism are on the March', 20 January 2001. On the US influence, see E. Ashbee, 'The US Republicans: Lessons for the Conservatives?' in Garnett and Lynch, *The Conservatives in Crisis*, pp.29–48.
86. 'We will Champion the Vulnerable'. Speech to the Conservative Spring Forum, 24 March 2002.
87. M. Garnett and P. Lynch, 'The Tribulations of a Quiet Man: Iain Duncan Smith and the Conservative Party', paper to the Political Studies Association Conference, 2003, provides a survey.
88. 'Public Services are Our Greatest Mission', 10 October 2001, and 'Conservatives will Make Policy from Principle', 17 January 2002.
89. Nicholas Ridley Memorial Lecture, 21 November 2002.
90. *Daily Telegraph*, 3 January 2003.
91. 'A Fair Deal for Everyone', 16 March, and 'Conservatives are Committed to a Fair Deal', 26 June 2003.
92. 'The First Conservative Government of the 21st Century'. Speech to the Centre for Policy Studies, 31 October 2003.
93. 'Public Services Come First', 24 March 2002.
94. *Independent*, 19 February 2003.
95. BBC News, 10 September 2003, <http://news.bbc.co.uk/>.
96. 'The Necessary and Sometimes Painful Process of Modernisation', 5 November 2002.
97. *Guardian*, 9 October 2003.
98. 'A Party Broad in Appeal and Generous in Outlook'. Speech to the 1922 Committee, 6 November 2003, and 'I Will Lead this Party from the Centre'. Speech at Roehampton, 6 November 2003.
99. 'A Clear Conservative View of Government', 14 October 2004.
100. Walters, *Tory Wars*, p.127.

8
Social Morality

Bruce Pilbeam

'People tend to tie themselves in knots these days trying to explain what Conservatism is. Are we libertarian, authoritarian, vegetarian or rotarian?'[1]

For students of contemporary British Conservatism, this observation is one with which much sympathy is likely to be felt – trying to pin down exactly what Conservatives believe today can indeed be a trying task. This is at least the case with moral issues. Are modern Conservatives simply *laissez-faire* libertarians, for whom morality is just another matter to be left to individual choice? Or is the 'real' face of Conservatism that of a dogmatic traditionalism, dedicated to the bolstering of authority in an effort to stem the tide of modern permissiveness? When it comes to Conservatives' engagement with moral issues in recent times – and even if the choice is not simply between libertarianism or authoritarianism – it is certainly often difficult to identify a great deal of consistency.

In fact, today moral questions commonly prove to be among the most troublesome for Conservatives to address. Whenever contemporary Conservatives intervene in moral debates, regarding matters such as 'family values' or 'law and order', this frequently embroils them in embarrassing controversies from which they experience great difficulties extricating themselves; qualifications, retractions and U-turns often follow soon-regretted bold assertions. This explains why many have come to prefer avoiding discussing morality altogether, or at least issues of 'personal morality'.

Yet at the same time, Conservatives continually find themselves drawn into moral disputes. A key reason for this is that modern Conservatism has signally failed to close down contestation over moral issues in the same way that it has done over others. Whereas in the economic sphere Conservatives may well take satisfaction in the fact that their basic views have largely triumphed – in the sense of having 'won' a widespread acceptance across the political spectrum that there is no alternative to market-based capitalism – in relation to that of morality, no similar dominance has been achieved. Having defeated the traditional left on the battleground of economics, Conservatives continue to face an array of opponents, such as feminists and gay rights activists, fiercely challenging them in the moral arena.

Indeed, the view of many conservative commentators is that modern British society has come wholly to reject traditional morality: post-war trends such as the rise in rates of divorce, the increasing social acceptance of 'alternative lifestyles' and the dwindling of respect for traditional values and institutions, are all taken as evidence of a deleterious moral decline. Over the last few years, we have thus been treated to a deluge of doom-mongering by conservative journalists, philosophers and think-tank pamphleteers, predicting (or simply describing) the 'abolition of Britain'[2] or offering an 'elegy' for a traditional English way of life that has now passed into history.[3]

Similarly pessimistic assessments by American conservatives regarding their society have provoked talk of the need for a 'culture war' to reassert traditional values and standards. British conservatives have generally been less forthright than their American counterparts in using the language of war, yet many have sought to fight similar battles. However, what is especially interesting about the jeremiads produced by British conservatives is the extent to which blame is laid at the door of the Conservative Party, not only for failing to prevent the enervation of traditional morality, but also for actually facilitating it. In their descriptions of moral decline, many such accounts are one-sided and hyperbolic in tone; nonetheless, they still offer useful correctives to common perceptions of the Conservative Party as unambiguously committed to the assertive promotion of traditional values.

It will therefore prove useful to consider the views of conservatives with both a large and a small 'c', that is, within and outside the Conservative Party. As such, this chapter will take as its central theme the importance of recognising that, by intent or otherwise, the Conservative Party has failed to fulfil the aspirations of conservative moralists. Yet what is also clear is that this is not because of any straightforward social libertarianism; as will be seen, Conservatives have been responsible for many highly illiberal 'law and order' policies. Instead, what will be shown is that there has frequently been a disparity between Conservatives' rhetorical endorsement of traditional values and their ability (or determination) to prevent long-term social trends moving in directions opposite to those desired by traditionalists.

However, to begin with it is necessary to reflect in more detail upon the major strands of thought within modern Conservatism, to consider how its libertarian and authoritarian (as well as 'vegetarian' and 'rotarian') tendencies have manifested themselves over the post-war era.

Libertarians versus authoritarians, 'modernisers' versus 'traditionalists'

[W]hat do we believe in? ... [W]e believe in both liberty and authority. These are the twin pillars of Conservatism.[4]

In the debate highlighted at the start of this chapter, over the conflicting demands of liberty and authority, the most obvious answer to the question of where Conservatives stand is to note that Conservatism is a 'broad church' ideology that accommodates both poles of this dispute. Indeed, many Conservatives profess the need to appreciate that liberty and authority are jointly important. This is indicated, for example, in the above quotation, from a speech by Conservative Party co-chairman Liam Fox, in which he argues that a core aim of Conservatives is finding a stable equilibrium between liberty and authority. What is supposed to guide us in our search for this balance is, Fox contends, morality.

Nonetheless, since there are clearly many occasions when liberty and authority may conflict, it remains important to understand that different types of Conservative have, at different times, typically prioritised one of these values over the other. For this reason, it is necessary to consider the issue of ideological factions within the Conservative Party. One of the most useful ways to understand this is provided by W.H. Greenleaf's argument that the British 'political tradition' is characterised by a conflict between the two approaches of libertarianism and collectivism (with this conflict played out in all political parties, not just the Conservative Party).[5] Libertarian and collectivist perspectives will frequently clash, though at any particular moment, one will likely be dominant.

How, then, has this been evident within post-war Conservatism? To begin with, collectivism may be found within various strands of argument. The first to consider is that of 'One Nation' or 'progressive' Conservatism, whose proponents avow a desire to chart a 'middle way' course, seeking to ameliorate social conflict and acquiescing to such developments as the emergence of the welfare state. Equally, One Nation Conservatives do not simply set their faces against modern social trends that may run counter to traditional moral prescriptions. In broad terms, this approach informed the philosophy of the post-war Conservative Party under all of its leaders from the 1940s through to the 1970s. Insofar as a libertarian strand remained with Conservatism during this period, it did so largely at the margins.

Since the ascendancy of the New Right in the 1970s, most analyses have identified a polarisation of the debate, pushing the arguments for both liberty and authority much further, supplanting (if not entirely destroying) earlier One Nation approaches. On the one hand, the rise of an aggressively individualist, free market neo-liberalism seemed to pull the Conservative Party in a much more libertarian direction, and on the other, that of an authority-centred traditionalist conservatism seemed to pull it in a more authoritarian one. What united them was their rejection of previous One Nation approaches, either for being too accepting of the welfare state's erosion of liberty or for insufficiently recognising the importance of strong moral authority.

Yet since each perspective offered different understandings of society's problems, proposed remedies also differed. For example, High Tory journalist Peregrine Worsthorne – writing on the cusp of the Thatcherite 'revolution' – diagnosed the malady of post-war corporatism as being not (as neo-liberals believed) that it gave individuals too little freedom, but that it gave them too much, leading to rising crime and social disorder. What was required, therefore, was 'not so much a splendid libertarian crusade as an ugly battle to restore some minimum of public order'.[6] It is this concern for the maintenance of social order that leads traditionalist conservatives to demand the defence of traditional values and collective institutions. In terms of policy prescriptions, while neo-liberals usually demand a rolling back of the state, to preserve order traditionalist conservatives have regularly argued for a strengthening of its authority.

For neo-liberals, the implications of a thoroughgoing individualism might seem to be that, in Margaret Thatcher's famous declaration, 'there is no such thing as society'.[7] Such a view would appear to suggest that any order that arises does so purely spontaneously. What is particularly significant about this is that, to many critics of Thatcherism, zealous free market individualism is principally what captured, or 'hijacked', the Conservative Party in the 1970s and 1980s, and has been the dominant strand within Conservative ideology ever since. This is important for present concerns because the unfettered free market is often held by critics to be responsible for a 'hollowing out' of social morality, in undermining the vitality of collective institutions and a common moral culture. In other words, if there has been a moral decline over the post-war era, Thatcherite Conservatives may be partly to blame. This argument will be returned to later.

At this stage, what it is necessary to question is whether many Conservatives have ever actually believed in a pure, unadulterated individualism. Even the most resolute intellectual proponents of free market beliefs (such as Friedrich von Hayek) have typically recognised the need for non-economic cultural supports for the market to function. Similarly, few Conservatives have ever been full-bloodied libertarians when it comes to non-economic issues. Most notably, modern Conservative devotees of economic liberalism, from Enoch Powell to Margaret Thatcher, have strongly believed in the collective of the British nation. Moreover, they have often expressed great concern about social disorder and 'demoralisation'. A good example of this is to be found in one of the seemingly most libertarian texts produced by a contemporary Conservative, *Saturn's Children* by Alan Duncan (and Dominic Hobson) which, in arguing strongly against the modern state's expansion, devotes much attention not only to the great 'loss of liberty' this has entailed, but also to the 'loss of virtue' caused by its creation of welfare dependency and erosion of individual responsibility.[8] Such Conservatives therefore seem to agree with traditionalists that the moral fabric of modern Britain has fallen into disrepair, even if disagreeing in placing primary blame for this on the state.

In fact, it is a commonplace among modern Conservatives that there is no contradiction between seeking greater liberty in the economic sphere and stronger moral authority in the social. It is also noteworthy how many Conservatives since the Thatcher era have appeared defensive when confronted by accusations of being uncaring individualists, with frequent efforts made to correct 'misinterpretations' of the 'no such thing as society' thesis. For example, in the mid 1990s, Michael Howard attempted to argue that when Thatcher made this declaration, 'far from extolling the virtues of a selfish and irresponsible individualism, she was in fact advocating the duties of neighbourliness'.[9] What she was arguing against, Conservatives insist, was a state-centred approach to social problems, when instead these are best dealt with by families and communities.

For anti-statist Conservatives who are nonetheless concerned with morality, a central aspect of their argument is that it is not just any type of individual they wish to see thrive if individuals are freed from the state's oppressive tutelage. This can be seen in possibly the most interesting intellectual defence of Thatcherism, that presented by Shirley Letwin.[10] Indeed, Letwin's argument is that the Thatcherite project was less an economic enterprise than it was a moral one, with Thatcherism's goal being to assert a very particular understanding of the individual, one that embodies specific 'vigorous virtues' (it is worth noting here that the idea of 'virtues' is specifically preferred by many conservatives to that of 'values', as the former is believed to imply a much more robust and definite approach to morality). A virtuous individual is someone who is 'upright, self-sufficient, energetic, adventurous, independent-minded, loyal to friends, and robust against enemies'.[11] In simple terms, it is all a question of character, about being what would once have been called a 'gentleman'.

This, then, is the significance of Thatcher's infamous attachment to Victorian values (or virtues – Thatcher herself points out that, although she often spoke of Victorian values, she originally used the phrase 'Victorian virtues').[12] What is also notable about Letwin's argument is that it is not posited from any purely abstract standpoint and its conclusions are not argued necessarily to possess any universal validity – instead, the Thatcherite project is understood to be a specifically British one. Thus, Letwin claims, what underpinned Thatcherism (and was vital for its success) was a distinctive 'British morality', with long historical roots and based upon the type of vigorous virtues Thatcherism sought to defend.[13] The peculiar combination of qualities that make up the British character is what enables the British to combine 'freedom with order' so successfully, the virtues they possess allowing them to coexist harmoniously without requiring any great sacrifice of liberty, in a way that other societies have failed to do. In other words, it is owing to the specific nature of Britain's national culture that British society is able to enjoy a stable balance of liberty and authority.

However, what is important to recognise next is that debates have moved on since the Conservatives' ejection from office. More recently, analyses of the treatment of moral issues within the Conservative Party have identified a different type of split to the divisions usually identified during the New Right's heyday: that is, between 'modernisers' and 'traditionalists' or, as some have put it, between 'mods' and 'rockers'.[14] Traditionalists are those who seek to retain conventional, morally absolutist standpoints, whereas modernisers are those who embrace more socially liberal views, adopting a more accepting and inclusive approach to alternative lifestyles and values. The key figure in the modernising camp is Michael Portillo, seen as having experienced a Damascene conversion from hardline Thatcherite to compassionate conservative, while traditionalists, like Norman Tebbit and Ann Widdecombe, have continued to be defenders of the old flame.

It might be thought that modernisers are simply returning to a pre-New Right, One Nation Conservatism, but this fails to take into account two crucial factors. First of all, being a moderniser on social issues does not necessarily mean abandoning Thatcherite stances on all others; it does not, for example, preclude retaining a strong attachment to free markets. Yet second, and even more important, is understanding why this modernising tendency has emerged.

To do so, it is useful to begin by considering a more cynical view of recent developments, as is offered by Matthew Paris: 'the media's portrayal of the tribal warfare within the Opposition as being between "inclusivist" modernisers and "traditionalist" moral conservatives is pure fantasy. I know my old party. Almost all Tories are moral conservatives.'[15] On this view, it is not so much that modernising Conservatives are genuinely socially liberal, but that they have come to realise that, publicly at least, it is necessary and expedient to present themselves as such.

In fact, for Conservatives, 'modernisation' might best be understood as a politically motivated form of pragmatic relativism (rather than as a principled commitment to tolerance). Thus, instead of the philosophy of modernisers representing a return to any earlier tradition of Conservatism, it should be understood as rooted in a specifically contemporary context, being a response to changing social realities that have made British society sceptical of absolutist moral positions. What many Conservatives have evidently calculated, regardless of their personal beliefs, is that if wider society is no longer willing to condemn single mothers, abortion or homosexuality, how can they continue to do so and still hope to win elections?

The next issues to consider must therefore be how conservatives have understood the changing nature of post-war social morality and what the responses of the Conservative Party to this have been.

Rolling back the permissive society?

The favourite social causes of our generation – unrestricted abortion, easy divorce, radical education, sexual equality, homosexual law reform, the end of censorship and the abolition of capital punishment – have all been victorious. In every single case, the warnings of the crustiest and stupidest conservatives now turn out to have been sober and accurate prophecies.[16]

This assessment of the legacy of the 1960s, by conservative journalist Peter Hitchens, highlights an important aspect of conservative understandings of post-war moral decline. For many, the 1960s was the decade in which the seeds were planted for all that has subsequently gone wrong with Western democracies, in ushering in the 'permissive society'. This era witnessed not only an increased acceptance of practices such as abortion and homosexuality, but also changes in their legal statuses; for example, the 1967 Abortion Act legalised abortion (though not, contra Hitchens, as an 'unrestricted' right) and the 1967 Sexual Offences Act decriminalised male homosexuality (though only for men aged over 21).

During the 1970s and 1980s, this decade was therefore frequently invoked by Conservatives – whether of the crusty and stupid variety or not – in their analyses of social disorder. For example, following the inner-city riots of the early 1980s, Thatcher asserted that 'we are reaping what was sown in the Sixties. The fashionable theories and permissive claptrap set the scene for a society in which the old virtues of discipline and self-restraint were denigrated.'[17]

However, many Conservatives believe that matters have since deteriorated even further, thanks to the rise of 'political correctness'. What this means, they perceive, is that it is not just that values and lifestyles once considered deviant have become widely accepted as 'normal', but that traditional values and institutions are now frequently castigated as the truly aberrant and immoral. In understanding this development, particular targets of Conservatives' wrath are feminists, who are accused of so demonising the traditional family as an oppressive institution (by inflating fears about domestic violence, rape and child abuse) that it largely seems to figure in public discussions today only as something to be vilified.

While political correctness may demand a relativistic approach to alternative lifestyles and values, it also appears to imply the construction of new types of rigid moral code, transgressions against which attract the kind of severe censure that contravening traditional moral prescriptions no longer does. Norman Tebbit, a long-time scourge of permissiveness, finds this even in once dependably conservative institutions, dismayed by what he believes to be the fact that the modern Church scarcely recognises any sins but those of racism, sexism and homophobia.[18] This assessment signifies what is most worrying for such Conservatives, that political correctness is not just a belief system promoted by a left-wing minority, but a corrosive ideology that has permeated every branch of society; this includes not only the Church, but also the legal and education systems.

How, though, did such developments come to pass? Much blame is, of course, apportioned to the left, especially for propounding – in Thatcher's words – 'fashionable theories', such as progressive educational doctrines and overly 'lenient' approaches to crime. Yet in New Right accounts, Conservatives of the consensus era are also held responsible, for failing either to prevent or reverse the rise of permissiveness. Indeed, in the late 1950s and early 1960s, during R.A. Butler's tenure as Home Secretary, the Conservatives actually introduced a moderately liberal agenda, relaxing the law in areas such as obscenity, gambling and licensing hours. Equally, when in opposition during the 1960s, individual Conservatives supported liberalising measures around abortion and homosexuality (even if there were also strong Conservative voices in opposition). Most notably, when the Conservatives returned to office in 1970, the Heath Government did little to undo the moral and cultural changes wrought in the previous decade and nor did it repeal the major pieces of liberal legislation enacted by the preceding Labour Government.

However, what is particularly noteworthy about conservative discussion of the permissive society is the very fact that it continues to this day. The New Right was attacking the 1960s back in the 1970s, yet the Hitchens article from which the quotation with which this section began was drawn dates from 1998. What this illustrates is that, even after 18 years of the Thatcher and Major Governments' reforms, many conservatives believe that the legacy of the 1960s has still not been undone. For this reason, it is necessary to examine exactly what Conservatives did in the 1980s and 1990s to try to roll back the permissive society.

The Thatcher Governments certainly took action to attempt to restore public order and the authority of the state. Thus, the police enjoyed major increases in funding and manpower, and various pieces of legislation (including the 1982 Criminal Justice Act, the 1984 Police and Criminal Evidence Act and the 1986 Public Order Act) were passed, giving police extended powers – for example, of stop and search – and allowing tougher sentences to be passed by the courts. Such measures clearly demonstrated a rejection rather than embracing of social libertarianism.

Yet leaving aside the repressive nature of these efforts, what is of most interest here is how little they truly addressed the concerns of moral conservatives. Indeed, for those who believe the causes of social disorder are essentially moral, a 'tough' approach to law and order may be as ill-suited to providing a real solution to the problem as a 'soft' one. Arguing just so, conservative sociologist Christie Davies points out that spending more money on police and putting more people in jail has not succeeded in reducing crime.[19] This is because, he argues, fundamentally the problem is not amenable to conventional 'law and order' policies: the reason most people do not commit crime is not because they fear punishment, but because they understand that it is wrong.

From a conservative standpoint, Davies' analysis makes sense. At any rate, if Thatcher's own belief was that it is the denigration of the 'old virtues' that explains antisocial behaviour, she ought as Prime Minister to have recognised that strengthening the courts and the police was unlikely to achieve conservatives' desired end; whatever else they may be capable of, judges, the police and prison officers cannot actually make society virtuous. Davies' own argument is that, if the root cause of social disorder is the decay of virtue and, he suggests, a decline of national character, we need to 'think less about policemen and jails' and instead focus on areas of policy like education, if we wish to create 'honest, peaceable and undestructive citizens'.[20]

However, in looking beyond law and order initiatives, it is much harder to identify what Conservatives concretely achieved in the 1980s in 'remoralising' society. Perhaps the clearest example of Conservatives' 'success' was the incorporation of Section 28 into the 1988 Local Government Act, which forbade local authorities promoting homosexuality. Other examples include the provision of the 1986 Education Act that sex education should be taught with due regard to moral considerations and the value of family life. Yet such measures have to be viewed in context. For instance, despite their belief in the importance of upholding the value of the family in sex education, the Conservatives' most significant campaign around sex became the promotion of 'safe sex' over fears around AIDS. This was much to the displeasure of moral campaigners outside the Conservative Party, as well as many within, who saw this as a morally neutral message against 'unsafe' sex, when to them the real problem with AIDS was sex outside of marriage in general and gay sex in particular. In truth, the government's campaign was far from morally neutral, in promoting a generalised climate of fear around sexual behaviour, yet this did not address the specific qualms of moral conservatives.

More generally, the wider context can be understood by considering Hitchens' list of his generation's favourite social causes: if they remain 'victorious', it is at least partly because the Thatcher Governments did little to reverse their advances. As Martin Durham has shown in detail, the Conservative Party under Thatcher kept its distance from external moral campaigning organisations, such as anti-abortion and anti-obscenity groups, many of whom were disappointed to find their favourite social causes not taken up by the government.[21] Demands to repeal or revise the liberal legislation of the 1960s met with little success. Although in 1990 the time limit for permitting abortions was reduced from 28 to 24 weeks, this hardly satisfied anti-abortionists who had been agitating vigorously throughout the 1980s. Furthermore, despite Section 28, there was never any question of the government actually recriminalising homosexuality. Other campaigns, such as those to prevent contraception being given to girls aged under 16 without parental consent, also failed to win government support.

So why did the Conservatives not pursue a more determined moral agenda, given the belief of even the Prime Minister herself of the baleful effects of permissiveness? One argument is that the Thatcher Governments were more concerned with fighting other battles, especially in the realms of economics and foreign affairs, leaving cultural conflicts a much lower priority. Yet what also has to be taken into account is that, while many changes in the spheres of politics and economics worked in Conservatives' favour during the 1980s (such as the left's declining ability to persuade people to support its agendas), many social trends were much more to their disadvantage (such as the weakening status of the nuclear family). This made it much harder to argue for programmes of remoralisation than to argue for programmes of economic or political change.

To understand this, it is useful to return to the argument that Thatcherism itself, in advancing free market policies, was responsible for undermining social morality. This charge is levelled by critics from both the left and the right. Typical of these arguments is that offered by Melanie Phillips, who contends that under 'the Thatcher/Major regime, the Conservatives became debased liberals and promoted a political culture of atomised and irresponsible individualism which has done untold damage to our society',[22] destabilising institutions like the family and weakening belief in notions such as the existence of a common good. Even if this was unwitting, Conservatives therefore undermined the key structural supports of traditional morality: if institutions like the family have been so enervated as to make them unable to sustain traditional values across society, Conservative politicians cannot resurrect these values simply by assertion. It has already been seen that few Conservatives have ever espoused a purely individualistic philosophy, yet the essence of critics' arguments is that there is nonetheless a contradiction between economic liberalism and social conservatism that Conservatives themselves do not recognise. Many Conservatives, of course, reject this indictment. For example, David Willetts has formulated a theory of 'civic conservatism', based on the idea that liberal economics can be complemented by a communitarian emphasis upon strong associational activity, in many respects specifically to counter the accusation that the operations of the market inevitably weaken the integrity of communities.[23]

However, regardless of whether or not Willetts' argument is compelling, what remains clear is that the social structures traditionally depended on by Conservatives – such as the family, the Church and the nation – have undergone significant changes in recent decades, in ways that make it far from certain that they any longer straightforwardly support a conservative morality. Several of these will be considered in more depth below. At the very least, in devoting its energies to attacking the collective institutions of the left, such as trade unions, the Thatcher Governments can be accused by conservative moralists of neglecting the interests of those collective units cherished by the right.

In any case, since the Thatcher period, difficulties in addressing moral issues have become even more acute for Conservatives. Analyses of the Major era often suggest that it represented an attempt to present a 'softer', more socially concerned Conservatism, though initiatives such as the 1994 Criminal Justice Act (which restricted the right to protest and eroded the right to silence) militate against this interpretation. Most notable, though, was John Major's call for a 'Back to Basics' campaign at the 1993 party conference, which was widely viewed as meaning a crusade to revive traditional moral values. This was denied by Major himself, and no such crusade emerged, though it was the resignation of various ministers for the 'immorality' of their involvement in sexual and financial scandals that ultimately led to its being abandoned. Still, the question traditionalists might ask is, why was 'Back to Basics' *not* a call for the launching of a culture war? The answer is that, with social values continuing to move further away from those of traditionalists, by this stage there was little confidence among most Conservatives that such a war could be won.

Indeed, since the Conservatives left office, and with memories of the 'Back to Basics' debacle still prominent in Conservatives' minds, the chances of Conservative leaders advocating comprehensive programmes of moral rehabilitation have grown even slimmer. In fact, even tough law and order stances, once the safest of grounds for Conservatives, now cause them many difficulties. For example, when Ann Widdecombe, as Shadow Home Secretary, proposed a 'zero tolerance' policy on drugs at the 2000 party conference, despite receiving the loud applause of the party faithful, this led to widespread denouncements from outside the Party (including from the police) and to other Conservative MPs rapidly distancing themselves from it. Soon even the then Party leader, William Hague, was to be found backtracking from supporting the proposal. Again, this had little to do with social liberalism and much to do with fears of reducing Conservatives' electoral prospects even further, especially with the young.

Instead, the distinctive social agenda of post-Major Conservatism has centred upon the idea of 'compassionate conservatism', to which all three subsequent party leaders have proclaimed a commitment. This notion is consciously modelled on American conservative formulations, as a supposedly more inclusive form of conservatism. In policy terms it means, for example, devolving responsibility for delivering social policies to the institutions of civil society, such as voluntary and faith-based bodies (in tackling problems like drug abuse and family breakdown), rather than relying upon the heavy hand of the state. Significantly, a major text setting out the 'twelve principles of compassionate conservatism', published under Iain Duncan Smith's leadership, was entitled *There Is Such a Thing as Society*,[24] in an attempt to persuade us of modern Conservatives' conversion from harsh Thatcherites to sensitive humanitarians.

However, whether the approach is 'hard-headed' or 'soft-hearted', Conservative programmes depend upon the wider institutions of society. At this point it will therefore be valuable to consider probably the most important of these for Conservatives, the family.

The family or families?

> [W]e admire those many people who are doing an excellent job raising children on their own ... Our society has changed. For good or ill, many people nowadays do not marry and yet head stable families with children. For a younger generation, in particular, old taboos have given way to less judgemental attitudes to the span of human relationships ... The Tory party is conservative and not given to political correctness. Still the party never rejects the world that is. Tolerance is a part of the Tory tradition.[25]

The Conservative Party has repeatedly proclaimed itself to be the party of the family, especially during the Thatcher era. For example, the Conservatives' 1979 manifesto identified 'Helping the Family' as one of their five key tasks in restoring Britain's fortunes.[26] However, the question for modern Conservatives is, should a single model of the family be privileged or, as those like Portillo have come to argue, can a range of models be valued by tolerant Conservatives? In other words, should Conservatives stop talking about the family and instead talk about families?

Until very recently, it would have been unnecessary to ask this question. In the past, invocations of the 'family' would immediately conjure up the image of the traditional nuclear family: a monogamous, heterosexual married couple living with their children. During the 1980s, when single parents were mentioned by Conservatives it was usually not to express admiration for the excellent job that they did in raising their children; more commonly, it was to chastise them for precisely the opposite, as well as for their parasitism upon the welfare state. By contrast, modernisers appear willing to accept as legitimate not only single-parent families or cohabiting heterosexuals, but even gay couples as well.

One fact that is impossible to dispute is that major changes to the constitution of the British family have occurred, at least partially as a result of what Portillo describes as less judgemental attitudes to the span of human relationships. For example, the annual number of marriages in the UK fell from around 459,000 in 1971 to just over 286,000 in 2001, while over the same period, divorce rates rose from just under 80,000 to 157,000.[27] As a result of such changes, between 1971 and 2003 the proportion of households containing the traditional family unit (a couple living with dependent children) fell from 35 per cent to 22 per cent of the total; at the same time, single-parent households rose from 3 per cent to 5 per cent. Perhaps the most troubling statistic for traditional-ists is the growth of births outside of wedlock, which rose from 12 per cent in 1980 to 41 per cent in 2002. These changing facts about their potential voters undoubtedly help explain modernising Conservatives' rediscovery of tolerance.

Yet it is necessary also to understand why traditionalists so cherish the nuclear family. One useful account is provided by conservative phil-osopher Roger Scruton. According to Scruton, the importance of the family derives from the fact that it is the first institution through which the social world is perceived and is therefore crucial in the formation of identity.[28] The traditional family establishes a link between genera-tions, binding the individual within the web of past and future history, cultivates a sense of belonging and acts as a natural source of the values of stability, order and continuity that individuals take with them when relating to wider society. In fact, Scruton believes that, thanks to the nature of family life, 'however vociferously people may declare their attachment to other ideologies, in their most solemn innervations they are naturally conservative'.[29]

The family is also valued by many Conservatives for its ability to inculcate virtue; as Letwin argues, the family was important for Thatch-erism because it is a key means by which the vigorous virtues are passed down from generation to generation.[30] Another of Letwin's contentions is that, since one of the prime virtues is self-sufficiency, this should apply to the family itself, implying that it should be as independent as possible. Yet this point highlights a particular difficulty for Conservatives, which is well identified by Willetts: 'Conservatives value the family because of its independence from the state yet they often find themselves tempted to use government policy levers so as to support it, or prop it up, or encourage it.'[31] In fact, one of the most significant conservative texts on the family produced during the Thatcher years, *The Subversive Family* by Ferdinand Mount (at the time director of the Prime Minister's Policy Unit), argued strongly against government intervention, seeing the family as a site of resistance against the expansionist state.[32]

The problem here for Conservatives is illustrative of the difficulty faced by all Conservative arguments that favour civil society's institutions over the state, especially for the delivery of their social policy goals. This may be an appealing argument for Conservatives when such institutions are functioning in ways of which they approve, yet what about when they are under threat or in a 'demoralised' condition? Moreover, should modern social trends simply be left to run their course, even if this means the nuclear family's disintegration, without asking the state to intervene? Phillips is one writer concerned about demoralisation who is disturbed that the Thatcherite view, as expressed by writers like Mount, seemed to amount to little more than the belief that 'the best thing to do with the family was to leave it alone'.[33]

It has already been seen how many supporters of the traditional family were disappointed at the failure of Conservatives to undo the achievements of the 1960s, but just as bad in many of their minds was the fact that Conservative policies of the 1980s and 1990s appeared to help accelerate detrimental trends. One such critic, Patricia Morgan, argues that changes made to the tax and benefit system severely disadvantaged the two-parent family.[34] For example, Conservatives during the Thatcher and Major eras allowed the value of Child Benefit to fall in real terms (which in any case was far less beneficial to two-parent families than the older tax allowances for children) and similarly the value of Married Couples Tax Allowance; equally, they continued to make available to lone parents benefits that were denied to married women (or men) who stayed at home but whose partners went out to work. Also to the great consternation of pro-family campaigners, the 1996 Family Law Act introduced the concept of 'no fault' divorces, in their view further undermining the institution of the family.

The vital question remains, though, of whether it is necessary for Conservatives to insist that the nuclear family is the ideal model. The assumption of modernisers is that it is possible for Conservatives to substitute for this demand that of supporting all types of family. One argument against this is suggested by the view presented by John O'Sullivan (a former adviser to Margaret Thatcher) who argues that non-traditional identities are not only parasitical upon but also adversarial towards traditional ones.[35] For example, although gay families 'mimic' the form of traditional families, since the way that gay identity defines itself is in opposition to the supposedly repressive nature of traditional ones, there is an inherent tendency for them to be antagonistic towards traditional families. In other words, there may simply be no possibility of peaceful coexistence between different family models – being tolerant towards alternative ones may simply help fuel a growing disdain for the traditional family.

This argument parallels conservatives' fears about political correctness and feminism noted earlier. Yet even if many Conservatives might resist these types of argument, it remains far from certain that non-traditional families are capable of fulfilling the roles that they expect of traditional ones. As traditionalists argue, the tightly-knit arrangement of the nuclear family is most clearly suited to binding the individual within the social fabric in the way Conservatives' desire, not to mention transmitting their favoured virtues between generations; the looser, more easily revocable bonds of other family types are far less likely to perform either of these functions.

So while it may be possible for Conservatives to accept a diverse range of family models as legitimate – and doubtless find it electorally difficult not to – this may be at the price of abandoning one of the key supports of Conservatism itself. What remain to be examined are the other structures that have also traditionally sustained a conservative morality.

The death of Tory England?

England has been forbidden – and forbidden by the English.[36]

As seen, for British conservatives morality is intimately bound up with national identity, as expressed in such notions as a 'British morality'. In particular, many see a common national morality as requiring a common national culture. Yet as the 1990s progressed – and even before the fall of the Major Government – observers began to identify as a serious problem for Conservatives a range of challenges to traditional conceptions of national identity, that together were responsible for the actual or imminent 'death of Tory England' or 'break-up of the conservative nation';[37] since 1997, these phrases have become ubiquitous within commentaries.

Of course, fears about threats to national identity have been a central concern of post-war Conservatism. Especially notable for many years were those of Conservatives bitter at the loss of Empire, for whom British identity was an imperial one. Moreover, immigration from the Commonwealth provoked anxieties about the 'swamping' of British culture, most notoriously in the speeches of Enoch Powell in the 1960s and 1970s (whose arguments against the free movement of immigrants into Britain indicated that, when it comes to preserving national identity, even free marketeers can believe that individual liberty must be constrained).

Concerns about non-white immigration, even if expressed less aggressively than Powell's, were more than just the preserve of a few marginal figures. After all, the Commonwealth Immigrants Act of 1962 had already been introduced by a Conservative Government some years before Powell achieved his notoriety, revealing its acceptance of the belief that non-white immigration needed to be controlled (with no attempt made to restrict, for example, Irish immigrants). Similarly, both Heath's and Thatcher's Governments also introduced restrictive legislation. Further anxieties about the erosion of national identity since the 1950s have, of course, increasingly centred on the menace posed by the project of European integration.

What is significant about both of these perceived dangers – immigration and Europe – is that they indicate how post-war Conservatives have projected the problems of national identity on to external sources. Yet the easy scapegoating of immigrants and European federalists for the undermining of traditional national identity, which has led many Conservatives to expend their energies attempting to keep these perils at bay, means that they have frequently overlooked the fact that the real causes of this undermining are much closer to home.

Conservative recognition of these domestic sources is revealed by Scruton's appreciation that what he calls the 'forbidding' of England is something that the English have done to themselves (for Scruton, the idea of a *British* nation is a fiction). Thanks, traditionalists argue, to the spread of doctrines such as political correctness, multiculturalism and moral relativism – not to mention a widespread cultural 'dumbing down' – most of the key institutions and traditions of 'Tory England' command little respect. Whether or not the reasons conservatives identify for this are correct, it is evident that those like the monarchy, the (old) House of Lords and even the flag and the currency are today rarely esteemed and often disparaged.

Moreover, many established institutions are positively hostile to Conservatives. As Thatcher discovered, if once the Church of England was the

'Tory Party at prayer', by the 1980s many within the Church were quite prepared to criticise Conservatives for the damage wrought by their free market policies upon society. Yet the deeper problem for contemporary Conservatives is that neither the Anglican Church nor the Christian religion – which many Conservatives have seen as the prime source of the virtues that they value – any longer possesses much social authority. As John Gray observes, British cultural conservatives neglect 'one very large and, for them, very awkward fact ... that "traditional Christian morality" is for most people in Britain today not even a historical memory'.[38]

However, there is an even greater difficulty for Conservatives. Over much of the post-war era, Conservatives' implicit assumption was that, despite menaces to national identity from without (or internally from the left), the majority of native Britons – or at least those of middle England – could be depended on as possessing a broadly conservative outlook. The major problem for Conservatives today is the fact that, if there ever was in Britain a conservative (moral) majority, this is quite clearly no longer the case.

Efforts to reassert traditional ideas of national identity in recent times have tended to meet with minimal enthusiasm outside Conservative circles. On the one hand, the least subtle – such as the 'cricket test' devised by Tebbit in 1990, which suggested that people from ethnic minorities could be considered truly a part of the nation only if they supported the England cricket team[39] – meet with widespread dismissal. On the other, efforts at presenting less inflammatory conceptions rooted in tradition are frequently simply platitudinous or anodyne – such as John Major's attempt to evoke nostalgia for a Britain of warm beer, green suburbs and old maids cycling to communion (in a speech delivered in 1993).[40]

What all this means is that in future, Conservatives will likely continue spending much time attacking Europe, as well as asylum-seekers, since they have basically lost the major domestic battles over cultural identity; yet this being the case, these attacks will remain essentially displacement activities.

Conclusion

The contemporary political and social landscape is radically different to the one that existed at the beginning of the post-war era; nonetheless, Conservatives can be judged to be both victims and creators of the problematic circumstances in which they today find themselves. Social morality has shifted in ways which many Conservatives disapprove of, yet these shifts are partially Conservatives' own responsibility, whether as the unintended consequences of the promotion of free market policies or because of Conservatives' inability or unwillingness to resist challenges to traditional values. However, if with the decline of the nuclear family, secularisation and the loss of faith in traditional institutions the social foundations of Conservatism have been undermined, Conservatives are left with a stark choice. Either they can try to fight against prevailing trends, and in so doing threaten to consign their party to political oblivion, or they can adopt the cause of 'modernisation'. In pursuing this latter strategy, the main difficulty for Conservatives (apart from convincing people of their sincerity) is that they may lose the ability to present a distinctive alternative – why vote for a Conservative Party spouting rhetoric about inclusion and social justice, when New Labour has been providing voters with the option of a party that does this for many years? The crucial question then becomes not 'What is Conservatism?', but 'What are Conservatives for?'

Notes

1. B. Johnson, *Lend Me Your Ears* (London: HarperCollins, 2003), p.377.
2. P. Hitchens, *The Abolition of Britain* (London: Quartet Books, 1999).
3. R. Scruton, *England: An Elegy* (London: Pimlico, 2001).
4. L. Fox, 'Conservative Policy Forum Swinton Lecture: Liberty and Authority – A Conservative Equilibrium', Conservative Party Conference, Bournemouth, 4 October, 2004.
5. W.H. Greenleaf, *The British Political Tradition*, Vol. I and Vol. II (London: Methuen, 1983).
6. P. Worsthorne, 'Too Much Freedom', in M. Cowling (ed.), *Conservative Essays* (London: Cassell, 1978), p.150.
7. In an interview given to *Woman's Own* magazine (October 1987).
8. A. Duncan and D. Hobson, *Saturn's Children: How the State Devours Liberty, Prosperity and Virtue* (London: Sinclair-Stevenson, 1995).
9. *Observer*, 16 October 1994.
10. S. Letwin, *The Anatomy of Thatcherism* (London: Fontana, 1992).
11. Ibid., p.33.
12. M. Thatcher, *The Downing Street Years* (London: HarperCollins, 1993), p.627.
13. Letwin, *The Anatomy of Thatcherism*, pp.336–8.
14. See E. Vaizey, 'Mods and mockers', *Guardian*, 22 November 2000.
15. M. Paris, 'The Tories need to kiss and make up', *The Times*, 24 August 2002.
16. P. Hitchens, 'The Legacy of the Sixties', *Prospect*, 28 (1998), p.14.
17. *Observer*, 28 March 1982.
18. N. Tebbit, 'There is such a thing as society', *The Spectator*, 25 November 2000, p.16.

19. C. Davies, 'Law and Order: Back to Fundamentals', in D. Anderson and G. Frost (eds), *Hubris: The Tempting of Modern Conservatives* (London: Centre for Policy Studies, 1992).
20. Ibid., p.19.
21. M. Durham, *Sex and Politics: The Family and Morality in the Thatcher Years* (London: Macmillan, 1991).
22. M. Phillips, *All Must Have Prizes* (London: Little, Brown, 1996), p.326. A similar argument is forwarded by John Gray – see *The Undoing of Conservatism* (London: Social Market Foundation, 1994).
23. D. Willetts, *Civic Conservatism* (London: Social Market Foundation, 1994).
24. G. Streeter (ed.) *There Is Such a Thing as Society* (London: Politicos, 2002).
25. M. Portillo, *The Ghost of Toryism Past: The Spirit of Conservatism Future* (London: Centre for Policy Studies, 1997), pp.18–19.
26. *The Conservative Party Manifesto* (London: Conservative Party Central Office, 1979).
27. All figures taken from Office for National Statistics, *Social Trends 34* (London: The Stationery Office, 2004), pp.25–36.
28. R. Scruton, *The Meaning of Conservatism* (Basingstoke: Palgrave Macmillan, 2001, 3rd edition), pp.129–31.
29. Ibid., p.131.
30. Letwin, *The Anatomy of Thatcherism*, p.35.
31. D. Willetts, 'The Family', in D. Kavanagh and A. Seldon (eds), *The Thatcher Effect* (Oxford: Clarendon Press, 1989), p.265.
32. F. Mount, *The Subversive Family* (London: Cape, 1982).
33. Phillips, *All Must Have Prizes*, p.305.
34. P. Morgan, *Farewell to the Family?* (London: IEA Health and Welfare Unit, 1995).
35. J. O'Sullivan, 'Conservatism and Cultural Identity', in K. Minogue (ed.), *Conservative Realism* (London: HarperCollins, 1996), p.39.
36. Scruton, *England: An Elegy*, p.247.
37. See J. Gray, 'The Strange Death of Tory England [1995]', in *Endgames* (Cambridge: Polity Press, 1997) and B. Schwarz, 'The Break-Up of the Conservative Nation', *Soundings*, 7 (1997).
38. Gray, *Endgames*, p.129.
39. *The Times*, 21 April 1990.
40. *Guardian*, 23 April 1993.

9
Inequality

Kevin Hickson

'Conservatives, if they talk about freedom long enough, begin to believe that that is what they want. But it is not freedom that Conservatives want, what they want is the sort of freedom that will maintain existing inequalities or restore lost ones, so far as political action can do this.'[1]

The political thought of the Conservative Party has been little analysed, at least in comparison with the Labour Party. Emphasis has instead been placed on the pragmatic nature of the Conservative Party, reinforced by the supposed non-ideological nature of conservatism itself and the utterances of many leading Conservatives that the Party lacks ideology or as it is often expressed is the party of 'common sense'. A frequent approach of those who do analyse the political thought of the Conservative Party has tended to be descriptive, listing the features most associated with British conservatism.

This chapter seeks to explore the political thought of the Conservative Party since 1945 and argues that those who emphasise the non-ideological aspects of the Party miss key features of Party doctrine. Moreover, it is argued that even in those accounts that do seek to uncover the underlying principles of the Party, there has been a neglect of one value which, according to this author, has been a consistent feature of the Party's thought.

It is argued that the Conservative Party has held a steady commitment to the principle of 'inequality'. Often this does not appear like an ideological commitment at all since there has been a varying degree of inequality present in British society – in terms of social stratification and income and wealth distribution – since 1945. Therefore what could be seen as an objective of the Conservative Party has often been interpreted as pragmatism, the maintenance of the status quo or a rebuttal of the Labour Party's (at times shaky) commitment to greater equality. However, as this chapter will seek to argue, there has been a principled defence of inequality by the Conservative Party. This has taken various forms, from theological or 'natural' arguments for inequality to an argument that individual freedom and social and economic equality are incompatible objectives. Therefore, the Conservative Party has sought at different times and in different ways since 1945 to limit the impact of egalitarian policies or even to reverse them.

One further point should be made at this point which is that if we see the Conservative Party as having a central commitment to inequality, that Conservative politics is *about* inequality, then it would be possible to see a greater degree of continuity in Conservative Party politics since 1945 than is often asserted. What would appear to be the very different stances taken by 'One Nation' and 'New Right' Conservatives towards economic and social policy broadly could in fact be similar in that they both have a commitment to 'inequality'.

The chapter begins by discussing several approaches within the academic literature towards the balance between ideology and pragmatism within the Conservative Party. It will then examine the core positions set out in this book – 'traditional Toryism', 'New Right' and 'One Nation'. It is demonstrated in the chapter that these positions share a similar attitude to inequality.

Ideology and pragmatism in the Conservative Party

Several Conservative politicians have described the non-ideological nature of their Party's politics. This can be traced through each generation of Conservative politicians since 1945. As the key figure in the post-war reconstruction of the Conservative Party, R.A. Butler has described politics as being the 'art of the possible'.[2] One key thinker in the 1950s, Quintin Hogg spoke of the limits of political action and of human knowledge. This was partly because society was 'organic' and could not be captured in its complexity by abstract ideologies and also because man had a limited capacity for knowledge and was capable of doing bad as well as good.[3] What mattered was therefore a cautious, pragmatic politics. Ian Gilmour has also claimed that a key feature of Conservative politics is its pragmatic nature: 'British Conservatism ... is not an "-ism". It is not a system of ideas. It cannot be formulated in a series of propositions, which can be aggregated into a creed. It is not an ideology or a doctrine.'[4]

Indeed, this is his main objection to 'Thatcherism' – which is seen by him as being ideological. This emphasis on pragmatism has led to a concern with power. This view has been stated by Francis Pym: 'by combining a strong motive for unity with a firm refusal to let ideology threaten it ... the Conservative Party has a strong instinct for power'.[5]

The most sophisticated statement of this approach has been made by Michael Oakeshott, who characterised Conservative politics as being 'anti-rationalist'.[6] Rationalism was an ideologically based politics. It was a politics based on an abstract concept such as equality or liberty. Instead, Oakeshott argued that since this approach was not capable of capturing the full complexity of the organic society and could not be understood outside of the tradition in which these ideas were formulated a more desirable approach to politics would be one rooted within a recognisable tradition, which would entail operating within national identities. Such an approach has led to a distinction between 'ideological' politics and 'realist' politics. The drift towards economic and social planning after 1945 could be seen as a break with a recognisable British political tradition inspired by socialist ideology. The Thatcher Government after 1979 could therefore be seen as a reassertion of 'realism' since it was an attempt to reverse the drift of post-war politics and return to the British political tradition.[7] Some Conservative commentators then argued that the Major administration after 1990 was ideological since the policies of that government were based on economic liberal ideas rather than Conservative realism as the Thatcher Government had been.[8]

An alternative approach has been presented by Jim Bulpitt, who sees the essence of Conservative Party politics as one of statecraft.[9] According to Bulpitt, when academics focused on the ideology of the Conservative Party they were really looking at the wrong thing. At the other end of the spectrum were those who saw the Conservative Party as being a pragmatic entity. These approaches had both been used to explain the politics of Thatcherism. So there were those who were sympathetic to the 'New Right' and saw in Thatcherism the implementation of 'New Right' ideas in a consistent way. Moreover, critics of the 'New Right' also saw Thatcherism as the consistent implementation of 'New Right' ideas and were critical of Thatcherism on exactly those grounds. Hence, Tory 'wets'[10] were in agreement with left-wing commentators[11] in seeing Thatcherism as the consistent implementation of 'New Right' ideology. There were also a number of essentially journalistic critics of Thatcherism who regarded it as lacking in consistency.[12]

Bulpitt's approach was closer to those who regarded Thatcherism as being essentially pragmatic, but he sought to place this within the Conservative Party tradition, which was one characterised by the consistent application of 'statecraft'. Bulpitt states: 'what is statecraft? The crude answer is that it is the art of winning elections and achieving some necessary degree of governing competence.'[13] The significance of Bulpitt's analysis is the emphasis given to state autonomy and the control over 'high' politics. The Conservative Party from the time of Salisbury had sought to maintain central government control of things regarded as 'high' politics such as foreign affairs and increasingly as the Twentieth Century progressed macroeconomic policy also. Other areas of policy, characterised as 'low' politics would be left to local government.[14] The aim of the Conservative Party should therefore be to win elections, maintain control of 'high' politics and leave 'low' politics to others. The central state would retain power over key areas of decision-making and the authority of the state could be maintained by not getting embroiled in 'low' politics, thus minimising the number of policy areas it would be responsible for and the number of controversies in which it would become embroiled and thereby allowing a greater chance for the Conservative Party to maintain power.

There were several elements to statecraft.[15] First, successful party management. Leaders will seek to position themselves above the Party and will not normally become involved in intra-party disputes thus maintaining a degree of personal authority. Second, the Party will seek to devise a winning electoral strategy. This would involve the formulation of a policy package capable of winning electoral support and stimulating party activists.

Third, achieving political argument hegemony. This would entail achieving a situation in which the arguments made by party leaders would have easy predominance in elite debate regarding what was perceived as a problem and how the government would tackle it. Hence the Party leadership would seek to define not just its policies but also the terrain over which political arguments would be made.

Fourth, achieving governing competence. This would mean being able to demonstrate that the party in power has implemented its policies and managed the polity. Finally, a further winning electoral strategy. Although these appear to be sequential, they are not, since they would be occurring together.

The significant point for purposes of this chapter is that the idea elevates the 'pragmatism' seen within many accounts of the Conservative Party to a process of statecraft. The Conservative Party has had a consistent statecraft since Salisbury, of which Thatcherism was only the latest phase (at the time when Bulpitt was writing). The subsequent difficulties of the Major Government and the condition of being in opposition since 1997 can be seen as the failure to find a successful post-Thatcher statecraft.[16] Ideology only has a limited role within the Conservative Party. Although ideology will be present it does not have importance in itself but only as a means of securing successful party management, winning elections, securing political argument hegemony and demonstrating governing competence. Ideology is therefore only one feature of statecraft and is subservient to it. If successful statecraft means changing ideology – defined in terms of the underlying values of political action – then so be it.

Thus we have in the idea of statecraft perhaps the most sophisticated account of why the role of ideology is limited within the Conservative Party. There are, however, at least three criticisms of the notion of 'statecraft' in the academic literature.

The first is that Bulpitt takes what has been called a 'unidimensional' approach to politics. That is that he emphasises one aspect of change – the political – over others such as the ideological and the economic. Moreover, his approach takes little account, or so it is argued, of the international and the way that that impacts on national politics. What may be argued is that it assumes a greater degree of state autonomy than is often present. This view has been made most clearly by David Marsh,[17] who argues for the need to develop a multidimensional approach examining how different factors impact on one another. Although there is some truth in this critique, it is possible to defend the 'statecraft' idea from these points of criticism. Statecraft should be viewed as an examination of how the Conservative Party has sought when in power to insulate itself from social, economic and international pressures and how it has sought to manipulate them in order to maintain some degree of governing competence. It would then become a value judgement as to how successful the Conservative Party had been in its 'statecraft', with Bulpitt stating that the Party had been broadly successful in its pursuit of statecraft, while others could reach a different view. In short, the 'statecraft' approach should not be seen as 'unidimensional'.

The second point of criticism would be to say that Bulpitt states that there is a much greater degree of continuity of 'statecraft' than was in fact the case. Instead, it is possible to see several 'statecraft' strategies in existence since the time of Salisbury. Even if 'statecraft' is seen as a key feature of Thatcherism it would be possible to see a very different form of 'statecraft' than that of Salisbury. Indeed, some conservative critics of Thatcherism have based their criticism on exactly this point. According to Salisbury, a successful government was one that did little.[18] Although claiming to be about reducing the role of the state, Thatcherism would in fact mark a continuation of policy activism since the state would be required to change economic and social institutions to bring about the free market society that Thatcherites wanted. Hence some 'traditional Tories' regarded the 'New Right' as being as firmly a break with the minimal politics tradition as the 'One Nation' approach.[19]

The third criticism is that Bulpitt allows greater importance to be attached to those aspects of Conservative Party policy after 1979 that support the 'statecraft' thesis than others. Hence Evans and Taylor note that the importance of monetarism was exaggerated.[20] Monetarism could be seen as being a key part of 'statecraft' since it was about granting the centre a greater degree of state autonomy by removing it from the need to negotiate with the trade unions over incomes policy. Keynesianism meant that the state would become embroiled with economic actors such as the trades unions. Monetarism provided a theoretical argument that the state could manage the economy on its own through control of the money supply. This proved difficult in practice so the Conservative Government after 1979 kept changing its monetary policy in an attempt to control the money supply. Monetarism could therefore be seen as being a part of Conservative Party statecraft rather than a commitment to economic liberalism.[21] However, as Evans and Taylor go on to say, the Conservative Party after 1979 also pursued a number of other policies that could not be so easily subsumed within a concern with 'statecraft'. Policies such as privatisation, reform of the welfare state, and so on, could be seen as complex and embroiled the party in power in many controversies and sometimes questioned their governing competence.

It is this last point which raises what I wish to argue is a fundamental weakness in the 'statecraft' approach. That is that it reduces the salience of 'ideology' within the Conservative Party. There are many values held by Conservatives, which sometimes conflict. For example, the tension between 'traditionalists' and 'liberals' within the Party over issues of social morality recently. However, I also wish to argue that the Party has a more widely shared belief in *inequality* which has underpinned various economic and social policy programmes since 1945. Rather than seeing the Conservative Party as being *about* statecraft, it would be better to see it as being marked by an underlying commitment to inequality. Statecraft is of course important since the Conservative Party has shown a tendency to successfully find ways of winning elections and staying in power often with a degree of higher public faith in its competence than the Labour Party. However, it would, I wish to argue, be wrong to subsume ideology within statecraft. Instead, statecraft would be better seen as the way in which the Conservative Party has successfully pursued its ideological objectives at any one time.

I wish to examine some of the key thinkers and publications associated with each of the key positions identified in this book of the Conservative Party since 1945: 'One Nation', 'traditional Toryism' and 'New Right'. Although these positions can be seen as being distinct in that they all hold different attitudes as to what the economic and social policies of the Party should be, they all hold to a similar anti-egalitarianism.

One Nation

The loss of the 1945 general election was a major turning point for the Conservative Party. The result, or at least the scale of the defeat, came as a shock and senior figures sought to reform the organisation and policies of the Conservative Party. This would probably have been unsuccessful had Churchill not allowed modernisation to occur. It was therefore a mix of ideological and pragmatic factors that led the Conservative Party to accept many of the reforms of the Attlee Government. However, the role of R.A. Butler is usually seen, rightly, as the key to change within the Party. The modernisers saw the policies of the Disraeli and Baldwin Governments as the most suitable basis for future policy. They argued that the aim of the Conservative Party should be to promote 'One Nation' and to accept social reform as a means of reducing poverty and moving towards a more united society. Norton and Aughey argue that this in fact meant a distortion of the ideas of Disraelian Conservatism since the post-war reconstruction of the Party involved the acceptance of a larger and more centralised state than earlier Conservatives were prepared to accept.[22] However, in broad terms it may be possible to see some continuity within these two strands of Conservatism since they were both on what has been termed the 'healer' side of Conservatism – using government, either local or national, to alleviate social distress. Hence reformers within the Party after 1945 have been described as 'One Nation' Conservatives.[23]

At first, it would appear that 'One Nation' Conservatives, in their acceptance of the welfare state and mixed economy, would be likely to have a more favourable attitude towards notions of social and economic equality. However, it can be seen that key figures within the 'One Nation' approach to Conservatism were united in their opposition of equality as a political principle. They remained committed to hierarchical social and economic structures and saw 'equality' as something to which the Labour Party were committed. Hence, although it may be possible to see a broad-based consensus of policy after 1951, with the Conservatives accepting much of what the previous Labour administration had done, there remained no ideological consensus with the idea of 'equality' showing a fundamental dividing line between the two major parties.[24]

Hence, while the Labour Party 'revisionists' such as Hugh Gaitskell and Tony Crosland were busy arguing that socialism was about equality,[25] several of those seen as being on the 'left' of the Conservative Party were rejecting the idea of equality as being fundamentally against the principles of Conservatism. Hence David Clark, a leading member of the post-war Research Department and a key 'moderniser' along 'One Nation' lines, argued that inequality was natural: 'inequality of natural ability results in class. Some men will always rise superior to others. In a group of men pursuing common purpose, whether it be a nation or a family, a factory or a farm, there must always be those who exercise authority and those who obey.'[26] For post-war Conservatives therefore there was to be an acceptance of the state, much enlarged during the Second World War and by the Labour Government of 1945–51, but an explicit rejection of 'equality'. This can be seen in the stance taken on policy by leading Conservative thinkers, so for example, Hogg made a categorical distinction between poverty and inequality much similar to those associated with the New Right during the 1970s and argued that equality should not be a factor in education reform, where Hogg defended both public schools and grammar schools.[27]

A similar stance towards equality can be seen in the writing of a later prominent Conservative 'One Nation' thinker, Ian Gilmour.[28] Gilmour argued that a belief in inequality is a core tenet of Conservatism. He argues that since a basic Conservative belief is freedom and since equality is a threat to freedom then Conservatives must reject equality. Equality is an ideological abstraction and since it lacks precise meaning must be something which is arbitrarily imposed. Although Gilmour sees the elimination of poverty as a Conservative objective, equality is dismissed as something which is the concern of socialists. Gilmour also sees inequality as desirable and natural as an underpinning for the family and for economic activity. There is much in Gilmour's view of equality that could be found in a traditionalist or New Right approach, although he would be accepting of much greater government involvement in the economy and society. Similarly, contemporary politicians who hold to the 'One Nation' position reject the idea of equality. For example, Alistair Burt argues that Conservative politics is concerned with freedom, markets, enterprise and choice, and so even those on the 'left' of the Party do not commit themselves to the value of equality.[29]

Traditional Toryism

The essence of traditional Toryism is social order coupled with a strong sense of English nationalism. The mechanism through which these principles are achieved has changed dramatically so that at the start of the twentieth century, as Andrew Gamble[30] has commented, traditionalists were committed to economic protectionism. This was the idea promoted most notably by Joseph Chamberlain who called for economic ties with the colonies to be protected against outside trade in order to maintain social order and national prestige, at that time bound up with the Empire. Although this view was still present in the post-war period as some Conservatives opposed all measures of decolonisation, by the 1960s it had effectively been replaced with a free market approach, most associated with Enoch Powell.[31]

A second division within the traditionalist approach is between elitists and populists. The elitist approach was to maintain social order while preserving the traditional political and social elites. This entailed developing ideas and images with which the masses could identify while allowing the elites to govern. The alternative approach was a populist strategy that would bring the masses into the political fray to bolster the Conservative electoral position. At first, there was some scepticism of mass democracy, most notably seen with Lord Salisbury, while a more populist approach could again be seen with Powell from the 1960s. However, this should not be seen as too rigid a distinction since even some 'populists' such as Powell have maintained a strong respect for traditional institutions. The elite approach has declined largely with the decline of 'deference' but can still be seen, prominently in the writings of Peregrine Worsthorne.[32] What links these two positions is a belief in the 'character' of the English (more than British) people, who seek to defend the essential traditions of life.[33]

However, what should again be clear is that underpinning these differences is a belief in the virtue of inequality. The elitist approach most clearly demonstrates this belief. The main argument for the 'aristocratic principle', as Worsthorne calls it, is that the aristocracy are the best people to govern. Since they have a strong sense of public duty and have independent financial means, whereas politics conducted by those further down the social order means the rise of 'career politicians' who are interested in financial and personal gain and in so doing follow the Party line and/or promote arguments for change, which means that the strong sense of tradition is lost. The principle of inequality is defended not just in terms of social order and economic necessity but also for the maintenance of a 'decent' politics.

The more populist approach also sees the need to defend economic and social inequalities explicitly. In so doing, the traditionalist approach uses all political arguments available to defend such inequalities. So Powell and the so-called Peterhouse Group associated with Maurice Cowling, John Casey and Edward Norman, drew on the neo-liberal arguments of Friedrich von Hayek in order to defend inequalities. This led to them being described as a 'Conservative New Right' since they combined traditionalist approaches with economic liberalism. However, although some of these individuals remained committed to Thatcherite policies after 1979, others became critical on the grounds that the Thatcher Governments were 'ideological', as discussed below.

This points to a further element of traditionalist Toryism, which is the 'anti-rationalist' nature of politics. Politics based on abstract principles should be rejected in favour of a politics derived from and respectful of political traditions. There were anti-rationalist arguments put forward in favour of English national identity, as seen in the anti-immigration stances adopted during the 1960s and respect for traditional political institutions as seen in Powell's rejection of House of Lords reform. For some this marked a major distinction between traditional Toryism and the politics of the New Right, which was seen as being based on abstract (liberal) principles.

This in turn led to a further defence of inequality as seen in the opening quotation from Maurice Cowling. Inequalities are not just sought by those who would 'benefit from inequalities of wealth, rank and education but also by enormous numbers who, while not partaking in the benefits, recognise that inequalities exist and, in some obscure sense, assume that they ought to'. They assume that they ought to because 'they are accustomed to inequalities, inequalities are things they associate with a properly functioning society and they do not need an ideological proclamation in order to accept them'.[34] It was this appeal to custom, 'common sense' and natural order that should be at the heart of the Conservative appeal in its defence of inequality. Inequality and privilege did not need to be based on abstract principles and could not be refuted by rational politics since they were the natural way of things.

New Right

The essence of the New Right, or at least the economic liberal New Right if we exclude those traditionalists who endorsed Thatcherism, is the restoration of economic freedoms lost in the post-war drift to collectivism. Both Labour and Conservative administrations had been responsible for this drift and so the dedication of Hayek's *Road to Serfdom* to the 'socialists of all parties' struck a chord with free market Conservatives.[35] Economic collectivism and social liberalism were seen as going together in the post-war period. The New Right could therefore be seen as opposing post-war trends. However, the emphasis on economic freedom was to be much more significant with those thinkers such as Keith Joseph who are usually seen as being 'New Right'. To many of those with a more traditionalist outlook, this emphasis on freedom was a concession to rationalist or ideological politics, a concession specifically to liberalism. There were some therefore associated with the *Salisbury Review* in particular who distanced themselves from the New Right and from the Thatcher Governments that they had initially supported because they regarded the drift in policy as being essentially *liberal*,[36] while others who also held similar views were keen to distance themselves from the New Right from the outset.[37] The extent to which the New Right can be seen as united around free markets and social conservatism as suggested by some academics has been exaggerated, since the former was stronger among many of those closest to Thatcher, while those who held to the ideas more commonly associated with traditional Toryism had mixed views on the Conservative Governments after 1979.

Perhaps the main distinction between the traditional Tory approach and the New Right was therefore the prioritisation attached to market freedoms. For the New Right, other things would emerge from the extension of free markets, whereas for traditionalists the emphasis on freedom was seen as being a concession to liberal ideology; instead the market was a means of restoring social order and state authority. An essentially free market attitude was nevertheless a part of both the traditionalist and New Right approaches by the late 1970s.

One of the first Conservatives to promote a distinctive economic liberal argument therefore was Keith Joseph, who had been influenced in particular by the writings of Hayek and who came to have a substantial impact on the programme of the Thatcher governments after 1979 as well as on Thatcher herself.

The arguments presented by Joseph and others were essentially that the market was the mechanism through which individual liberties could be extended. The argument went that there was simply too much equality by the 1970s and that the aim of public policy should be to restore lost inequalities. However, rather than seeing inequality as desirable for social order or as seeing it as 'natural' so as not requiring an intellectual defence as with the traditionalists, the New Right sought to articulate a clear intellectual argument in favour of greater inequality, a defence which was based on the arguments of Hayek, and to a lesser extent Nozick.

Joseph made clear his defence of inequality in a number of speeches throughout the mid to late 1970s, culminating in his book with Jonathan Sumption, *Equality*, written before the 1979 general election but published afterwards.[38] He argued that the demand for greater equality was based not on a clear conception of social justice, since, following Hayek, he argued that such a conception could not be identified, but rather on negative human sentiments of greed and envy. The demand came not from those who held the higher incomes but from those at the bottom who were envious of the success of others. Higher incomes were needed as incentives to work harder, perform more difficult tasks and to take risks. The reduction of pay differentials had resulted in the loss of skilled workers, managers, entrepreneurs, and so on, to other countries, notably the United States, which had larger differentials and lower rates of direct taxation. Incentives were therefore necessary and desirable economically and the reduction of inequalities was a barrier to economic efficiency.

Moreover, Joseph argued, greater inequality would be socially desirable, not just for those at the top who would benefit from lower rates of taxation, but also the poor in at least two ways. First, the higher rates of economic growth would allow the incomes of the poorest to rise more quickly than through means of direct redistribution through the state, what was called the 'trickle down' effect. Second, the poor would also benefit from realising that work would have greater financial benefits than social security. Greater inequality and reform of the taxation and social security systems would benefit the poor and reduce the 'poverty trap' and 'dependency culture', by restoring individual responsibility.

Finally, the New Right thesis, as developed within the Conservative Party by Joseph, claimed that calls for greater equality were based on conceptual confusions in at least two ways. First, it confused the meaning of what it was to be in poverty. Poverty was an 'absolute' condition caused by either having too low an income or misuse of that income that would otherwise be sufficient. Instead, many commentators were seeing poverty as 'relative', that is that people were in poverty if their income fell below a certain proportion of the average incomes at any given time. This view, according to Joseph, was a misguided attempt by mainly left-wing social policy experts to justify the pursuit of greater income equality. People were not poor, he argued, as a result of being unequal. Moreover, since there was very little 'primary' poverty in society, that is to say that income levels were sufficient to meet basic needs given current levels of social security, then most poverty was the result of people misusing the income they had and the aim should be to reform the attitudes and behaviour of those in poverty. This distinction between the 'deserving' and 'undeserving' poor was one which reconnected the traditionalists and the economic liberal New Right.

The second conceptual confusion made by those who wanted greater economic equality was over the nature of freedom. This argument was based on a distinction between 'negative' and 'positive' freedom, or between the freedom from deliberately imposed external constraint and the freedom to do something. The concept of 'positive freedom' had been used by egalitarians to justify the further redistribution of resources to the poor in order to reduce inequalities. However, 'real' freedom, for Joseph, was freedom from coercion and so had nothing to do with resources. Direction over who should own what was therefore seen as irrelevant, and Joseph declared that 'poverty is not unfreedom'.[39]

It should be pointed out that these arguments face a number of criticisms, and social democrats have sought to justify the link between freedom and resources and the call for greater economic and social equality. More significantly for the purposes of this chapter, the case for greater inequality as presented by Joseph was criticised by traditionalists within the Party for placing too much emphasis on freedom. Freedom was a liberal and not a conservative value. This view can be identified in Worsthorne's statement that what Conservatives were concerned about was: 'not so much the lack of freedom as its excessive abundance'.[40] What traditionalists opposed was the general argument that freedom was desirable since a Conservative view of human nature showed that freedom should be constrained, while others argued that the role of the state would still be too large and too purposive under the New Right, despite its attempts to withdraw the state from many of the commitments entered into after 1945. Although Joseph argued that self-restraint was the basis of freedom and that therefore freedom and authority were not in conflict, it could be said that the tensions between freedom and authority continued at least at an ideational level for some time, and still do in the tensions within the Party between the so-called 'mods' and 'rockers' over issues of social morality. The use of arguments put forward by Hayek by Joseph was of concern to those more well versed in the traditionalist approach to state authority and social order.

Conclusion

The above, necessarily brief, discussion of the main intellectual positions within the Conservative Party since 1945 reveals many points of conflict, between those who favoured greater state intervention in the economy and those who wanted greater use of the market, and between those who favoured more individual freedom and those who wanted more social discipline in particular. However, underpinning all of these differing outlooks was a shared belief in the virtues of a society marked by social and economic stratification; that is, by inequality.

The 'One Nation' position could be seen as the most economically interventionist and socially progressive tradition of Conservative Party thought. However, a consistent theme was that inequality was both necessary and desirable. The traditionalist approach again regarded inequality as essential to the maintenance of state authority and social order. The New Right regarded inequality as essential to an efficient economy and to individual freedom. Moreover, there was some overlap in these positions since not all of those who believed that freedom and inequality were incompatible were of the New Right, similar arguments can be found within those more associated with the 'One Nation' approach.[41]

Where individuals and the different traditions diverged was over the amount of inequality that was deemed desirable and the justification for wanting inequality. The 'One Nation' position was accepting of the mixed economy and much of the welfare state introduced after 1945 while wanting to limit further drift towards collectivism, believing that further reductions in inequality would be undesirable; something that can be seen in the record of the Conservative Governments after 1951. By the 1970s, when the tensions with the New Right emerged, the 'One Nation' position could be characterised as not wanting to reduce any further than current levels economic inequalities. This contrasted with both the traditionalist approach and the New Right who both wanted to reverse post-war trends, to increase inequality. Both had in mind some form of earlier society they regarded as desirable, one marked by wider inequalities and one which had been lost in the post-war drift to a more equal society. For traditionalists this involved restoring a declining social hierarchy, whereas for the New Right it was less significant to restore a specific social class since those who were the most economically productive would automatically rise up within an economy characterised by having good incentives.

The reasons for wanting more inequality also differed depending on which tradition is examined. More traditional justifications for inequality involved family, social order, the authority of the central state, religious arguments, and so on. What can be seen as being significant about the New Right is the more directly economic justifications for greater inequality and in the greater emphasis attached to individual freedom. Although there had been concern expressed about the threat to individual liberty posed by equality since 1945, the New Right, drawing on the arguments of intellectuals such as Hayek and Nozick, emphasised much more clearly the (perceived) threat. Arguably, despite the criticisms made of the New Right by traditionalists and 'One Nation' Conservatives concerning the degree of emphasis placed on individual liberty, the New Right were able to present the clearest intellectual defence of inequality made by the Conservative Party since 1945.

Contemporary Conservatism shows the continuing commitment to inequality. There has in fact been little direct reference to inequality made by the Conservative Party in opposition since 1997, perhaps because it has not been a major part of the Labour Government's domestic objectives since 1997 either. The Conservative Party has remained broadly united around a much more pro-market stance than when last in Opposition. Debates relating to social policy have been held within a much more market-orientated discourse, and major debates over Europe and social morality have reopened older disputes over the nation, freedom and order without reopening any debate over the level of inequality deemed desirable within contemporary society. In short, inequality is much wider now than in 1979, largely as a result of a successful New Right policy framework, and there is little questioning of this by any section of the Conservative Party.

The purpose of the above discussion has not been to address the content of 'One Nation', traditionalist and New Right thought in any detail since space is not available and this has in any case been done extensively elsewhere. However, two conclusions can be made from this broad survey. First, despite many differences between these positions, there is one idea which is common to all and is notable as a continuous unifying principle within the Conservative Party, and that is inequality. Second, given that the Conservative Party can be said to have a unifying principle, it is possible to reassert the notion that the Party is 'ideological'. Rather than seeing pragmatism or 'statecraft' as the thing which binds together the Conservative Party, it could instead be argued that the apparent pragmatism is a concern to find the most appropriate (popular) arguments to justify widening (or at the very least maintaining current) inequalities.

Notes

1. M. Cowling, 'The Present Position', in M. Cowling (ed.), *Conservative Essays* (London: Cassell, 1978), p.9.

2. R.A. Butler, *The Art of the Possible* (London: Hamish Hamilton, 1971).
3. Q. Hogg, *The Case for Conservatism* (Harmondsworth: Penguin, 1947), pp.7–30.
4. I. Gilmour, *Inside Right: A Study of Conservatism* (London: Quartet, 1978), p.121.
5. F. Pym, *The Politics of Consent* (London: Hamish Hamilton, 1984), p.192.
6. See M. Oakeshott, 'Rationalism in Politics' and 'On Being Conservative' both in his *Rationalism and Other Essays*, ed. T. Fuller (Indianapolis: Liberty Press, 1991).
7. See K. Minogue, 'Hyperactivism in Politics', in Cowling, *Conservative Essays*, and S. Letwin, *The Anatomy of Thatcherism* (London: Fontana, 1992).
8. This view was expressed in several essays in K. Minogue (ed.), *Conservative Realism* (London: HarperCollins, 1996).
9. J. Bulpitt, 'The Discipline of the New Democracy: Mrs Thatcher's Domestic Statecraft', *Political Studies*, XXXIV (1986), pp.19–39.
10. For example, I. Gilmour, *Dancing with Dogma* (London: Simon and Schuster, 1992).
11. For example, S. Hall and M. Jacques (eds), *The Politics of Thatcherism* (London: Lawrence and Wishart, 1983).
12. For example, P. Riddell, *The Thatcher Government* (London: Martin Robertson, 1983).
13. Bulpitt, 'The Discipline of the New Democracy', p.21.
14. See also J. Bulpitt, *Territory and Power in the United Kingdom: An Interpretation* (Manchester: Manchester University Press, 1983).
15. Bulpitt, 'The Discipline of the New Democracy', pp.21–2.
16. As analysed by Andrew Taylor in this volume.
17. See P. Kerr and D. Marsh, 'Explaining Thatcherism: Towards a Multidimensional Approach', in D. Marsh (ed.), *Postwar British Politics in Perspective* (Cambridge: Polity Press, 1999).
18. See P. Marsh, *The Discipline of Popular Government: Lord Salisbury's Domestic Statecraft, 1881–1902* (Brighton: Harvester, 1978).
19. N. O'Sullivan, 'Conservatism, the New Right and the Limited State', in J. Hayward and P. Norton, *The Political Science of British Politics* (Brighton: Harvester, 1986).
20. B. Evans and A. Taylor, *From Salisbury to Major: Continuity and Change in the Conservative Party* (Manchester: Manchester University Press, 1996).
21. Bulpitt, 'The Discipline of the New Democracy', pp.30–3.
22. P. Norton and A. Aughey, *Conservatives and Conservatism* (London: Temple Smith, 1981), pp.68–83.
23. The distinction between 'warriors' and 'healers' was made in P. Cosgrave, *Margaret Thatcher: A Tory and her Party* (London: Hutchinson, 1978).
24. K. Hickson, 'The Postwar Consensus Revisited', *Political Quarterly*, 75:2 (2004), pp.142–54.
25. Notably, C.A.R. Crosland, *The Future of Socialism* (London: Cape, 1956).
26. D. Clark, *The Conservative Faith in the Modern Age* (London: Conservative Political Centre, 1947).
27. Hogg, *The Case for Conservatism*.
28. Gilmour, *Inside Right*, especially pp.121–95.

29. Interview in the House of Commons. I am grateful to David Seawright for this information.
30. A. Gamble, *The Free Economy and the Strong State: The Politics of Thatcherism* (Basingstoke: Macmillan, 1988) and A. Gamble, 'An Ideological Party', in S. Ludlam and M. Smith (eds), *Contemporary British Conservatism* (Basingstoke: Macmillan, 1996).
31. My discussion of Enoch Powell has benefited considerably from S. Heffer, *Like the Roman* (London: Weidenfeld and Nicolson, 1998).
32. P. Worsthorne, *The Socialist Myth* (London: Cassell, 1971) and *In Defence of Aristocracy* (London: HarperCollins, 2004).
33. See Arthur Aughey in this volume.
34. Cowling, 'The Present Position', pp.9–10.
35. F.A. von Hayek, *The Road to Serfdom* (London: Routledge, 1944).
36. From those who contributed to the volume *Conservative Essays* edited by Maurice Cowling, Roger Scruton was later to criticise the Thatcher Governments on these grounds. See in particular, R. Scruton, *The Meaning of Conservatism* (Basingstoke: Macmillan, 1984). Others who contributed to that volume were also critical, notably John Biffen and Peregrine Worsthorne, on different grounds, while others remained more sympathetic including Cowling himself, Shirley Robin Letwin and Kenneth Minogue.
37. See, for example, O'Sullivan, 'Conservatism, the New Right and the Limited State'.
38. K. Joseph and J. Sumption, *Equality* (London: Murray, 1979). See A. Denham and M. Garnett, *Keith Joseph* (Chesham: Acumen, 2002) for a discussion of the writing and publication of *Equality*.
39. Joseph and Sumption, *Equality*.
40. P. Worsthorne, 'Too Much Freedom', in Cowling, *Conservative Essays*, pp.141–54.
41. Similar arguments against equality could indeed be found in Gilmour's writing, thus showing some area of convergence between the 'One Nation' Conservatism that he was defending and the New Right he was criticising.

Part Three
Commentaries

10
Traditional Toryism
Simon Heffer

When J. Enoch Powell said (as he often did) that he was 'born a Tory', many who heard him understood as well as he did what he meant by the term.

As reinterpreted by commentators and thinkers among Powell's contemporaries, like T.E. Utley or Maurice Cowling, it came to represent more than simply a belief in upholding the status quo. It was about, essentially, institutions.

It was a vision of a society composed of such institutions, ruled and governed by them, associating through them, and drawing strength and self-confidence from their sense of continuity. The political philosophy that stemmed from this almost instinctual belief was essentially about the treatment and stewardship of those institutions, some of which were metaphysical or abstract. It was about preserving a society not so much in aspic, as in a condition where opportunities for improvement could be taken without ever risking instability or revolution.

The Conservative Party that Powell joined in 1946 as a brigadier back from the war, and with the ambition to become a politician, was in a state of shock after its heavy election defeat the previous year. It had lost, as is well known, not merely because of its association with the 'Men of Munich' who had led Britain so blindly in the 1930s, but also because it offered no coherent or compelling and distinct vision for the future. Indeed, it was hardly to do so until the late 1970s – the election victories of 1951, 1955, 1959 and 1970 being based on a programme that owed more to the socialist consensus than any sense of traditional Tory values. Of course, Mrs Thatcher's victory in 1979 owed much of its strength to her importation of nineteenth-century economic liberalism to her ideology. However, Powell, in embracing in the mid 1950s what came to be monetarism long before Milton Friedman invented it, had reached that point by applying the traditional Conservative distrust of the state.

Yet economics has little place in traditional interpretations of Toryism precisely because the traditional Tory left those sorts of things principally to the workings of the market and of private enterprise. Where the old Tory approach diverged most from Liberalism in the nineteenth century was in matters of trade – free trade versus protectionism – and in Liberalism's innate belief in the perfectibility of the individual through a process of progress and the extension of more and more liberty. The essential pessimism of the Tory position harks back to feudalism, and was seen in the paternalism of the Tories of Disraeli's era. It was a pessimism about the rate at which the uneducated classes could improve themselves, and which led to the belief that they needed a strong hand from above to guide them until the distant day when, perhaps, they might be masters of their own destiny.

This, of course, dictated a strong role for institutions: and for the concept that institutions are a repository not merely of values but of wisdom. Such institutions – and let us begin at the top with the Church and the Monarchy – are, in the Tory's view, inseparable from and inevitable in an old country. All attempts at modernisation must at some stage reach an accommodation with the living monuments that history has left to us. Any Tory administration that seeks to do otherwise will not be in the same tradition, and will run the risk of being branded opportunist rather than Conservative.

Since secularisation took hold in Britain in the second half of the Victorian era, the Tory Party's association with the Church has become more and more flexible. In its turn, the established Church has become more radical in its politics. Since the Liberal Party of Gladstone and Asquith was relegated to third place in our political scheme of things after 1922, the Church has tended to divide along the lines of the main parties.

Social conservatives are now rarer and rarer. Eclipsed by an apparently far larger group who view capitalism – an inherently Tory doctrine – as being the means to take the bread out of the mouths of deserving people, rather than the opposite. For this reason, Toryism in the twentieth century became increasingly more secular, as the established Church became less and less relevant to it and more out of sympathy with it. This meant that, while never engaging in open hostility with the institution of the established Church, the Tories looked for their institutional lead to temporal rather than spiritual quarters.

This meant, first and foremost, complete support for a constitutional Monarchy, and a constitutional set-up at the apex of which stood (or rather sat, enthroned) the Monarch. That is why, in 1993, there was so much shock among many Tories when a Conservative Prime Minister, in political trouble, secured an agreement from the Queen that she would pay income tax.

Since the Queen's remuneration through the civil list had always been gauged according to the fact that she paid no tax, and since the revenues from the Crown Estates had gone to the Exchequer in lieu of tax since 1937, this was an entirely gratuitous and unnecessary move. Tories feel they share an ethos with the Monarch, not of the upholding of a rigid class system (in which neither royalty nor Tory politicians appear to have believed for several generations) but of public service and *noblesse oblige*. Above all, they feel the Monarch is an apolitical figurehead who unifies and symbolises the nation: and traditional Tories, above all, believe in nation.

Sovereignty, in both senses of the word, is at the heart of this belief. The notion of the Queen in Parliament, making for the nation laws with the consent of the nation's people, is central to the traditional Tory idea of democracy. That, similarly, is why many Tories have been so offended by the notion of a foreign power – the European Union – making laws for Great Britain. Powell also expressed his scepticism of the United States, which he thought had a long-term project to destroy British imperial power. It is also why they have been so offended by attempts to reform the House of Lords, thereby upsetting a constitutional balance that Tories believe (with some justification) worked well throughout the twentieth century after the showdown of 1911. Mainstream Tory thinking accepted after 1911 that the House of Lords could not, in an era of universal suffrage, flout the will of the House of Commons. After 1945 the Salisbury–Addison convention – named after the Shadow Leader and Leader respectively of the House of Lords – ensured that the Tory-dominated Lords would not seek to defeat any legislation by a Labour Government that was a manifesto pledge, and which therefore demonstrated that it had behind it the will of the people.

More to the point, by the end of the 18 years of Tory rule up to 1997, the Lords defeated the government in that period just under 300 times, demonstrating its independence as an institution, its vigour in the constitution, and its value as a revising chamber. Tories believe that the Monarch should retain her reserve powers, notably that of choosing a Prime Minister (however much of a technicality that is these days) and of being able to dissolve or refuse to dissolve Parliament. They also accept Bagehot's view of her right to warn, advise and be consulted about the activities of her government by her Prime Minister. Believing though Tories do in the rightness of democracy, they are also sophisticated enough to see that for a country to function properly and without harmful divisions, there must be some semi-permanent non-democratic element within the constitutional framework. The Monarch is one such, but the House of Lords is another.

In the era before the removal of most hereditary peers, those hereditaries who did attend were by definition committed public servants, and (under the Salisbury–Addison convention) did nothing to impede the will of the House of Commons. That, for most Tories, was as close to perfection in constitutional matters as one was likely to get.

For much of the last three centuries, belief in nation was synonymous with a belief in the Union. In the 1970s most Tories were firmly against the idea of devolution. The majority, English component of British Toryism held this belief in an entirely selfless way: England was disadvantaged financially by the Union and, in modern times, ceased to derive any strategic benefit from it. With this Labour Government, the Union as it had pertained since 1707 has come to an end. But since for the Tory the root of his belief, or the framework for it, must be the nation state, this has meant for many a transference of belief in the nation of Great Britain to that of belief in the nation of England. Scottish Tories – of whom there are still a few left – are in a position that is now anomalous, and may yet become like that of a Unionist in the republic of Ireland. For English Tories their nationalism is not based on race or ethnicity, but on culture and a community of interest among all the people of England. As with much in Tory philosophy it has reached this point by evolution rather than by convulsion, thought it has had to be a faster evolutionary process than most would have liked.

Other institutions are important to the Tory, either as being part of the legitimate authority of the state or as being the structure through which an orderly social existence is led. The Armed Forces, with their credo of strict loyalty to the Crown, are obvious in this respect; so too, in a metaphysical way, is the rule of law. Further down the institutional hierarchy – but not remotely lacking in importance or significance to the traditional Tory – was the institution of the family. Even once Toryism diverged from the Church, Toryism's instinctive belief in Christian values and morality held fast. The ideal – more these days in principle rather than in practice – was that of the married family, of children born in wedlock.

It remains, for many Tories, an incarnation of Burke's notion of the little platoons all acting according to a common creed, all contributing to the maintenance of the nation and the upholding of its values. Toryism always had built into it an understanding of compassion and social service. However, these were duties performed by individuals, not by the state. Families, and often extended families, supported their members whenever necessary. Aristocrats and landowners provided employment, shelter and care for staff and tenantry. The well-to-do were encouraged, for traditional Christian reasons, in acts of charity to assist those worse off than themselves. Welfare was built on human obligations rather than state compulsion: it was symbolic of the way in which Tories felt things ought to be done. Hereditary and inheritance, whether in grand or humble families, were regarded as vital precepts, essential to the continuity of institutions and of the nation.

What traditional Toryism is viscerally opposed to is what modern *soi-disant* Tories and others call 'inclusivity'. This is not because of prejudice or bigotry; it is because the nation, to their minds, depends for its continuance as a distinct entity on having a clearly defined culture and values. Within such a society there is room for other ways of life and outlooks, and an obligation in a free society to respect and tolerate those that are within the law. However, the Tory upholds, in his idea of the nation, a monocultural society that accepts other cultures at the margins, rather than the notion of the multicultural society, which would dilute and end the traditional conception of the British nation.

Many of these values persisted way beyond 1945, through the invention of the welfare state, through the near-destruction of the old aristocracy and landed estates, through an era of high taxation and death duties, through obsessions with multiculturalism (now abandoned, officially, by the Chairman of the Commission for Racial Equality) and so-called 'alternative' lifestyles, and through the Conservative Party's love affair with something called 'Europe'. In a climate driven ever more by the findings of focus groups, it will be interesting to see whether or not any trace of them can remain for very much longer, except in the theoretical musings of a dwindling number of Tory intellectuals, and the hearts of millions of people who feel that no political party now speaks properly to them.

11
New Right
John Redwood

The 'New Right' as it is commonly represented is a contradiction in terms. Conservatives are by nature cautious, sceptical and adverse to radical change. We need a good reason to overturn an institution or convulse a tradition. 'New Right' is often little more than a term of abuse thrown at some of us by our detractors. They want to create an impression of revolutionary Conservatives, people who wish to hurl brutal change at society whilst claiming there is no such thing as society.

In the demonology of the left there are two very different strands to the so-called 'New Right'. The first is individualistic capitalism, and the second is authoritarian social engineering. It would be difficult to combine these two positions in one mind and impossible in one coherent piece of thought. Indeed, the Conservatives' detractors and some Conservatives themselves have made a battle out of these two positions. The 'modernisers' or 'mods' ally social liberalism to individual freedom-loving capitalism. They have been represented by Michael Portillo, Francis Maude and others in the parliamentary party and spoken for by Michael Gove amongst the commentators. They have moderated their enthusiasm for unalloyed capitalist freedoms by also believing in more state spending on health and education. The social authoritarians or 'rockers' take the view that the state should intervene to influence the pattern of family life, to control the unruly, to regulate drugs and to disapprove of homosexuality. Ann Widdecombe is the only alleged fully signed up 'rocker' generally identified. The theoretical underpinnings of her position come from the Catholic Church.

What is remarkable about this largely phoney battle is that neither side have produced great thinkers or extended essays to set out their positions. In neither case does the work extend beyond some newspaper articles and other ephemera. I doubt that people will be arguing the toss between Conservative 'mods' and 'rockers' in ten years time, let alone in a hundred.

The New Right as freedom-loving supporters of enterprise and individual endeavour are more fully rooted in the Conservative tradition, and do have their mentors amongst the intellectual giants and advocates amongst more recent thinkers. In 1950 and 1951 a successful Conservative Party campaigned to set the people free, offering a bonfire of controls and promising to get rid of many of the wartime rules and rationing. Edward Heath rode to victory in 1970 on a policy of economic liberalism, based on the results of the Selsdon conference in Opposition. Conservatives have been most successful over many years when they have opposed too large a state, opposed nationalisation and stood up for freedom.

Their first hero would be Edward Heath of the 'Selsdon man' vintage. The crucial Shadow Cabinet before the 1970 general election pledged the Conservatives to reversing some nationalisations of the Labour era and to driving an agenda that was friendly to business and effort. Instead the government did the opposite, raising taxes, increasing state intervention in business and imposing a stunning array of controls for a peacetime economy. The right spurned their fallen idol, Edward Heath. They remain wedded to Milton Friedman and the Chicago school, favouring monetary solutions to controlling inflation, and supply-side policies to promote growth.

Margaret Thatcher and Keith Joseph in the 1970s re-learnt the lessons in defeat that Edward Heath forgot in power. They looked to the works of Friedrich von Hayek for their guiding philosophy. Lord Blake offered more active encouragement, bringing together a group of young academics to publish *The Conservative Opportunity*. In it we set out how we needed to free the country from so much state spending and intervention – we needed to set the people free. John Patten, Vernon Bogdanor and Peter Sinclair were all young Oxford dons who contributed.

I wrote 'Public Enterprise in Crisis', 'Equity for Everyman' and 'Controlling Public Industries' to establish the case for denationalisation. I worked through the Centre for Policy Studies, where Alfred Sherman, the director, was a keen exponent of less government and an important intellectual influence on Keith Joseph. I was aided by a committee of thinkers and business people – together we worked through each industry in turn, deciding what should be done to improve its performance and lessen its reliance on the taxpayer.

As the 1980s advanced, so Thatcherism took shape. John Hoskyns ran a small Policy Unit for Margaret which concentrated on trade union reform. The Centre for Policy Studies helped them, and Norman Tebbit provided the political cutting edge to see through the main programme and to give it voice in the country. Modern Conservatism believed in giving unions back to their members and in breaking the monopoly stranglehold of some shop stewards and trade union officials over important industries or public services.

I ran the larger Policy Unit after the 1983 election victory. I persuaded Margaret Thatcher to undertake a major privatisation programme, starting with Telecoms and going on to sell two thirds of the industries brought into the public sector by Labour. It was a huge shift in economic power. It brought in substantial proceeds to the Treasury, allowing the government to reduce income tax rates from 98 per cent to 40 per cent to foster enterprise. It soon transformed the industries themselves. We also had to give the Prime Minister advice on the dreadful miners' strike, which tested the new union laws almost to destruction but in the end resulted in industrial peace on a scale the UK had not known for many a long year.

In 1987 I published *Popular Capitalism* which set out the case for what we had been doing. It showed how the large programme of council house sales, the sale of shares in public enterprises to employees, the encouragement of many more small businesses, and the promotion of some worker buy-outs was creating a new nation of owners. The idea was to break down the old barriers between the few with property and the many without, by creating a whole nation of owners directly participating in the wealth of the nation.

Under Brian Griffiths the Policy Unit turned its mind to educational and health reform. Only limited progress was made before the Leader was ejected by the MPs. Brian and his colleagues turned to American and continental models for public service reform, in particular admiring the works of Alan Eindhoven on health organisation.

In the 1990s the so-called 'New Right' took up the cause of Euroscepticism. The parliamentary and press battles over the Maastricht Treaty pushed Europe into the forefront of UK political debate. John Major's refusal to allow a free vote on the issue, and insistence that we sign the Treaty, split the Party and created an active Eurosceptic choir in Parliament. As the 1990s moved forward they looked to the European Foundation, to the British Management Foundation and the Bruges Group to publish and research the big issues that arose from our membership of the EU.

I wrote *The Death of Britain?* in 1999. Andrew Marr, Christopher Hitchens and Simon Heffer also published on the same problem. We asked, in our different ways, was Labour's constitutional revolution, unleashing regional government and attacking the House of Lords, just part of the process of Europeanisation, preparing us for the eventual superstate? I became a strong advocate of keeping the pound and restoring democratic control over fishing and farming here in the UK, breaking from the Major Government to make this case, and set it out in books and articles from 1995 onwards. I could not believe that a Conservative Prime Minister could even dally with the idea of destroying the pound and submitting to so much more Brussels decision-making. I set out the case for a free Britain in *Our Currency, Our Country* and the sequel, *Just Say No*.

Euroscepticism itself contained a range of different motives and characters. Some enthusiasts for the cause were from the traditional left, horrified at the capitalist elements in the EU scheme that would become mandatory as the EU strengthened its grip. Some, like Frank Field, were Labour moderates who believe strongly that important matters of government should be settled democratically in the UK. Some are freedom-loving Conservatives, who oppose the EU as the latest and most dramatic example of overmighty government meddling with our lives. Others are strong nationalists, believing in our country and opposing the eclipse of its right to self-government. The 'New Right' are just part of the crowd of objectors to the flexing muscles of the EU. The EU is a backward-looking old-fashioned protectionist club. The lower tax, lighter regulatory models of government in the US and Asia will prove much more successful over the years ahead. The relative importance of the EU in the world economy will halve over the first 50 years of this century as the relative outperformance of the US and Asia is allied to the declining population of the continental countries. Why should the UK accept political union with countries that wish to look inwards and back, rather than taking a global perspective and understanding that too much government causes poverty and stress?

The authoritarian strand of 'New Right' thinking was attacked by Labour in Opposition, but some of it has been adopted by them, at least in their rhetoric, in government. Labour was unhappy about the so-called attack on single mothers under John Major. His 'Back to Basics' campaign was meant to be a set of policies to bring back traditional teaching and policing, but was misrepresented by Labour as a new moral crusade in favour of monogamy, the family and faithfulness. Labour both lambasted Conservatives for failing to live up to these invented high standards, and attacked us for wishing to involve fathers more in the upbringing of their children. Conservatives made the case for the Child Support Agency (CSA), an institution designed to seek at least a financial contribution from a father estranged from his family for whatever reason. Labour tried to represent this as an 'attack on single mothers'. Subsequently they expressed support for the general principles of the CSA, and despite its unpopularity with many families and the many teething troubles it experienced, Labour kept it once in power.

The authoritarian strand supported tax incentives to buttress the married family with two parents supporting their children. It favoured advocating this as the best or normal system, against a background of more and more family breakup. Supporters were unhappy about the idea of lowering the age of consent for homosexual practices, or for removing the restraint on local government from advocating homosexuality as a lifestyle. Many followed the general Catholic approach of restricting or banning abortion, recommending childbirth in wedlock and proposing that the state should be on the side of such arrangements rather than being neutral in the face of the kaleidoscope of views on how we should live now.

At the same time there was controversy over whether there is any such thing as 'society'. The left-wing critics of the party took a phrase of Margaret Thatcher's out of context and tried to portray her and all her works as being hostile to the whole idea of community and helping thy neighbour. In this they did her a grave injustice, and misunderstood the traditional and Christian underpinnings of her beliefs. Mrs Thatcher took a dislike to social engineers, sociologists and bogus social scientists peddling a debased form of Marxism. She rightly eschewed class analysis as a way of understanding or solving social problems. She always believed in society, and saw it in Burkeian terms, favouring the small battalions and voluntary associations rather than massive extensions of state power to try to solve social problems. In this she was not New Right but old Tory.

David Willetts, an adviser in her Policy Unit in the 1980s, decided to accept some of the left's criticism on her behalf at a later stage, and reminded Conservatives that we do traditionally believe in community. Most Conservatives, whether right, left or centre, always have believed in community. Our Party has a strong tradition of charity, voluntary work and working to create a political community through service and debate.

Today the political landscape is largely determined not by the 'New Right' or the old left, but by the split in the government between Blair and Brown. Both genuflect to parts of the Conservative tradition and look to parts of the Conservative coalition for some of their voting support. Both are muddled in their thinking and both eclectic in their intellectual influences.

Both seek to talk Tory, Blair more than Brown. Brown talks Tory on competitiveness, the success of the US economic model, and the need to encourage people to work and the need to get people off benefits. Blair talks Tory on the US alliance, on the need to offer people choice in public services, and the need to involve the private sector in public sector delivery.

Neither deliver Tory. Both end up spending and taxing more than Conservatives would recommend. Both expand the public sector mightily. Both support substantial increases in intervention in all aspects of social and economic life. Both move us inexorably closer to the European model whilst using words that imply they value the US model instead. Some Conservatives think we should choose between Blair and Brown. They used to favour Blair – he looks more like a Tory and uses more Tory language. More recently they have come to like Brown's independent Bank of England and tough talk of cutting the costs of government.

The truth is that Conservatives should be swayed by neither. Neither will deliver anything that we can recommend or enjoy. They tell us Europe is coming our way, then sign yet another treaty or constitution giving away yet more power from the UK. They tell us they will cut the costs of government, whilst continuing to hire huge numbers of supernumerary public sector workers. They allowed Blunkett as Home Secretary to adopt nationalist and authoritarian language about immigration and crime, whilst following a policy that does the opposite.

The 'right' is sometimes said to include fringe parties that campaign on single issues connected to nationalism. It is difficult to understand why the British National Party is thought to be right-wing, when its appeal is rather stronger to former Labour voters and when it wishes to strengthen the use of state power in its chosen areas. Its racism affronts all mainstream political parties. Nor is it easy to understand why Euroscepticism is seen as a right-wing movement. It covers the political spectrum, and is especially popular with Bennites who strongly believe in the need for a democracy in the UK to settle our differences and encourage social progress.

The 'New Right' is more a construction of its opponents than a reality. There is no 'New Right' club, no 'New Right' parliamentary faction, no 'New Right' organisation within the Conservative Party. Labour confuses its attacks by believing there are both extreme *laissez-faire* economic thinkers and authoritarian social thinkers who have united to produce a single philosophy that informs the phantoms of the 'New Right'. There have always been free enterprise and authoritarian social strands in Conservative thinking, just as there have been economic interventionist strands and social liberal strands. Today the believers in economic freedom are in the ascendancy, whilst most Conservatives adopt a pick and mix approach to social liberalism or authoritarianism.

12
Centre
Francis Maude

Introduction

It's a confusing business in today's political landscape trying to calibrate positions on the left–right axis. The whole political spectrum in terms of left and right has narrowed significantly in the last ten years, with the gap between the two parties now much more akin to that in the United States and on the continent. The centre of gravity is in a different place, but the range is comparable. Issues that were the red meat of politics 20 years ago have simply been taken out of contention: inflation, state ownership, nuclear weapons, penal taxation rates, even support for the capitalist system. Once issues of the most heated debate, these are now beyond dispute.

This erosion of the differential between the parties has of course occurred because Mr Blair's New Labour deliberately sought to move towards the Conservative Party. He concluded that for Labour to be electable they needed to offer a high degree of continuity with the Conservative Government they were seeking to replace. So began the process of Labour 'stealing the Conservatives' clothes', a cause of enormous anxiety to Conservatives ever since it began in 1994.

For some the only response is for Conservatives to move ever further away from Labour, believing that at all costs we must 'differentiate' ourselves from Labour. Others draw the reverse conclusion: that if Labour have achieved electoral success by occupying the 'middle ground', then that proves that success lies there for us as well.

These are twin fallacies: the 'clear blue water' fallacy and the 'middle ground' fallacy. Fallacies because they both flow from a cynical standpoint.

They both seek to address the question: 'How do we get elected?' But the right question is: 'What do we want to do when we are elected?' Campaigning tactics should flow out of the action plan for government, not vice versa.

And another thing. Both of these fallacies seek to define a Conservative position by reference to our opponents. That must be wrong. Surely we should establish our position by reference to our beliefs. I don't think my beliefs have changed much over the 20-odd years since I was first elected. But the problems to which those beliefs must be applied have changed seismically. It is this question that we have to answer: 'What does a modern Conservative Party have to offer twenty-first-century Britain?' When we establish that, we will know how to make ourselves appealing to modern Britain.

Essentials of the modern Conservative Party

First, we have to understand modern Britain and twenty-first-century Britons. We need to grasp how society has changed. We need to understand how people live their lives; how they want to live their lives; what they wake up worrying about; what they hope for and what they fear. We need to understand why so few people are engaged with conventional party politics, and why so many have tuned out altogether. People want politicians to be less partisan, more honest, less opportunistic than they believe we currently are.

So we should set out our stall in a very straightforward way. We think Britain has a stronger society as well as a more cohesive society when the state does less, preaches less, regulates less and taxes less. We think that when the state does less, people do more, not just for themselves and their families but for each other and for their communities. We think that decisions are best made by people themselves, or when that is not possible, by bodies as close to the people as possible. We believe in people being as independent as possible. We believe that society has a duty to ensure that no one is abandoned to abject poverty or deprivation; and that it is an affront to us being a united country for there to be pockets of desperate poverty in some of our great cities. We believe that Britain must be internationalist in outlook, never isolationist.

And we do not believe that Conservatism equates to 'individualism'. In the 1980s, during the great battle of ideas against socialism, we properly opposed collectivism. But the alternative to state collectivism is not individualism. This is a false opposition. The alternative to state collectivism is people doing things themselves, voluntarily. And most of what we do is done in groups.

Yes, we believe in the liberty of the individual. We believe in trusting individuals to choose. We believe in individual responsibility. And we believe in the individual's ability to make a difference to their own lives and the lives of others around them. But most of what we all do, day by day, is done in groups – the family, at work, sports, church or voluntary organisations. We don't do that much completely solo.

So we do believe there is such a thing as society. That the strength and cohesiveness of society flows from what people do, not what the state does. And most of what people do is done together, in groups, in communities, in that fantastically complex tapestry of voluntary organisations – so-called 'intermediate institutions' – that together combine to form society.

So how did it ever become possible for Conservatism to be caricatured as a selfish creed; as the doctrine of me-first, greed is good, look after number one? It is of the essence of Conservatism that we think much better of people than that. It is because we trust people to do good things, to help each other, to work for their communities, that we believe that over time the state should increase its activities by less than the nation's activity increases. It is because we *don't* believe that people are mean and greedy and selfish; because we *don't* believe that most people want to walk by on the other side of the road when they see someone in need.

So we believe in society – and we also believe in communities. Localism, the belief in dispersing state power away from the hub to the rim of the wheel, was the forgotten theme of Conservatism in the 1980s and 1990s. Take it back far enough and you have 'Court and Country', when Tories were the country party; the party resisting the centralised concentration of power in Whitehall. By instinct and tradition we should be decentralisers.

And we have to show that we are really seriously committed to public services. Yes, we do believe that the state should over time do less. But it has become too easy to caricature that preference as a dogmatic determination to privatise everything that moves, and our belief that a private sector in health and education should exist as a visceral dislike of the public sector. There are many structural problems in the way public services are organised today. They urgently need reform. But our approach must show convincingly a passionate desire to make them work better, rather than an enthusiasm for helping people to exit them. The Conservative answer is to surrender central control in favour of the users of the services, and to substitute the rule of local professionals for the diktat of Whitehall bureaucrats and politicians.

This localism in action has to be given real edge in our approach to local government. In office we seriously eroded local government. The perfectly understandable concern about extreme left-wing control seemed to justify dragging ever more power to the centre. That's because far too little financial responsibility lies with councils. Some 75 per cent of town hall budgets comes directly from Whitehall. In no other comparable country does the central government share of local spending rise even above 30 per cent. Find a way to slash at least some local authorities' dependence on Whitehall, and increase their dependence on local people and businesses, and we will have begun to revive civic responsibility in the community.

Conservatives should stand for social justice as well. But isn't social justice a concept from the left? From the left, yes. But not the property of the left. For Conservatives as much as anyone it should be unacceptable for there to be pockets of entrenched deprivation, with communities locked into an apparently unbreakable cycle of failure.

But whereas for the left it is the responsibility of the organs of the state to alleviate this disadvantage, Conservatives believe that these social obligations cannot simply be contracted out to the state. Paternalism got a bad name among Conservatives in the 1980s, but the notion of social obligation should be central for us. That the strong have a duty to support the weak, the rich to help the poor, should be a fundamental tenet.

We must be a party for all Britain and all Britons, no matter on what side of the tracks they were born, whatever their origin, their gender, the colour of their skin or their sexual orientation.

This desire to represent the whole country has to come from deep within. It is about attitude and outlook. It is how we feel about ourselves and our fellow citizens. It should be part of our soul. Respect for all, male, female, rich, poor, old, young, black, white, gay, and straight. This is not about 'pandering to minorities' or trying to build a 'rainbow coalition', as some charge. It is about being a decent party.

Today many couples decide not to marry, yet form stable families with children. These are not way-out people on the fringes of society. We cannot be a party of choice, yet seem to want to deny people the choice of how to organise their relationships. Seeming to rail against cohabitation makes us look as if we are clinging desperately to a rose-tinted past. Gay couples, cohabiting couples, unmarried parents, all exist. Conservatives must recognise that plenty of good citizens who are the lifeblood of a neighbourly society choose to live in all kinds of relationships. It does not make them bad people. It was encouraging that most Conservatives supported the recent Civil Partnerships Act. Some thought it a deeply un-Conservative measure, antagonistic to family values. Now that we are a society where there is a genuine respect for people's sexuality more and more same-sex couples want to take on the shared responsibilities of a committed relationship. It is in all our interests to encourage the voluntary acceptance of such shared responsibilities. The state's support for such publicly declared commitments recognises that society is stronger and more stable when people live in settled relationships and households.

We should never forget that in 1979 we had more support among voters aged under 35 than voters aged over 35. Could we persuade them today? Without doubt. Today younger people are more sceptical about government and the ability of government to improve their lives than my and preceding generations were. They simply do not believe that the state is going to provide for them. And at the same time they're much more self-confident about their own ability to make a difference. They don't want to be preached at; they want to be given the space to make their own decisions about how they live their lives.

And they want the state to concentrate on the things that only the state can do and give them more space to run their own lives. Not because they're selfish and want to look only after number one. Mostly they do want to help others and are quite amenable to the Conservative argument that freedom and prosperity confers obligations on everyone to help others.

But we have to cut through their cynicism about politics and politicians. We need the chance to persuade them that we mean it; that we will do it; and that we will do it not because it serves some narrow sectional interest but because we believe it creates not just a better and more vibrant economy, but also a more cohesive and compassionate society.

13
One Nation

Damian Green

No intellectual tradition in British Conservatism has a more distinguished pedigree than 'One Nation'. No other political phrase has flourished for so long as a desirable cover for political activity. The phrase, and the ideas to which it is attached, stem from Disraeli's novel *Sybil*, whose purpose was to attack the division of Britain into 'Two Nations', the rich and the poor. Disraeli's purpose was to show that there were no inherent divisions in society, and that the Conservative Party's objective was to represent all sections and groups. He committed the Party to 'the elevation of the condition of the people' as its ultimate aim, and it is the attempt to achieve that sweeping ambition which has been the underlying driver of successive generations of 'One Nation' thinkers and politicians.

An understanding of One Nation Conservatism starts from the realisation that its adherents are fighting battles on two fronts. They need to fight two natural tendencies inside the Conservative Party: the attractiveness of pure reaction and the ideological enticement of purely market solutions. At the same time they must be outward looking, seeking to convince those who are not Conservative that there are genuinely Tory solutions to social problems which are both distinctive from the offerings of the left and more effective.

The basic One Nation propositions have remained the same. A One Nation Conservative will regard it as a duty of government to take active steps to relieve poverty and its attendant social ills, and will not assume that an unfettered free market will perform this task. He or she will believe that individualism is not enough, and that a Tory Government should encourage the creation of a strong civil society through active measures to help family, voluntary and community action in the many areas covered by 'social services'. So One Nation Conservatism is not afraid to use state power, but will only use it as a last resort if it is clear that private measures will not suffice, whether taken individually or by groups which naturally cohere within society. A One Nation Conservative regards a social conscience as a necessary tool for a decent and effective politician, not as the embarrassment it sometime appears for those on the hard right of Tory politics. One Nation Conservatives have always recognised that Tory values have to be adapted to changing external circumstances, and that progressive Conservatism is not the oxymoron that many on the left would wish it to be. Ian Gilmour said that 'the fundamental concern of Toryism is the preservation of the nation's unity, of national institutions, of political and civil liberty, and not the achievement of some ideological victory'.

In short, One Nation Conservatism enables the Conservative Party to reach places and people it would otherwise fail to reach. R.A. Butler, a central figure in the development of this tradition, said he was keen to make it 'perfectly possible to be literate, rational, well-informed and a Tory'. Ian Gilmour wanted to prevent a Conservative 'retreat behind the privet hedge into a world of narrow class interests and selfish concerns'. Both of these rather high-minded quotes have particular relevance in the early years of this century, as the Conservative Party struggles to attract supporters beyond its core vote.

The One Nation approach has infused the politics of many Conservative leaders since Disraeli. Between the wars Baldwin made peace with organised Labour after the General Strike and encouraged modest social reform in the 1930s. In the same period Harold Macmillan wrote the *Middle Way*, which became the template for much of his economic policy when he became Prime Minister in the 1950s. Reading the *Middle Way* today its interventionist economics seem shocking to a Tory of any stripe. But even then Macmillan simply wanted to improve the performance of the private sector so that it could concentrate on what it did best, while the state dealt with social problems such as old age where private sector solutions were not available.

Macmillan's underlying insight was that if Conservatives seemed not to care about the problems of the old, sick, and poor, they would be unelectable (and would deserve to be). Even under the wartime coalition there were stirrings of progressive Conservative thought, notably from the Tory Reform Group (a name later to be revived). When the 1945 electoral nemesis arrived, as a verdict not on Churchill but on the hard-faced image the Tories had retained from the late 1930s, revival was made swift by the rapid adoption of One Nation policies in opposition. Macmillan and R.A.

Butler led the way in the early years, and the Industrial Charter of 1947 marked a clear break from previous Conservative economic and social policies. It accepted that government had a responsibility to maintain a 'high and stable level of employment', and accepted a mixed economy, while opposing nationalisation 'in principle'.

The potential for confusion in this recipe was addressed squarely by one of the most powerful informal groups ever formed inside the Party – the One Nation group. This initially brought together nine MPs elected in February 1950, including Edward Heath, Iain Macleod and Enoch Powell. The future divergence even between those three indicates that simplistic analysis of this group, or of One Nation thought generally, as being on the 'left' of the Party is wrong. More importantly, the writings of the group during the 1950s, such as the pamphlets *One Nation*, *Change is Our Ally*, and *The Responsible Society*, set out a distinctive Conservative position which rejected *laissez-faire* economics and socialism alike. The original *One Nation* pamphlet praised the Conservative contribution to the development of the welfare state, but concluded that the pendulum had swung too far towards state intervention. In welfare policy, *One Nation* argued for selective rather than universal solutions. More generally, the group argued that the state did have a role in welfare provision, but that in order to create the wealth that could pay for it there was a need for greater competition and freedom for private commerce. The press release accompanying *The Responsible Society* said the group was 'concerned with the political process of restoring a proper balance between the power of the state and the rights and initiative of the individual'.

It is the language of balance which is the key, and it was this sense of balance that became dangerously lost in subsequent debates within the Party on the direction of policy. Many of the One Nation group became the Party establishment in the 1960s and 1970s, a period which ended with the failure of the Heath Government in 1974. Edward Heath had become Prime Minister on a rigorously right-wing programme, but transformed his government into a (then) orthodox Keynesian administration, without ever damping down the fires of industrial conflict. The defeat of 1974 set the Conservative Party on a course when One Nation ideas were dismissed as semi-socialist and explicitly rejected by the leadership, while those who held them were barely tolerated.

Fatefully, Sir Keith Joseph, as courteous an intellectual as can ever have held high office in the Conservative Party, said in 1974 'it was only in April 1974, that I was converted to Conservatism. I had thought that I was a Conservative but I now see that I was not one at all.' Less gentle souls subsequently took this argument as a basis to argue that those who held by One Nation ideas were simply not Conservatives, and should therefore leave the Party. For the 18 years of Conservative rule under Margaret Thatcher and John Major this did not seem to matter, but the habit of anathematising Conservatives who did not hold to the current orthodoxy, a habit which the party had largely avoided in its previous history, has caused huge damage in the long term. The Party developed its own 'betrayal myth', in which Heath and others on the centre-left of the Party, having reneged on his original manifesto, were not to be trusted in anything.

By 1997 the One Nation tradition was much better represented at the very top of the Party (John Major, Michael Heseltine and Kenneth Clarke) than at any other level. Since then successive new intakes of MPs have reflected a much more New Right tone, and inevitably the previous generation of leaders have retired from the front line. The Conservative-supporting newspapers have themselves moved to the right, and since they provide the background for Conservative Party members and strong supporters this has helped to make One Nation arguments less visible. The effect in the early years of Opposition was that the intellectual firepower of those in the One Nation tradition tended to be used largely on the debates about Europe. The leading proponents of One Nation Toryism were also mainly in favour of the Party's traditional pro-European stance, at a time when the centre of gravity of the Party shifted increasingly into the Eurosceptic camp, and at the margins towards a desire to leave the EU altogether. The need constantly to fight over the Europe issue meant a narrowing in the public impression of what the One Nation tradition stood for, which was damaging to the image of One Nation Conservatives among Conservative activists. The vitriolic style of the internal battle contributed to the impression that the Conservatives were becoming divided and extreme (at one point Margaret Thatcher referred to One Nation Conservatives as being 'no nation Conservatives') which was electorally disastrous.

The effect of this ideological war was also damaging for the intellectual self-confidence of the Party. Conservatives had always prided themselves on being able to draw inspiration from the past experiences of the nation, and through this process to recast immutable values in a modern form. The radical Thatcherite analysis claimed that the Party was simply in error for most of the period between 1945 and 1975, and that success therefore lay in cutting Conservatism off from its roots. This may be a successful prescription for a party of the left, but rejecting the past is a peculiar and uncomfortable stance for a party that calls itself Conservative. The search for a new consensus which included all Conservative traditions in a suitable balance has been the Grail quest of modern Conservative thinkers.

By the early years of this century a paradoxical position had been reached when the leading figures in the Labour Government regularly claimed that they were now the Party of One Nation, to their clear electoral advantage, while the Conservative Party agonised about its future direction. The eternal problem of how Conservatives should adapt to a changing country resurfaced in debates between 'modernisers' and 'traditionalists', with issues such as the role of women to the fore, both in wide terms such as how to organise child care in a society where most women choose to work, and in the narrow sense of trying to persuade Conservative associations to select women candidates (as well as those from ethnic minorities – another under-represented group in the parliamentary party). Because many of the leading modernisers were also strong Eurosceptics, there has up to now been no easy fit with the main One Nation protagonists, even though the modernising agenda is a good example of adapting Conservatism to new trends – that permanent wish of One Nation Conservatives. Similarly, another new set of ideas has developed based on Christian principles, and associated most strongly with Iain Duncan Smith. These ideas are particularly concerned with social policy in the inner cities, and the possibility of using voluntary groups, often faith-based, to help the most disadvantaged. Many of these ideas fit well in the One Nation tradition, and may prove another route to reviving the strength of that tradition inside the Party.

The period from the late 1990s onwards has been a time when One Nation voices and ideas have been furthest away from the central thrust of Conservative policy. It has also been the time when the Conservative Party has been furthest away from the affections of the British people. This is not a coincidence. But there are now some signs that the need yet again to recast the One Nation ideals in modern form is being recognised as a necessary condition for Conservative recovery. The countervailing forces within the party are still strong, but if they can be overcome it will be possible to see how the Conservative Party could once again become the natural home of One Nation thinking, and thereby the natural party of government.

Conclusion

Kevin Hickson

The rationale for the book was to allow for a discussion of the main ideological positions within the Conservative Party since 1945 – traditional Toryism, New Right, centre and One Nation – without making an overall evaluation. Therefore, by way of conclusion, this chapter intends to point to some of the main themes from the preceding chapters and to allow readers to make their own judgements.

A discussion of the political thought of the Conservative Party points to some contemporary dilemmas that the Party faces if it is to regain its position as a serious contender for government. These can be stated briefly as relating to the leadership, the broad stance over economic and social policy, social morality, Europe and the constitution.

The first dilemma for the contemporary Conservative Party relates to the leadership. This has been a feature of the Party since at least the late 1980s with the removal of Margaret Thatcher. Her successor, John Major, had a difficult leadership faced by rebellions, particularly over Europe, and the Party appeared to be unmanageable. Divisions became more apparent and some were even prepared to risk electoral loss, effectively forming an Opposition within the same party. This position has been reinforced by the experiences of William Hague and Iain Duncan Smith. Both sought to manage the internal divisions within the Party and to push for change in order to make the Party appear more relevant to the needs of the electorate. However, in so doing, both Hague and Duncan Smith, and also Major before them, were accused of betraying the Thatcherite legacy. The current Leader, Michael Howard, was seen as a more effective campaigner and parliamentarian who could best challenge the dominance of Blair. However, after a year as Leader, Howard's opinion poll rating was no higher than that of Duncan Smith when he was ousted. In a recent poll the Conservatives (30 per cent) were 8 per cent behind Labour and Howard's personal rating (33 per cent) was also 8 per cent behind that of Blair. This led to media reports of the Party's disappointment with the current Leader.[1] Howard is therefore seen as failing to make inroads into Blair's support base despite the fact that the Prime Minister has been subject to lower satisfaction ratings since the Iraq War.

The leadership issue may well have thought to have been resolved by those within the Party with the choice of Howard, but there is now once again speculation over the time he still has available as Leader. There are two factors that seem important here. The first is that the next general election is likely to be in the spring of 2005 and so there is unlikely to be a change of Leader in the short time available. Howard may well survive if the Conservative Party does better than expected in the next general election. The other is that it is not clear who the alternatives to Howard are. The leadership issue may well be settled therefore for the foreseeable future, by default. This is important since the Leader can shape the future direction of the Party.

The preceding chapters also point to a set of policy dilemmas for the Conservative Party. The first of these again may well be more settled by the absence of alternatives. This relates to the broad stance over economic policy. There is now a broad consensus within the Party, pointed to in a number of chapters in this book as well as by a wider number of commentators. Many in the Party now accept the substantial role for the market introduced by the Conservative Governments after 1979. Some, mainly those of a New Right persuasion, want to see further use of markets, especially in what was left of the central state by 1997: mainly the provision of healthcare and education. Nobody seems to dispute the current balance between public and private from the other direction – there is no serious call for the increased use of the state. This is so even among the 'modernisers' who call instead for the increased use of voluntary activity to strengthen 'community' and achieve 'social justice'. The progressive position in the contemporary Conservative Party is therefore substantially different from the position held by those such as Ian Gilmour in the late 1970s and early 1980s who were critical of the Thatcher Government's efforts to reduce the role of the state. There is therefore a degree of consensus within the Party over economic policy.

Given the greater degree of ideological consensus over the free market within the Party, the major disputes have been over social morality and Europe. Here, of course, the divisions have been much greater. The debate over social morality has recently been characterised as one between the 'mods' and the 'rockers', with the former advocating a more liberal attitude to social issues and the latter being opposed to such an attitude, which they regard as an erosion of traditional social morality. This in fact is a longer-standing debate between social liberals and social conservatives within the Party. However, the main force behind the development of a more social liberal attitude has sometimes appeared to be the need to attract votes, and consequently the modernisers have been accused of lacking principles and are criticised as such by the traditionalists while also failing to convince those outside the Party who would welcome a more genuine conversion to social liberalism. Simon Heffer argues in this book that a 'tougher' stance to social issues may well win more votes, but it may also be the case that a more convincing social liberalism within the Party may be more effective in its electoral appeal.

The debate over Europe is essentially one between those who are favourable to closer integration and those who are more sceptical. This is a complex issue for the Conservative Party since it goes to the heart of national identity and the meaning of sovereignty and national identity, crucial for a party of the right. It is not just a left–right issue and there are different justifications – political and economic – for a more sympathetic or a more sceptical attitude. The issue is therefore one that has divided the Party and consequently a key factor in its failure to appear a credible alternative government. Moreover, the emergence of a Party more openly committed to British withdrawal from the European Union may well have an electoral impact (for better or worse). The centre of gravity within the Party though has moved in a more sceptical direction and the pro-Europeans have become increasingly marginalised.

The dilemma for the Party on constitutional matters may appear less relevant to the Conservative's electoral fortunes, but a major area of policy radicalism under New Labour, at least initially after 1997, has been constitutional reform, and this has again impacted on the Conservative Party. Those who see the defence of the traditional constitutional structures as central to their politics, although intellectually coherent, are very much a minority, and the Party in Scotland and Wales in particular has shown flexibility in working within devolved structures as a means of electoral revival. However, a number of issues have been left unresolved by New Labour's programme of constitutional reform, such as the future composition of the House of Lords or the process of devolution in England. So far there has been little discussion of the future of the constitution within the Party and there are many issues to be resolved here also. A clear choice exists between a reactionary attitude that seeks to go back to the constitutional arrangements that existed before 1997, a conservative attitude that seeks to embed the post-1997 reforms, and a radical stance that seeks to largely change the constitution in order to restore the traditional principles that underpinned the existing constitution.

For those looking for answers, or even for an overall argument, this short conclusion will be disappointing. Indeed, it may well be that these 'answers' are not yet available since many of the debates have yet to be settled. This suggests that there is scope for a more thoroughgoing debate over policies and ideas. In undertaking this process of revision, two factors are crucial. First, the Party must be able to distinguish itself from the Labour Government, not easy considering how New Labour has so effectively captured the centre ground. This could either mean a shift to the right to create 'clear blue water' between the parties, but it could also mean presenting itself as the party of social diversity and individual liberty given the current government's stance on law and order issues in particular. The second consideration is that whichever position the Party settles on, it must appear genuine in order to capture electoral support. With each of the commentaries claiming the best arguments for the future revival of the Conservative Party, there is scope for good debate.

Note

1. Figures reported in Alan Travis, 'Tories back to days of Duncan Smith', *Guardian*, 18 November 2004. This article also stated that most Conservative members asked thought that Labour was more in tune with the average views of voters, that one in four thought that the Conservative Party could not win the next general election and that a more sceptical attitude towards the EU was needed. Similar articles appeared in other newspapers.

Select Bibliography

Amery, L.S. *Thoughts on the Constitution* (Oxford: Oxford University Press, 1947; 2nd edition 1953)

Baker, D. and Seawright, D. *Britain For And Against Europe* (Oxford: Clarendon Press, 1998)

Balniel, Lord, Carr, R., Deedes, W., Fletcher-Cooke, C., Fort, R., Harrison, B., Joseph, K., Longden, G., Low, T., Ramsden, J. and Rippon, G. *The Responsible Society* (London: Conservative Political Centre, 1959)

Barry, N. *The New Right* (London: Croom Helm, 1987)

Barry, N. *Welfare* (Buckingham: Open University Press, 1999, 2nd edition)

Barry, N. 'The Rationale of the Minimal State', in A. Gamble and A. Wright (eds), *Restating the State* (Oxford: Blackwell, 2004)

Biggs-Davison, J. *Tory Lives* (London: Putnam and Company, 1952)

Blake, R. *The Conservative Party from Peel to Major* (London: Arrow Books, 1998)

Blake, R. and Patten, J. (eds), *The Conservative Opportunity* (London: Macmillan, 1976)

Boyson, R. *Centre Forward: A Radical Conservative Programme* (London: Temple Smith, 1978)

Bulpitt, J. 'The Discipline of the New Democracy: Mrs Thatcher's Domestic Statecraft', *Political Studies* xxxiv (1986)

Bulpitt, J. 'The European Question: Rules, National Modernisation and the Ambiguities of *Primat der Innenpolitik*', in D. Marquand and A. Seldon (eds), *The Ideas that Shaped Post-War Britain* (London: Fontana, 1996)

Butler, A., Baker, K., Brittan, L., Goodhart, P. and Alison, M. (eds), *One Nation at Work: By the One Nation Group of MPs* (London: Conservative Political Centre, 1976)

Butler, R.A. *The Art of the Possible* (London: Hamish Hamilton, 1971)

Cecil, H. *Conservatism* (London: Home University Library, 1912)

Coleman, B. *Conservatism and the Conservative Party in Nineteenth Century Britain* (London: Edward Arnold, 1988)

Coleraine, Lord. *For Conservative Only* (London: Tom Stacey, 1970)

Cowling, M. (ed.), *Conservative Essays* (London: Cassell, 1978)

Critchley, J. 'Strains and Stresses in the Conservative Party', *Political Quarterly*, Vol. 44 no. 4 (October–December 1973)

Critchley, J. and Halcrow, M. *Collapse of Stout Party: The Decline and Fall of the Tories* (London: Victor Gollancz, 1997)

Cross, J.A. *Lord Swinton* (Oxford: Clarendon Press, 1982)

Denham, A. and Garnett, M. *Keith Joseph* (Chesham: Acumen, 2002)

Evans, B.J. *Thatcherism and British Politics, 1975–1999* (Stroud: Sutton Publishing, 1999)

Evans, B.J. and Taylor, A.J. *From Salisbury to Major: Continuity and Change in Conservative Politics* (Manchester: Manchester University Press, 1996)

Forster, A. *Euroscepticism in Contemporary British Politics* (London: Routledge, 2002)

Gamble, A. *The Conservative Nation* (London: Routledge and Kegan Paul, 1974)

Gamble, A. *The Free Economy and the Strong State* (London: Macmillan, 1988; 2nd edition 1994)

Garnett, M. and Aitken, I. *Splendid! Splendid! The Authorised Biography of Willie Whitelaw* (London: Jonathan Cape, 2002)

Garnett, M. and Lynch, P. (eds), *The Conservatives in Crisis: The Tories after 1997* (Manchester: Manchester University Press, 2003)

Geddes, A. *The European Union and British Politics* (Basingstoke: Palgrave Macmillan, 2004)

George, S. *An Awkward Partner: Britain in the European Community* (Oxford: Oxford University Press, 1998; 3rd edition)

Gilmour, I. *The Body Politic* (London: Hutchinson, 1971)

Gilmour, I. *Inside Right: A Study of Conservatism* (London: Hutchinson, 1977)

Gilmour, I. *Britain Can Work* (Oxford: Martin Robertson, 1983)

Gilmour, I. *Dancing with Dogma* (London: Simon and Schuster, 1992)

Gilmour, I. and Garnett, M. *Whatever Happened to the Tories? The Conservative Party since 1945* (London: Fourth Estate, 1997)

Goodhart, P. *Jobs Ahead* (London: Conservative Political Centre, 1984)

Greenleaf, W.H. 'The Character of Modern British Conservatism', in R. Benewick, N. Berki and B. Parekh (eds), *Knowledge and Belief in Politics: The Problem of Ideology* (London: Allen and Unwin, 1973)

Hayek, F.A. von *The Road to Serfdom* (London: Routledge, 1944)

Hayek, F.A. von *The Constitution of Liberty* (London: Routledge and Kegan Paul, 1960)

Hayek, F.A. von *The Mirage of Social Justice* (London: Routledge and Kegan Paul, 1976)

Heath, E. *The Course of My Life: My Autobiography* (London: Hodder and Stoughton, 1998)

Heffer, S. *Like the Roman: The Life of Enoch Powell* (London: Phoenix, 1999)

Hogg, Q. *The Conservative Case* (Harmondsworth: Penguin, 1959)

Holmes, M. (ed.), *The Eurosceptical Reader* (Basingstoke: Macmillan, 1996)

Holmes, M. (ed.), *The Eurosceptical Reader 2* (Basingstoke: Palgrave Macmillan, 2001)

Holmes, M. *European Integration: Scope and Limits* (Basingstoke: Palgrave Macmillan, 2001)

Johnson, N. *Reshaping the British Constitution* (London: Palgrave Macmillan, 2004)

Johnson, R.W. *The Politics of Recession* (London: Macmillan, 1985)

Joseph, K. *Stranded in the Middle Ground* (London: Centre for Policy Studies, 1976)

Joseph, K. and Sumption, J. *Equality* (London: John Murray, 1979)

Kedourie, E. *The Crossman Confessions and Other Essays in Politics, History and Religion* (London: Mansell, 1984)

Layton-Henry, Z. (ed.), *Conservative Party Politics* (London: Macmillan, 1980)

Letwin, S. *The Anatomy of Thatcherism* (London: Fontana, 1992)

Ludlam, S. and Smith, M. (eds), *Contemporary British Conservatism* (Basingstoke: Macmillan, 1996)

Lynch, P. *The Politics of Nationhood: Sovereignty, Britishness and Conservative Politics* (London: Macmillan, 1999)

Macleod, I. and Maude, A. (eds), *One Nation: A Tory Approach to Social Problems* (London: Conservative Political Centre, 1950)

Macmillan, H. *The Middle Way* (London: Macmillan, 1938)

Major, J. *John Major: The Autobiography* (London: HarperCollins, 1999)

Minogue, K. (ed.), *Conservative Realism: New Essays on Conservatism* (London: HarperCollins, 1996)

Moore, C. and Heffer, S. (eds), *A Tory Seer. The Selected Journalism of T.E. Utley* (London: Hamish Hamilton, 1989)

Murray, C. *Losing Ground* (New York: Basic Books, 1994; 2nd edition)

Norman, J. (ed.), *The Achievement of Michael Oakeshott* (London: Duckworth, 1993)

Norton, P. *The Constitution in Flux* (Oxford: Martin Robertson, 1982)

Norton, P. '"The Lady's not for Turning": But what about the rest of the Conservative Party?' *Parliamentary Affairs* (1990)

Norton, P. and Aughey, A. *Conservatives and Conservatism* (London: Temple Smith, 1981)

Oakeshott, M. *Rationalism in Politics and Other Essays* (London: Methuen, 1962)

Oakeshott, M. *On Human Conduct* (London: Oxford University Press, 1975)

Oakeshott, M. *Rationalism in Politics and Other Essays* (Indianapolis: Liberty Press, 1991)

One Nation, *One Nation 2000* (London: Conservative Political Centre, 1992)

One Nation, *One Nation: At the Heart of the Future* (London: Conservative Political Centre, 1996)

O'Sullivan, N. *Conservatism* (London: Dent, 1976)

O'Sullivan, N. 'Conservatism, the New Right and the Limited State', in J. Hayward and P. Norton (eds), *The Political Science of British Politics* (Brighton: Harvester, 1986)

Popper, K. *The Open Society and its Enemies* (London: Routledge and Kegan Paul, 1945)

Popper, K. 'The open society and its enemies revisited', *The Economist*, 23 April 1988

Powell, E. and Maude, A. (eds), *Change Is Our Ally* (London: Conservative Political Centre, 1954)

Pym, F. *Politics of Consent* (London: Sphere Books, 1985)

Quinton, A. 'Conservatism', in P. Pettit and R. Goodin (eds), *A Companion to Contemporary Political Philosophy* (Oxford: Blackwell, 1993)

Redwood, J. *Popular Capitalism* (London: Routledge and Kegan Paul, 1988)

Redwood, J. *Singing the Blues* (London: Politicos Publishing, 2004)

Riddell, P. *The Thatcher Government* (Oxford: Robertson, 1983)

Roberts, A. *Salisbury: Victorian Titan* (London: Weidenfeld and Nicolson, 1999)

Scruton, R. *England: An Elegy* (London: Chatto and Windus, 2000)

Scruton, R. *The Meaning of Conservatism* (London: Palgrave Macmillan, 2001; 3rd edition)

Scruton, R. *The Need for Nations* (London: Civitas, 2004)

Seldon, A. *Churchill's Indian Summer: The Conservative Government, 1951–55* (London: Hodder and Stoughton, 1981)

Seldon, A. (ed.), *The Thatcher Effect* (Oxford: Oxford University Press, 1989)

Seldon, A. (ed.), *How Tory Governments Fall: The Tory Party in Power* (London: Fontana, 1996)

Seldon, A. and Ball, S. (eds), *The Conservative Century: The Conservative Party since 1900* (Oxford: Oxford University Press, 1994)

Smith, P. (ed.), *Lord Salisbury on Politics* (Cambridge: Cambridge University Press, 1972)

Thatcher, M. *The Downing Street Years* (London: HarperCollins, 1993)

Turner, J. *The Tories and Europe* (Manchester: Manchester University Press, 2000)

White, R.J. *The Conservative Tradition* (London: Nicholas Kaye, 1950)

Willetts, D. *Modern Conservatism* (London: Penguin, 1992)

Willetts, D. *Civic Conservatism* (London: Social Market Foundation, 1994)

Worsthorne, P. *The Socialist Myth* (London: Cassell, 1971)

Worsthorne, P. *In Defence of Aristocracy* (London: HarperCollins, 2004)

Young, H. *This Blessed Plot: Britain and Europe from Churchill to Blair* (London: Papermac, 1999)

Index

Abortion Act (1967) 165
Acheson, Dean 10
AIDS 167
Alport, Cuthbert 72–4, 77, 85
Amery, Leo 98, 104
Amsterdam Treaty (1997) 117
Ancram, Michael 65
Anglo-Irish Agreement (1986) 118
aristocratic principle 186–7
Asquith, Herbert 198
Attlee, Clement 36, 53, 103, 184
Aughey, Arthur 2, 7–27, 126, 184
authoritarianism 158, 160, 161, 202,
    205–6, 207, 208

'Back to Basics' 143, 169, 205
Baldwin, Stanley 54, 71, 84, 184, 215
Ballymoney Free Press 7
Barber, Anthony 38
Barry, Norman 2, 28–50
Benn, Tony 38
Bentinck, George 23
Beveridge Report 35
Biffen, John 57, 62
Bill of Rights (1689) 93
Birch, Nigel 37, 138, 139
Blair, Tony 24, 28, 66, 152, 153,
    206–7, 209, 219–20
Blake, Robert 10, 13
Blunkett, David 207
Bogdanor, Vernon 203
Bow Group 57, 62, 82
Boyle, Edward 82
Boyson, Rhodes 105, 106, 108
Bretton Woods 38
British National Party (BNP) 207

Brittan, Leon 125
Brown, Gordon 206–7
Bruges Group 84, 204
Bulpitt, Jim 115, 125, 180–3
Burke, Edmund 22, 29, 93, 118, 143,
    200, 206
Burt, Alistair 84, 85, 185
Bush, George W. 149
Butler, R A 11, 36, 76, 79–80, 82, 83,
    166, 179, 184, 215, 216
Butskellism 36

Callaghan, James 61, 122, 135
Cameron, David 84
capitalism 4, 29, 32, 33, 34, 35, 45,
    46, 133, 137, 159, 198, 202, 205,
    209
Carr, Robert 60, 83
Carrington, Lord 60, 61, 62
Casey, John 118, 187
Cash, William 127
Castle, Barbara 34, 47
Cecil of Chelwood, Lord 98
Cecil, Lord Hugh 7, 9, 99
Centre (Conservative Party) 2, 219
    changing nature of 58–9
    changing social composition of 56
    current status of 65–6
    ethos of 52–3
    ideological 51–2
    relevance of 51
Centre for Policy Studies (CPS) 106,
    203, 204
Centre Forward 51
Chamberlain, Joseph 186
Chamberlain, Neville 53, 71

227

Oikophobia, 22
One Nation, 2, 3, 69–70, 102, 147,
219
criticism of New Right 46
European attitudes of 82–4, 118
inequality 179, 183, 184–6, 191,
192
legacy of Disraeli 70–3
One Nation group 51, 72–6
pamphlets 76–82
postwar consensus 34–6
social morality 160–1, 164
One Nation (1950) 74, 76–8, 87, 216
One Nation 2000 (1992) 81
One Nation at the Heart of the Future
(1996) 81–2
One Nation at Work (1976) 80–1
Operation ROBOT 137, 139
organic society 31
O'Sullivan, John 173
O'Sullivan, Noel 30
Ownership 44–6

Parliament 94, 96, 97, 100
Parliament Act (1911) 93, 99
Parris, Matthew 164
paternalism 34
patriotism 18–22, 24, 54, 144
Patten, John 106, 203
Peel, Robert 31, 71
pensions 47–8
permissiveness 158, 164–70
Peterhouse College, Cambridge 187
Pilbeam, Bruce 3, 158–77
Police and Criminal Evidence Act
(1984) 166
Popper, Karl 36, 96
populism 15–16, 186
Portillo, Michael 64, 145–6, 147–8,
163, 170, 202
postwar consensus 28, 29, 30, 34, 36,
42, 58, 133, 140, 184–5
Powell, Enoch 20–1, 37, 38, 57, 72,
74, 79, 83, 84–5, 118, 122, 138,
139, 140, 162, 174, 186, 187,
197, 198, 199, 216
Powellism 59
pragmatism 28, 126, 179–80, 181–2,
192

Pressure for Economic and Social
Toryism (PEST) 2, 82
Prior, Jim 61, 141
Privatisation 36, 37, 40, 44–5, 47, 145,
183, 204
protectionism 186, 198, 205
Public Order Act (1986) 166
Pym, Francis 51, 52, 53, 58, 59, 61–2,
180

Quinton, Anthony 30

Raison, Timothy 62, 98–9
Rannoch, Lord Pearson of 107
rationalism 29, 180, 187, 188
realism 11, 94, 180
redistribution 33
Redwood, John 4, 45, 47, 63, 202–8
Republican Party (USA) 145
Responsible Society, The (1959) 80, 83,
216
Ridley, Nicholas 84, 125
Rifkind, Malcolm 64
Rodgers, John 74, 83
Rolls Royce, nationalisation of 37
rule of law 93–4, 200

Salisbury–Addison convention 199,
200
Salisbury Review 188
Salisbury, Third Marques of 7, 8, 9, 16,
143, 181, 182, 186
Sandys, Duncan 77
Scottish Parliament 106–7
Scott, Nicholas 57, 62, 83
Scruton, Roger 8, 9, 21, 22, 31, 32–4,
39, 42, 45, 48, 108, 118, 171, 174
Seawright, David 2, 69–90
Section 28 167, 168, 206
'Selsdon Man' 37, 203
Sexual Offences Act (1967) 165
Shephard, Gillian 63
Sherman, Alfred 203
Sherman, Bill 82–3
Simon, Jack 71–2
Simons, Henry 32
Sinclair, Peter 203
Single European Act (1984) 48, 101,
117, 118, 119, 123, 124, 125, 127